THE
MAYERTHORPE
STORY

FROM AMBUSH TO AFTERMATH

The Mayerthorpe Detachment, February 11, 2005.
Top, L to R: S/Sgt. Gary Radford, Cst. Brock Myrol, Cst. Leo Johnston, Cpl. Jim Martin, Sgt. Brian Pinder, Cst. Clayton Seguin, Cpl. Jeff Whipple, Supt. Marty Cheliak. Bottom, L to R: Cst. Peter Schiemann, Cst. Cindie Dennis, stenographer Heather Heystek, office manager Pat Lakeman, Cst. Julie Letal, Cst. Joe Sangster. (*Mayerthorpe Freelancer*)

THE
MAYERTHORPE
STORY

FROM AMBUSH TO AFTERMATH

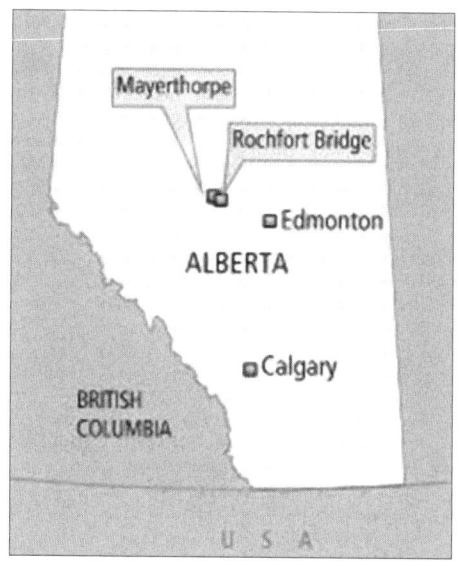

Robert Knuckle

GSPH

GENERAL STORE PUBLISHING HOUSE
499 O'Brien Road, Box 415
Renfrew, Ontario, Canada K7V 4A6
Telephone (613) 432-7697 or 1-800-465-6072
www.gsph.com

ISBN 978-1-897508-42-8

Copyright © Robert Knuckle, 2009

Design and layout: Magdalene Carson / New Leaf Publication Design
Printed by Custom Printers of Renfrew Ltd., Renfrew, Ontario
Printed and bound in Canada

Library and Archives Canada Cataloguing in Publication

Knuckle, Robert, 1935-
      The Mayerthorpe story : from ambush to
aftermath / Robert Knuckle.

ISBN 978-1-897508-42-8

      1. Police murders--Alberta--Mayerthorpe. 2. Royal Canadian Mounted Police--
Officials and employees--Crimes against--Alberta--Mayerthorpe. 3. Roszko, James.
4. Accomplices--Alberta--Mayerthorpe. 5. Trials (Murder)--Alberta--Edmonton.
I. Title.

HV6535.C33M38 2009   364.152'30971233   C2009-902730-5

For Our Grandchildren

Lakota Knuckle

McKinley Knuckle

Geneva Knuckle

Alexander Barthorpe

Samuel Chichakian

Joseph Chichakian

Silvana Chichakian

Contents

Author's Comments

THIS BOOK IS the culmination of my stories about the Royal Canadian Mounted Police. My earlier books were stepping-stones whereby I learned valuable lessons in style and structure. But more than anything, writing those books taught me the importance of incorporating as many interviews as possible to create a compelling narrative.

In July 2005, I was researching *In the Line of Duty, Volume II*, a compendium of all the members of the RCMP who have been killed in the performance of their duties and whose names are inscribed on their Honour Roll.

At that time, I was afforded the opportunity to interview the family members of the four Mounties murdered at Mayerthorpe, as well as other principals integrally involved in the story. Those interviews—and over fifty others since then—allowed me unprecedented access to sources whose intimate knowledge of the case was invaluable. Although the murders occurred in 2005, it is only now that the complete story can be told.

For over three years, its plot remained unfinished because the two men who were accused of being complicit in the Mayerthorpe murders had not been brought to justice. Then, in January 2009, both of these men, Shawn Hennessey and Dennis Cheeseman, pleaded guilty to manslaughter and were sentenced to prison for their crimes.

These men still hold out hope that their guilty pleas will be overturned and they then can proceed to a trial. Nevertheless, at this time I feel this complex tragedy is sufficiently resolved so that the story can be properly told.

Furthermore, this incident, as tragic as it may be, has left an indelible mark on the fabric of Canadian history and, as such, it deserves to be recorded for posterity.

I believe it is a story that belongs on the shelves of every library and school in our country—and beyond.

I hope those who read this book will find the story as fascinating as I did.

1 | Mayerthorpe

ON THURSDAY, MARCH 3, 2005, the worst case of police mass murder in the history of Canada took place near Mayerthorpe, Alberta. On that day, a disturbed lone gunman ambushed and murdered four young members of the Royal Canadian Mounted Police with a semi-automatic assault rifle that killed them all within a matter of seconds.

There is tragic irony in the fact that such a dreadfully momentous event should be associated with a place like Mayerthorpe, a small and obscure rural town located on Highway #43 about 145 kms (87 miles) northwest of Edmonton.

In fact, this tragedy didn't really happen at Mayerthorpe at all but out in the countryside much closer to the rural hamlet of Rochfort Bridge, a tiny crossroads community of sixteen houses and one restaurant located in the county of Lac Ste. Anne.

The reason this atrocity will forever be associated with the town of Mayerthorpe is that three of the four slain policemen were members of the Mayerthorpe RCMP Detachment.

There have been other cases of multiple police murder involving the RCMP. Thirteen were killed during the Second World War, but that was over a period of years. Eight were killed in the rebellion of 1885, but that, too, happened in armed conflict and took place over a span of three days.

Five RCMP members drowned in Lake Simcoe in Ontario in 1958 while on a late-night investigative mission to Georgina Island; their small boat capsized in the turbulence of a sudden storm. In 1963, four Mounties died in a plane crash at Carmacks in the Yukon.

In 1962, Constables Joseph Keck, Gordon Pedersen, and Donald Weisgerber were gunned down at Kamloops, British Columbia.

On several occasions, two Mounties have been murdered at the same time. In 1970, Sgt. Robert Schrader and Cst. Douglas Anson were shot to death while responding to a domestic dispute near

The March West, 1874.

MacDowall, Saskatchewan. The same fate befell Cpl. Barry Lidstone and Cst. Perry Brophy at Hoyt, New Brunswick, in 1978. Constables Robin Cameron and Marc Bourdages were shot and killed by a lone gunman near Mildred, Saskatchewan, in July 2006.

But Mayerthorpe retains the dubious distinction of being the worst case of multiple murder in the modern history of the RCMP.

What's more, it is also a fact that the Province of Alberta is disproportionately represented on the official RCMP Honour Roll that lists all the Mounties who have died in the line of duty.

To date, thirty-nine of the 220 members on the Honour Roll have died in Alberta. This amounts to 18 percent of all the Mounties who have died in the line of duty across Canada since the inception of the Force.

This high percentage can be partially explained by the fact that the Mounties have been stationed in Alberta longer than anywhere else in Canada. The Force was initially organized as the Northwest Mounted Police in 1873 to help keep the peace in Canada's North-West Territories, which at that time encompassed the District of Alberta. The major incident that spurred the formation of the NWMP was the massacre of twenty-five Assiniboine Indians by wolf hunters and whisky traders in May 1873 in the Cypress Hills close to the Alberta eastern border.

In July 1874, a contingent of 275 of these Mounties began their famous "March West" from Fort Dufferin, Manitoba, and ended their western trek by establishing their headquarters at Fort MacLeod in southern Alberta. The Force was then divided in two, with half of the redcoats travelling north to Edmonton. The following year, Fort Calgary was founded.

Ever since 1874, the Mounties have policed Alberta. In 1905, when Alberta became a province, the Mounties, in essence, became Alberta's provincial police. And the massive size of the province makes that a challenging task.

Alberta ranks as the fourth largest province in Canada after Quebec, Ontario, and British Columbia. It is a land mass only slightly smaller than the State of Texas, extending 1,223 kms (760 miles) from Montana in the south to its northern border with the Northwest Territories. From east to west, Alberta's maximum width is 660 kms (410 miles).

The only areas in the province that the Mounties do not police are some of the big cities like Edmonton, Calgary, Lethbridge, and Medicine Hat. A few smaller communities such as Camrose and Taber also have their own police service.

Consequently, throughout Alberta there are 2,200 Mounties stationed in 107 detachments, from Waterton Park on the Montana border to Assumption, just below the southern edge of the Northwest Territories.

In 2005, Mayerthorpe had eleven members working in its detachment office, two of whom primarily worked traffic control on busy Highway #43.

Two other nearby communities that play a significant role in this story also have RCMP detachment offices. Whitecourt, a town of 8,500 situated on Highway #43 just north of Mayerthorpe, had a twelve-member unit. Barrhead, to the east of Mayerthorpe with a population of 4,600, had nine Mounties working in their detachment. Although Barrhead has a bigger population than Mayerthorpe, the latter detachment has more demanding highway responsibilities.

Mayerthorpe sits quietly north of the densely populated Calgary–Edmonton corridor, where it is nestled among the rolling hills and widespread rural properties of central Alberta.

The town began its existence in 1919 with the building of a small Merchant's Bank of Canada on "Main Street." That was soon followed by the erection of Crockett's General Store and a small hotel. As a fledgling village, the community got its name from Robert Mayer, the first postmaster in the area, and from the suffix "thorpe," an archaic Old English term meaning "little village."

It was officially incorporated as a village in 1927 and has sustained its existence since then by providing agricultural goods and services to local farmers. Today, with a population of 1,600 it also serves as a bedroom community for the lumber mills in Whitecourt and nearby Blue Ridge.

Although the town's weekly newspaper, *The Mayerthorpe Freelancer,* was closed in 2008, the essence of the community can be best understood by scanning some of the articles in its back issues:

Celebrating Agriculture in Alberta
Farm Safety
Calving Season Springs to Life
Alberta Angus Breeder of the Year
Preventing Farm Accidents
Our Greatest Asset is the Farm Family

The advertisements are equally revealing:

Farm to Fork with Alberta Pork
Silver II Custom Harvesting
The Dependable Bulls of the Towaw Cattle Company
Cunningham Fertilizers
Ditner's Feed Service and Supply
Farms and Acreages for Sale

In 2005, the economy in Mayerthorpe was sluggish. However, there had been a time when the town was a bustling, thriving community supported by the sale of cattle, grain, and lumber.

But its commerce suffered a severe blow in 2003 when the threat of "mad cow" disease closed the U.S. border to Canadian beef and devastated the local cattle and trucking markets. That same year, the area suffered a major drought. Then, in 2004, the region was infested with grasshoppers that plagued the grain crop.

Since then, economic conditions have only marginally improved, but farmers, being a hardy and determined breed, have stayed the course and helped keep the town solvent.

The weather in Mayerthorpe is typically Canadian. Although the summers are warm and spring is usually pleasant, the winters there can be brutal. Temperatures of twenty below zero are common and there is usually at least one week every winter when the thermometer dips to thirty or thirty-five below. When this cold is combined with a nasty wind, the chill factor can become unbearable.

But the fall in Mayerthorpe is glorious.

Pastor Wendell Wiebe, the minister of the local Baptist Church and chaplain of the town's volunteer fire department, says, "The fall colours here are amazing . . . beyond anything I've seen in the world. And that includes the Maritimes, the United States, and the Philippines."

Living in a small community like Mayerthorpe has both its advantages and disadvantages. On the one hand, the townsfolk enjoy the benefits of everyone being close and knowing about each other. When someone is sick or suffering, the news spreads quickly and the neighbours rally 'round to help. On the other hand, that same social intimacy has the potential for generating gossip. And that can be destructive.

In this regard, it is Pastor Wiebe's observation that the people of Mayerthorpe are generally cautious and reserved. "I think that's natural in a small town. Everyone knows everyone else and they have learned to be prudent . . . cautious . . . in their conversation. There's a warm sense of family here but most folks are careful of what they say . . . and who they say it to."

From a physical perspective, Mayerthorpe is unspectacular. Viewed from a distance, the town presents an unimpressive profile of low-lying buildings, including a downtown section comprised of four blocks of insignificant stores on either side of its one commercial "Main Street."

The most imposing structure in the community is a huge grain elevator, no longer functional, that stands next to the town's rusting railway tracks. Although the elevator is obsolete, it has been declared a historical site and is being retrofitted to its original condition when it was a busy commercial enterprise in the early 1960s.

Elsewhere in town, amid clusters of modest frame houses, there are schools, four churches, the twenty-eight-room Haven Inn Hotel, the Co-op and Super A grocery stores, a Canadian Legion, a fire hall, a Case Equipment dealership, the Lariat Restaurant, a community outdoor swimming pool, an eighteen-hole golf course, and a vacant lot where the old arena once stood. Sadly, it was lost in a fire in 2008.

The most attractive building in the community is the modern, dark-bricked RCMP detachment office that was opened in 1985 and sits on the edge of town near the highway. It's a one-storey structure with offices, an interview room, a meeting/coffee room, a filing room, a communications area, and four cells for short-term stays.

In March 2005, the Mayerthorpe Detachment was run by Sergeant Brian Pinder, an experienced NCO. However, beginning on Monday, February 28, 2005, Sgt. Pinder had gone on a one-week holiday leave. Acting as commanding NCO in his place was Cpl. Jim Martin, thirty-eight, who had fifteen years' experience and had been at the Mayerthorpe Detachment since September 2001.

Mayerthorpe is a friendly place. Most people who go there soon discover something warm and welcoming about the local people that they quickly come to appreciate.

It is, however, a place where nothing very exciting seems to happen . . . nothing of any real consequence.

But on Wednesday, March 2, some ordinary, rather minor events began to play out that would change the town's image forever.

The day started out like any other. People showered, ate their breakfasts, and began going about their normal routines. Kids went to school, moms and dads went off to work, salesmen made their calls, folks at home listened to their radios.

Everyone in town was looking forward to the end of winter and the start of a new and rejuvenating spring. As the morning progressed, no one in Mayerthorpe could suspect that within twenty-four hours the name of their community would be known around the world.

That morning, bailiff Rob Perry phoned the Mayerthorpe Detachment and advised Cpl. Jim Martin that he was proceeding to James Roszko's farm on Range Road 75 near Rochfort Bridge.

Perry told Cpl. Martin he was going there to execute a warrant authorizing him to seize a white 2005 Ford F350 Super Duty pickup truck on behalf of Kentwood Motors of Edmonton. The car agency had been unable to confirm Roszko's credit status, and for two months Roszko had failed to reply to their repeated phone calls.

Perry also said that based on the information he had received about Roszko's being aggressive and abusive, he decided to bring his partner, Mark Hnatiw, along with him for protection. Hnatiw was a huge man standing six feet, four inches and weighing 240 pounds; he formerly had been employed as a prison guard.

Cpl. Martin advised Perry to be careful, because Roszko had been charged last August for damaging the tires on the two different vehicles that had driven onto his property. One car belonged to a meter reader; the other to a census-taker.

Jim Martin had handled the census-taker's complaint. It alleged that Roszko had damaged all four tires on her car. When Martin went out to investigate, he found that Roszko had made a spike belt by splitting a length of plastic plumbing pipe and embedding it with nails. Then Roszko laid the pipe down in front of the gate of the driveway leading onto his property.

Prior to the census-taker's complaint, Roszko had used the same spike belt to flatten three tires on the meter reader's vehicle.

When Martin went out and discovered the spike belt in Roszko's laneway, he charged him with two counts of mischief. Now Martin was waiting to testify against him at an upcoming trial scheduled for the spring.

Martin also warned Perry to watch out for Roszko's two vicious dogs that he often let loose to frighten unwanted visitors.

Peter Schiemann outside the Mayerthorpe Detachment, 2003.

Martin finished his conversation with Perry by telling him he would come out to assist him. Jim said he would leave right away and meet Perry at the gate of Roszko's farm.

When the corporal got off the phone, he asked Cst. Peter Schiemann, twenty-five, to accompany him out to Roszko's farm. They left the office quickly, got into a PC (police cruiser) and headed out of town toward Range Road 75.

En route, Martin radioed Cst. Julie Letal in her PC and asked her to meet him at Roszko's place.

She responded "Ten-four," and turned her cruiser towards Rochfort Bridge.

Jim Martin and Peter Schiemann chatted amiably as they drove out of town and turned right onto Highway #18.

Schiemann, who was tall and trim, was a pleasant and personable young man who loved being a policeman. He had graduated with flying colours from the RCMP Training Academy at Regina in November 2000 and was immediately posted to Mayerthorpe. Now, with more than four years of experience at the detachment, he was one of the senior constables in the unit.

Jim Martin says, "Peter was a really good cop. He was raised in a good family where he learned strong moral and ethical values."

In August 2004, he was assigned to Traffic Services at Mayerthorpe. This meant he became part of a team that included

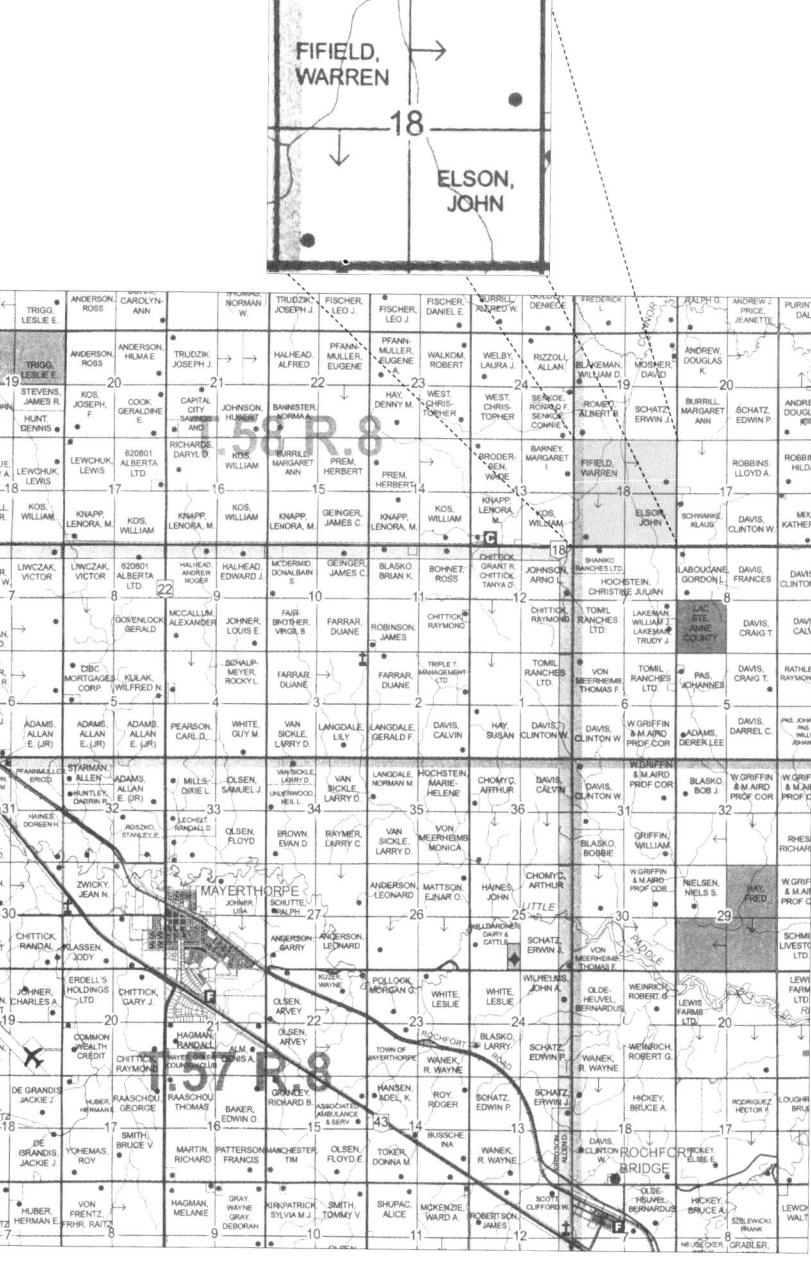

A partial plan of Lac Ste. Anne County showing the Fifields' three-quarter section relative to Mayerthorpe and Rochfort Bridge. The dot on the left of the property indicates the location of the Fifields' house; the dot on the right indicates James Roszko's farmstead. (Lac Ste. Anne County Office)

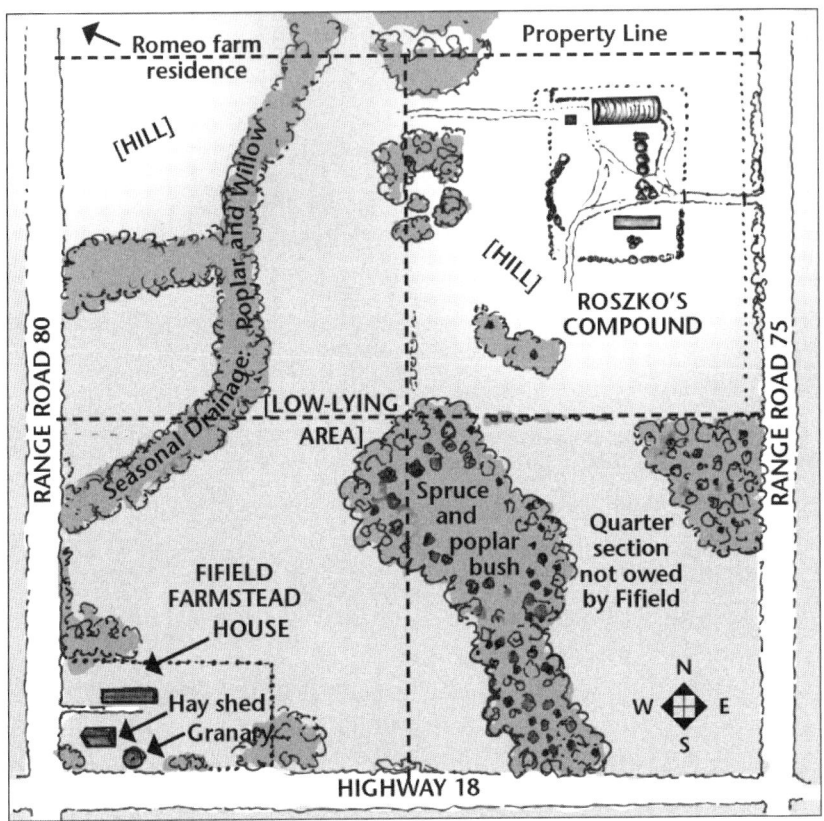

The Fifields' three-quarter section showing the Fifields' house on Range Road 80 and James Roszko's farmstead on Range road 75, plus the terrain, bush, and brush patches on the property. (Drawing by Magdalene Carson)

three members from Whitecourt who would patrol long stretches of both Highway #43 and Highway #32 in the area of the two towns and beyond.

Martin says, "On the way to Roszko's place, Peter and I talked about his recently being chosen for a special new 'interdiction crew' whose mandate was to target drug runners on the long stretch of highway to Grande Pairie. Peter had recently completed some projects at Jasper regarding interdiction and was looking forward to putting those theories into action. He was excited about that work. And he was very pleased with being selected for this special crew. Peter didn't brag or anything, but I knew that his being chosen was a notch in his belt . . . a real feather in his cap."

As they headed east along the highway, Martin briefed Schiemann on the task at hand.

Peter knew Roszko's name and his reputation. Everybody in the detachment knew about James Roszko. But they also knew that Roszko posed no great concern for the members. Roszko had a reputation of being nasty and threatening with everyone—everyone except the police. Jimmy Roszko often acted like he was crazy but he was smart enough to know he could only go so far with the police. He could be loud and foul-mouthed and aggressive with them, but he never dared to threaten them.

Roszko's farm on Range Road 75 was on part of his mother's and stepfather's three-quarter section, which equals 480 acres of land. His mother, Stephanie, and her third husband, Warren Fifield, lived in a house on Range Road 80, which is the next road west of James's. From their kitchen window, they could look north up the hill and see the back of James Roszko's farm. The view from James's hilltop property is delightful, with gently rolling farmland extending in a distant vista as far as the eye can see.

James Roszko's place really wasn't much of a farm. At the road, there was a locked gate across his laneway with a "No Trespassing" sign on it. The laneway ran about forty yards, and then there was another locked gate leading into his inner compound.

Inside the inner compound, there was a house trailer where he lived, an eighty-by-forty-foot steel Quonset hut where he worked, three 1,200-bushel galvanized steel granaries with conical tops, two gravity-drop gas tanks, a doghouse, and an old wooden shed at the southwest corner of his Quonset hut.

When Perry and Hnatiw pulled their black pickup to a stop in front of Roszko's locked gate, they spotted him in front of the smaller, "human" door of the Quonset. He was wearing a black baseball hat, blue jeans, and a dark jacket. Roszko clearly saw them but didn't acknowledge them. He turned and walked back into the Quonset.

Perry honked his horn several times but got no response.

Hnatiw says, "The next sighting of him was when he appeared by his pickup truck beside his house trailer. How he got there, I don't know. I didn't see him walking across the yard or anything."

Shortly after that, Roszko let loose two large dogs, one of which looked like a Rottweiler. Barking and growling, they came charging toward the bailiffs, who quickly retreated into the safety of their pickup truck. Roszko then went into the trailer.

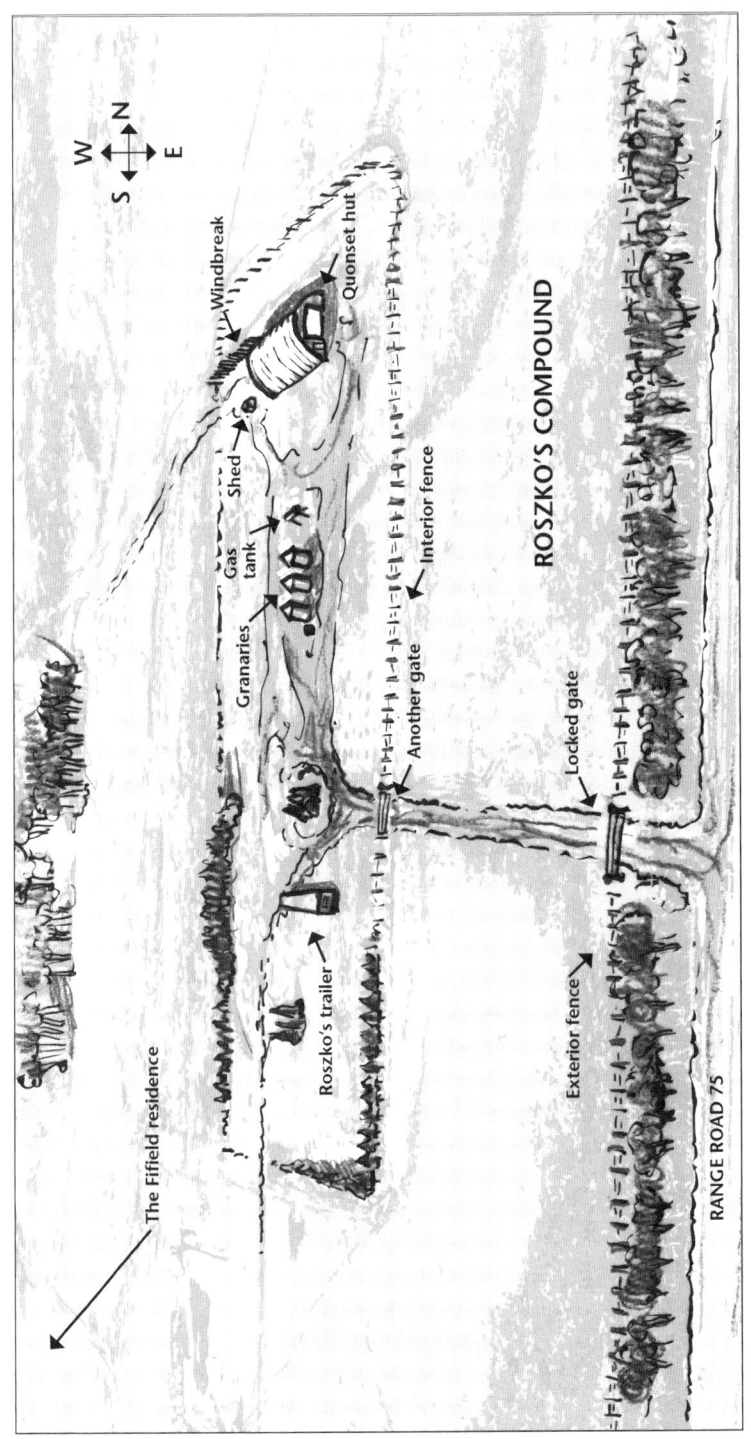

Roszko's compound on Range Road 75. (Roszko's trailer is in the position it was at the time of the killings.) (Drawing by Magdalene Carson)

An aerial photo of Roszko's compound showing the patches of bush and brush and the terrain nearby. (RCMP)

"We called the police again, 'cause that's when it started to get weird," says Hnatiw. "Then Roszko comes out, gets into the white pickup and drives south through a gate; then he stops at another one.

"We thought he was going to leave that way, but he didn't. He backed his truck up and came towards us and stopped at the inner chain-link gate. Then he let himself through the chain-link gate and before he got back in his truck he yelled at us, 'Fuck off!'"

After that Roszko climbed back in his pickup and drove west across the frozen fields.

Just as Jim Martin was turning his PC left onto Range Road 75, he received a second phone call from Perry, who reported their experience with the dogs.

"Hang on," Jim replied. "We'll be right there. Don't enter the property until we get there."

A minute later, at 3:40 p.m., Martin and Schiemann pulled up beside the bailiffs' truck.

After Rob Perry pointed out the direction in which Roszko had fled, Martin and Schiemann jumped in their cruiser and hurried away in an attempt to locate him.

Shortly after they left, Cst. Julie Letal arrived at the farm in her PC.

Martin and Schiemann sped south on the Range Road, had a quick look around Highway #18, surveying the yards of a few farms. Seeing no sign of Roszko, Martin headed north on Range Road 80.

Ten minutes before Martin and Schiemann made their turn north, Dianne Romeo, her daughter Buffy, her grandson Cooper Golden, her sister Dixie Mills, and her friend Crystal Loughran were out riding horses. Dianne and her husband, Bruce, own a spread immediately north of the Fifield property on Range Road 80. Dianne and her group had ridden north but now were returning south to the Romeos' stable.

She says, "All of a sudden I heard this motor roaring in the distance ahead of us. Because of the rise on the road, I couldn't see anything, but I knew someone was coming towards us at an awful clip.

"So we all edged over to the side of the road and I made sure my grandson's horse was edged over there, too.

"Then Jimmy Roszko came flying over the hill in his white truck. He kind of spooked our horses. Normally he doesn't drive like that . . . so fast and reckless.

"And it wasn't long after he went by that a police car heading south stopped us and said he was looking for Jimmy Roszko. He asked if we had we seen him.

"We told him what we'd seen . . . and then another police car [Martin's and Schiemann's] came speeding up from the south and the officers in both cars had a talk with each other. Then they both drove away.

"We wondered what they wanted Jimmy for. But it was none of our business, so we finished our ride and unsaddled our horses. That was about it."

When the two police cars separated, Martin decided it was more important that he and Schiemann return to the bailiffs at the Quonset hut. The other Mountie, Cpl. Jeff Whipple, continued his search for Roszko.

When Jim Martin and Peter Schiemann got back to Roszko's place, they had a brief discussion with Perry, Hnatiw, and Julie Letal about what they should do next. All the while, the dogs kept charging around inside the fence, barking and baring their teeth.

Martin checked with Perry and determined he had a duly authorized court order that allowed them to enter Roszko's property and permitted them to seize the Ford pickup truck.

The bailiffs said that Roszko might have fled the scene in the Ford pickup they had come to seize, but they couldn't be positive whether it was the actual vehicle.

They all decided the right move was to enter the property and see if the Ford pickup truck was still there.

The bailiffs used a bolt cutter to the cut the lock on the gate, and the five of them, wary of the dogs, advanced cautiously towards Roszko's inner compound.

When the dogs approached angrily, Cpl. Martin and Cst. Schiemann used pepper spray to back them off. Eventually they turned tail and scurried into an old grain storage shed at the southwest corner of the Quonset. There was a fair-sized doghouse beside the shed and Julie Letal used her PC to push the doghouse in front of the door to the shed. This effectively blocked the shed door and ensured the dogs could not get out.

To determine that the Ford pickup wasn't still on Roszko's property, the bailiffs decided to take a look inside the Quonset. To their surprise, they found that the small entrance door to the building—the human door—wasn't locked. There was a padlock hanging in the clasp of the human door but it wasn't snapped shut.

So in they went: Perry first, followed by Hnatiw, then Letal, Martin, and Schiemann.

The first thing that hit them was the powerful, distinctive odour of marijuana, which, in its growing stage, gives a smell similar to a skunk's discharge.

"Right off the bat," says Cpl. Martin, "you could tell there was a grow operation inside the building."

It was difficult to walk about in the Quonset. The dirt floor was cluttered with all kinds of automotive parts—axles, engine parts, dashboards, fenders, frames, and a number of tools. There were also two partially dismantled pickup trucks, a quad recreation vehicle, parts of several motorcycles, and a big Wermac generator on wheels.

Julie Letal recognized the Wermac generator as a stolen article from a photo that Cst. Cindie Dennis had shown her from one of her property files. The generator was valued at $30,000.

In the back (southwest) corner of the Quonset, there were two wooden-framed structures covered with black plastic sheeting. Above these structures was a platform that ran almost the width of the building.

Schiemann and Letal worked their way through the debris on the floor and peered into one of the plywood structures through an open flap in the plastic.

"There's a grow op back here, Corporal," Peter called to Jim Martin.

Jim Martin went to the back of the building and had a look through the flap in the plastic sheeting. Inside he saw hundreds of marijuana plants in various stages of growth.

"That's for sure!" he responded. "That's for sure."

Because the marijuana plants and the dismantled vehicles obviously indicated the building was the scene of criminal activity, Cpl. Martin immediately ordered everyone out.

"C'mon everybody," Martin shouted, "let's get out of here. There's no point in looking around any further. We need a search warrant."

As everyone filed out of the building, Cpl. Jeff Whipple pulled his PC up beside the Quonset. Then Constables Clayton Seguin and Brock Myrol arrived in their cruiser.

Martin contacted the Whitecourt Detachment office and notified them of the situation at Roszko's property, including the fact that Roszko had fled the scene in his white Ford pickup. He wanted all the detachments in the area to be on the lookout for him and arrest him on sight.

Throughout the afternoon, police cruisers patrolled the area near Roszko's farm, looking for him. Later in the day, a man who lived north of Roszko alerted the police that he'd seen James Roszko driving on a road near his farm. A cruiser was dispatched to look for him but was unable to locate him.

Subsequently, a province-wide dispatch called a "BOLO" (an acronym for Be on the Lookout For) was issued to locate and arrest James Michael Roszko. The bulletin was sent to every serving RCMP member from Wetaskiwin, south of Edmonton, to the borders of British Columbia, Saskatchewan, and the Northwest Territories.

Meanwhile, back at Roszko's farm, Jim Martin and Peter Schiemann prepared to leave the scene to return to the detachment office in order to prepare an application for a search warrant on Roszko's property.

In their absence, Martin ordered Julie Letal and Cst. Trevor Josok, a member of the Whitecourt Detachment, to stay on the property and secure the scene. Josok had arrived while the others were going through the Quonset.

Martin and Schiemann got back to the detachment office by four-fifteen p.m. and began the meticulous process of completing the search warrant application. In doing so, they had to be very careful to accurately specify the evidence they sought to retrieve from Roszko's Quonset hut and from his trailer.

When they were both satisfied that they had correctly met all the specifics for the search, Martin faxed the application to a Justice of the Peace in Edmonton.

While waiting for a reply, Martin and Schiemann started making phone calls to get resources lined up for the mammoth search operation that lay ahead. First of all, they needed an ample crew of members to search and secure the Quonset hut. This would require some assistance from the Whitecourt Detachment.

At 5:00 p.m., Martin put in a call to the Auto Theft Section at Edmonton Headquarters. Constable Steve Vigor, one of their specialists, took the call and listened as Martin outlined the situation at Roszko's farm.

When Martin had finished his summary, Vigor asked, "Do you need ERT?"

He was referring to Edmonton Headquarters' twelve-member Emergency Response Team, a specially trained and heavily armed assault unit that in some U.S. jurisdictions is called a SWAT team.

Martin replied, "No. The place is fully covered."

"Okay, then."

"When do you think you guys will be out here?"

"Well . . . considering the length of time it will take you to get the search warrant approved . . . and the limited lighting in the Quonset hut, I don't think there's much sense in us coming out right away."

"I think you're right."

"Okay, then. We'll be out first thing tomorrow morning," Vigor advised.

That was fine with Martin.

Shortly after that, Cst. Schiemann returned to the Roszko property with Cst. Brock Myrol, a recent graduate of the RCMP Training Academy in Regina. When they arrived, Cst. Josok departed.

Around six-thirty p.m., the two bailiffs returned to Edmonton, but before they departed, they placed a "Notice of Seizure" between the outside and inside doors of Roszko's mobile home.

By 7:55 p.m., the Edmonton Justice of the Peace had completed his review of the search warrant application and signed off on it, giving Martin authority to search and seize evidence from Roszko's Quonset hut and from the trailer in which he lived.

Martin then assembled a search team that included Constables Peter Schiemann, Julie Letal, Brock Myrol, Al Starman, and Joe Sangster — all from the Mayerthorpe Detachment.

Wednesday, March 2, was Brock Myrol's day off. However, when he heard about the marijuana operation and the chop shop activity that had been discovered on James Roszko's farm, he was eager to go out there and assist with the investigation. And, as it turned out, Cpl. Martin needed help checking out the property and the buildings.

Brock and his fiancée, Anjila Steeves, who were both new to Mayerthorpe, lived in a rented house in the town. As he prepared to leave for Roszko's place at 6:00 p.m., Anjila asked him, "Do you have your vest on?"

"Yes," he replied.

"Do you have it on right?"

"Yes. Why?"

"Because I don't want you to get shot."

Brock smiled. Then he was out the door and on his way to the detachment office.

By the time the entire search team arrived at Roszko's property, it was about eight-forty p.m. As soon as they got there, they began to scour the property for evidence and to record a list of the stolen items that would be used against Roszko in court.

One of the significant finds they located early in their search was a small stash of ammunition.

Around nine o'clock, Cst. Cindie Dennis of the Mayerthorpe Detachment brought out some pizza for the search crew. As she was rounding the corner onto Range Road 75, one of the pizza boxes slipped off the seat and dumped a pie face down on the floor of her vehicle. She pulled over and scooped up the topping and tried to put everything back in place.

"I did the best I could to make it look nice and normal.

"When I arrived at Roszko's Quonset, everyone was really hungry and wanted to get at the pizza right away. They didn't suspect anything was wrong, but I felt I had to tell them what had happened."

When Brock Myrol heard about her little misadventure, he hesitated briefly but then he said, "Looks all right to me." Then he grabbed a slice and dug in.

Cindie says, "They all must have been starving, because nobody gave it a second thought . . . they just started eating . . . and me, too."

Cindie recalls they put the pizzas on the hood of one of the police cars and stood around eating by the light from the Quonset hut.

"That's a lasting memory from that night . . . all of us huddled together eating pizza . . . nobody saying very much . . . just enjoying the pizza."

After their little break, everyone went back to work. And Cindie joined the search crew.

It soon became evident that the marijuana grow operation was larger than Cpl. Martin had originally thought. Consequently, shortly after nine-thirty p.m., he phoned Cpl. Lorne Adamitz of the Edmonton RCMP "Green Team," a specialized unit responsible for investigating large-scale drug operations, and advised him of the situation at Roszko's farm. Adamitz agreed to put together a unit immediately and said they would be on their way out there as soon as possible.

Then Martin called Tom Eichhorn, the owner of Uptown Auto Services in Mayerthorpe, to make arrangements to have some of the stolen property in Roszko's Quonset towed away and impounded as evidence.

Eichhorn, in turn, contacted two of his mechanics, Bruce Pearce and Kenny Poeter, and told them they were going to help the RCMP recover some stolen property. When Poeter found out their destination was Roszko's place, he says he was "a little worried," but he was curious, too. Pearce said the police gave them no indication that the assignment was any more dangerous than any other repossession, although Eichhorn did say that Roszko had fled the scene.

"I guess I felt safe, but I was nervous," Pearce says. "Nobody knew where he was. He could have been anywhere. We just basically wanted to get loaded and get out."

The mechanics describe the Quonset as having a cluttered, untidy interior with a sandy floor and unadorned walls.

As soon as they got there, they started removing some of the larger pieces of stolen goods. These included the Wermac generator, a 1997 motorcycle, two 1998 Honda motorcycles, a red 2003 GMC truck, a grey 2002 Ford F350 truck, a 1990 John Deere garden tractor, and a number of automotive parts.

As Martin and his crew kept searching and recording, Sgt. Brian Pinder, the NCO in command of the Mayerthorpe Detachment, arrived with coffee for everyone. Although Brian was on holiday leave, he had not gone away from the area. Upon learning of the situation at Roszko's farm, he placed himself back on duty and came out to the farm to check things out for himself. Martin gave him a thorough briefing on the progress of the investigation.

Brock Myrol was assigned to guard Roszko's trailer. When he looked inside he could see that the place was a mess. It was dirty and dishevelled and reeked of the smell of marijuana. During the search of the trailer, investigators found lists of all the RCMP members in the Mayerthorpe, Evansburg, and Whitecourt detachments, including their addresses and phone numbers plus the call sign and cell-phone numbers of their police cars.

They also found notes Roszko had made on every encounter he'd had with various police members.

Other items they discovered on the property included:

- Police scanners
- Wallets with various sets of identification, one containing $1,585 in cash
- Several sets of handcuffs and leg irons
- Seven long arms, i.e., rifles and shotguns

It was after midnight when Cpl. Adamitz and his "Green Team" arrived from the city. With him were RCMP Constables Al Gulash and Ray Savage, plus another member of the Edmonton City Green Team unit. It took them over two hours to dismantle the grow operation, and in the process they seized 280 marijuana plants, along with various items of grow paraphernalia. These included carefully recorded harvesting books and other documents pertaining to the science and care of growing marijuana.

By three a.m., the search was complete, except for the removal of the John Deere garden tractor, some automotive parts, chopped-up truck frames, and a truck shell that was outside the west end of the Quonset.

All of the police who searched Roszko's property that day were well aware that he had been in trouble with the law before. More often than not he had managed to wriggle his way out of being convicted.

This time, he was in very serious trouble and none of them were surprised.

2 | Roszko

JAMES ROSZKO WAS a violent, angry, emotionally unstable loner who had a widespread reputation for being an abusive bully and a sexual predator and pervert. He was also a man who hated the police and loved guns and knew how to use them.

These qualities of being violent, angry, unstable, a loner, and having a facility with a gun constitute the classic profile of a police killer.

RCMP files document case after case of instances where these types of men have murdered police officers.

In 1932, Albert Johnson, a reclusive trapper, who was a deadly shot with a rifle, was notorious for stealing gold from dead men's teeth. As the so-called Mad Trapper of Rat River, Johnson murdered thirty-one-year-old Cst. Edgar Millen during a chase-and-pursuit gunfight in the Northwest Territories.

In 1962, George Booth, thirty-two, a "mentally unbalanced" loner who reportedly could shoot the eye out of an eagle at sixty yards, murdered three young Mounties in a prolonged gun battle at Kamloops, British Columbia.

James Roszko.
(*Mayerthorpe Freelancer*)

In 1970, Wilfred Stanley Robertson, an odd little woodsman with a bad temper and deadeye aim, shot and killed two Mounties who had been called to a domestic dispute at his isolated shack in the Saskatchewan bush. He killed one Mountie at point-blank range. He shot the other, who was a long way off, through the glass pane of a window in his kitchen. As both men lay dying on his premises, Robertson sat down and finished eating his supper.

In 1978, a distraught loner named Leslie Crombie, who lived in a mobile home in rural New Brunswick, was being interviewed by two Mounties regarding a custody dispute over his young daughter. In the middle of the interview, Crombie excused himself, went into his bedroom, got his rifle, and came out shooting. He killed both policemen before they had a chance to draw their guns.

Dog master Michael Buday was shot and killed in 1985 at Teslin Lake, British Columbia, by Michael Oros, a psychotic loner who was a trapper and hunter.

In 2004, Jim Galloway, another RCMP dog master, was murdered in Spruce Grove, Alberta, by Martin Ostopovich, a desperately unstable man who was in possession of a number of high-powered rifles. Although Ostopovich was living with his wife, he was alienated from almost everyone.

These are just a few examples of murderers who have killed police suddenly and without provocation. All of them were loners, emotionally unstable, angry, and good with guns.

This same combination of characteristics fit James Roszko to a tee.

Roszko was born in 1959, the youngest of Bill and Stephanie Roszko's eight children. He was baptized as a Ukrainian Catholic at St. John the Baptist Parish near Rochfort Bridge and grew up attending church with his parents.

But when James was twelve years old, his mother left the family, and Bill, who is now deceased, had to raise the children on his own.

That seemed to be a pivotal point in his life. His father said, "James seemed to turn against religion then. That's when I began to see warning signs in his behaviour.

"I used to tell Jim to get ready [for church], but he fired back at me that I didn't need to preach to him because I was no preacher. I felt like I was between the devil and the deep blue sea. I used to pray that God would protect my youngest son, because when

James Roszko at his sister's home in Whitecourt, Alberta. (CBC)

I tried to reach out to him, he pushed me away."

Their relationship really soured when James was sixteen and Bill found a stolen gun in his room. And it deteriorated even further when Bill discovered James was using marijuana.

James's violent temper clearly came to the surface when, at seventeen, he learned that his mother had been badly beaten by an estranged male partner.

"Jimmy wanted to kill him," Bill said. "He went and took his mother to the hospital. I think this pushed him over the edge."

James's sister Josephine Ruel felt sorry for her brother. She said he went through a lot. "It started very young. We tried to let him know we'd help him. But he couldn't overcome it. I knew he was the one kid who needed more love than anyone else."

But Jimmy Roszko was hard for people to love.

Although he was only five feet five inches tall and 150 pounds, even as a teenager he was a snarling, snapping, foul-mouthed ball of anger who seemed to enjoy confrontation. Anyone who crossed him received a curse-laden tongue-lashing. And as he grew older, he began to bully younger people and threaten them.

As Mayerthorpe's number one problem child, he became a pariah in the community. Local people dubbed him a "ticking time bomb" and a "nut case."

As James grew older and got in more and more trouble with the law, most of his brothers and sisters stayed away from him. Some wanted nothing to do with him.

His family, his friends, even his lawyer say he hated the RCMP and blamed them for everything wrong with his life.

Roszko's Quonset hut as seen from his gate on Range Road 75.

Kim Connell, who is now retired from the RCMP, spent ten years of his police service posted at Mayerthorpe. He says, "Every time you met him, it was a violent confrontation. Even during routine traffic checks. A member would stop him and the argument would be on . . . the screaming and yelling and spitting."

In 1999, Brenda Storm, a bailiff, put on her body armour when she was sent to seize cattle on Roszko's farm. In her report she wrote: "Called a number of informants including the RCMP about this debtor. Learned he was quite dangerous . . . possibly in possession of a number of firearms. Has a long history of assaults . . . is known to have booby-trapped and used a spike belt to discourage vehicles."

After Brenda met him, she wrote: "One of the worst psychopaths it has ever been my misfortune to run into. His hatred for police was evident. He blamed all of his problems on the RCMP."

Roszko used to go into the local newspaper office of the *Mayerthorpe Freelancer* on a regular basis to complain about the police. He wrote letters to the editor complaining about the police's harassing him. He claimed the police were following him and he wanted them to leave him alone. But the paper never published any of his paranoia.

They did print one of his letters where he complained about the local veterinarian's being stopped for speeding when he was hurrying to save a dying calf.

But the woman who owned the sick calf sent in her own letter of reply saying that Roszko's description of the situation was inaccurate. Furthermore, she didn't need James Roszko speaking for her in the newspaper.

He would also try to put ads in the *Freelancer* saying terrible things about his enemies. Margaret Thibault, the newspaper's editor, says, "I guess he figured if I buy an advertisement, I can put whatever I want in it.

"I told him we had standards we followed and we would not accept libellous ads."

Margaret, like others in the community, found Roszko to be kind of a Jekyll and Hyde. He could be charming and reasonable for a while until he realized he wasn't going to get his way. Then he could turn into a monster. When he got mad he would vibrate and shake with anger.

One time he got very angry with Lorraine Dwyer, the *Freelancer* receptionist, who refused to publish one of the Christmas ads he had composed. It read: "Don't drink and drive, you might spill some."

When Lorraine turned him down, he began shouting and banging the glass top on the office counter.

Margaret came out of her office and said, "Stop that!"

James demanded to know what was wrong with his ad. Margaret explained, "Our paper doesn't condone drinking and driving. And we're not going to print it." Then she added, "And I don't want you behaving like that in here."

James seemed to cool down then and said, "I'm sorry. I'm just upset"

Although he'd stopped his ranting, Margaret says, "He still had that devil dancing in his eyes . . . like he was smouldering . . . ready to burst into flames."

But Margaret knew the secret to handling James Roszko. People had to stand up to him and show him they weren't afraid.

Margaret says, "There were grave concerns in the community about him hurting other people. He clearly had that capability. But that was a reputation he sought . . . and built up. He wanted to make people believe he was dangerous.

"I wasn't afraid of him. Apparently there was a list of places the police told him to stay away from. And the *Freelancer* was one of those places. I didn't think we needed to be on that list."

And there was a slyness about James Roszko. Especially when he wanted to induce local young men to come out to his farm. First of all he would choose the ones he thought he could manipulate and then he would ingratiate himself with them.

Once he became familiar with the person, he would invite him to come out and work on his farm for pay. When they got out there, he would make sure they had a pleasure-filled week by feeding them alcohol and drugs. Then he would engage them in acts of homosexuality. He used the automatic timer on his camera to take pictures of them performing drunken sex acts.

After that, he had them under his control.

He would tell them, "If you don't do what I want, I'll show people the pictures and tell them what you were doing out here."

Or he'd threaten them by showing them his guns and saying, "You talk to anyone and I'll take care of you."

It was all very clever. The only witnesses to what went on in his trailer were the ones participating in the action.

Seldom did anyone complain to the police, because most of these boys—and there were at least thirty of them over the years—were deathly afraid he would carry through on his threats.

The few who did lay charges would not show up in court to testify, because Roszko would contact them and threaten to kill them.

Margaret Thibault says, "That's how it went time after time. We saw charges laid; then saw the charges dropped."

On one occasion, Roszko dropped a boy off at the high school who was high as a kite on dope. The police happened to be right there and saw him stagger out of the car. They investigated and laid charges, but the young boy refused to take the stand as a witness against him.

James Roszko had become Mayerthorpe's worst nightmare.

And everyone in town knew it. Andria Gogan, the paramedic supervisor with Associated Ambulance says, "They kept putting him in jail and then he'd get out."

And it was common knowledge he kept guns at his farm. In spite of a court-imposed ban on Roszko's possessing firearms, the young people he invited to his farm knew he kept several weapons on his property. He would show them off to the boys and practise shooting in front of them, sometimes on targets 200 metres away. And they all could see he was a crack shot.

Between 1993 and 1998, the RCMP went to Roszko's farm three times with search warrants looking for illegal, unregistered weapons. They especially wanted to find the Heckler and Koch semi-automatic assault rifle that it was reported he had bought in the United States and smuggled into Canada twenty-five years before. But the Mounties were unsuccessful in their searches.

Retired RCMP Sergeant Cliff Wade says, "We didn't find the one we were looking for."

Another nagging concern for the police and the concerned citizens in the community was, how did Roszko support himself?

At one time, years ago, he had been employed. His most lucrative jobs were in the 1970s when he worked as a driller in the U.S. oilfields. After that, he ran a few head of cattle on his mother's farm. But in the last few years he seemed to survive with few resources, living alone with no livestock on the property on Range Road 75.

Rumours circulated about his Quonset hut and what he kept in it, but there was never any proof that something illegal was transpiring there.

An anonymous Mayerthorpe resident who doesn't want to be identified for fear that Roszko's allies might target him says that he worked on Roszko's property and knew him for twenty years. He believes that after Roszko was released from prison in August 2002 after serving time for sexual assault, he began working with a "small crew of career criminals" from the Mayerthorpe area.

Was it this group that was involved in the marijuana grow and the chop shop activity in his Quonset hut? Or was Roszko running this operation by himself?

With so many young men under his control, it's certainly possible that he was operating like Fagan,[1] sending the boys out to steal cars and trucks and anything else of value they could get their hands on.

---

1   From Charles Dickens's *Oliver Twist*; Fagan had a group of young boys who supported him through picking pockets and stealing.

Then again, Roszko was crafty enough to do a lot of illegal things on his own, without witnesses.

In one instance, he supposedly bought a new truck with very little money down but with high monthly payments. Roszko stripped the truck bare in his Quonset and sold the parts. Then he hid the demolished frame in the bush and made an insurance claim for his stolen truck.

As one Mayerthorpe resident remarked, "Oh, he had brains, all right. Except all his energy went in the wrong direction. He had extreme mental problems. He thought he was the centre of the world. And there was no connection between his head and his heart. He had no feelings for anyone except maybe his mother."

The best insight into James Roszko's troubled personality can be gleaned from his documented criminal history in the courts.

In total, Roszko was convicted on fourteen of the forty-four charges he faced during sixteen criminal prosecutions. Often several charges came from one particular set of circumstances. For instance, eighteen charges came from three prosecutions alone.

Many of the charges against him were either stayed or acquitted. That's because there were instances when the prosecutors lacked the evidence to proceed, or uncooperative and/or unreliable witnesses compromised the prosecutions.

Roszko's criminal history began on February 18, 1976, when he was seventeen years of age. That's when he was charged with two counts of break and enter, for which he was fined $150 on each count and placed on one year of probation.

In November of that same year, he was charged with one count of theft under $200 and fined $250.

On January 24, 1978, he received a suspended sentence and a probation order of eighteen months for one count of possession of stolen property and one count of break and enter.

In April 1979, he was charged with one count of making harassing telephone calls plus three counts of breach of his probation. Roszko was convicted and sentenced to thirty days in jail for the phone calls plus fifteen days for breach of probation to be served consecutively.

In December 1990, as a result of an argument with a school trustee over changes of a school bus stop, Roszko was convicted on one count of uttering threats to cause death or serious bodily harm and fined $250. At this time he was thirty-one years of age.

In March 1993, he pled guilty to two traffic tickets: driving without his seat belt engaged and having tinted windows on his truck, for which he was fined $25 on each count. That same day he was charged with causing a disturbance by using obscene language with the RCMP officer who gave him the tickets.

On June 17, 1993, Roszko, in turn, initiated a civil suit against Her Majesty the Queen and this same RCMP officer for "abuse of public office, false imprisonment, detention, and malicious prosecution." Roszko's lawsuit was dismissed on May 16, 2000, because he did not take the required legal steps to pursue the civil action.

On September 28, 1993, he was charged with one count of assault that was stayed when witnesses were mistakenly issued subpoenas for the wrong court date. The clerical error was only discovered when witnesses did not attend the court as expected.

In September 1993, he was charged with one count of impersonating an officer when he identified himself as an RCMP officer while attempting to trace a phone call. Roszko was acquitted because an essential witness in the case failed to attend the proceedings.

On December 1, 1993, James was charged with eight counts for a series of crimes allegedly committed between May 24, 1993, and December 1, 1993. These charges were based on a complaint by "Bradley," a pseudonym used to protect the identity of the complainant. The convoluted series of events pertaining to these charges is a good illustration of Roszko's bizarre homosexual relationship with a local boy.

Bradley, who worked on Roszko's farm, went on trip to the United States with him. They crossed the border illegally and drove to Utah, where Roszko purchased a Beretta 9mm handgun.

During the return trip to Canada, Roszko repeatedly asked to see Bradley's penis. When Bradley refused, Roszko pulled out the Beretta, loaded it, cocked the gun, and pointed it at Bradley's head. This assault continued for several miles until Roszko was pulled over for speeding. At that time, Bradley made no complaint to the highway policeman.

In early July 1993, Bradley claimed Roszko went to his home and pulled the gun on him again. At that time, Bradley testified that Roszko allegedly held him down on a bed and told him "he had a job to do," which was interpreted by Bradley to mean that Roszko was going to kill him. Then a friend of Bradley's came in and interrupted the assault. Bradley waited until his friend left then got a knife from the kitchen and stabbed Roszko in the jaw. Then Bradley took Roszko to the hospital

In October 1993, while Bradley was helping James put a replacement bumper on Roszko's truck, he reported that James offered him $10,000 to kill Roszko's enemy, a guy named "Conrad." Roszko made this offer twice. For this murder, James suggested Bradley use Roszko's rifle and he would supply Bradley with an alibi. Bradley refused these offers.

On December 1, 1993 during a chance meeting between the two men at Whitecourt, Roszko persisted in trying to speak to Bradley, who did not want to talk to him. However, after lengthy persuasion, Bradley agreed to come out to Roszko's farm to inspect one of James's vehicles. When Bradley arrived at the farm, Roszko told him he needed to drive out into the fields to check on his cattle. But he returned brandishing a shotgun and produced a set of handcuffs that he told Bradley to put on. When Roszko loaded the shotgun and began working the action it frightened Bradley and he complied with Roszko's demands.

Then a conversation ensued where James made it clear he was angry with Bradley because he had been avoiding him for the past month. James wanted to know what Bradley had been telling people about their relationship. When Bradley denied saying anything to anybody, Roszko hit him in the face. After a long and heated argument, Roszko released Bradley from the cuffs so they could have a fair fight.

When the fight was over, Roszko took Bradley to his house and said he still didn't trust him. James said he "needed something" to keep him from talking. So Roszko decided to use a camera timer and take pictures of the two of them engaged in a sex act, which he could use to prevent Bradley from talking. Bradley then performed oral sex on Roszko. However, Bradley was prepared to testify that he had agreed to the oral sex and the pornographic photos.

The trial commenced on June 3 in Queen's Bench at Edmonton before a judge and jury. But, as the Crown had anticipated, Bradley did not attend court to testify.

One week before the trial, Bradley fled to British Columbia. The Crown had a witness warrant issued and Bradley was arrested and brought back to Edmonton. Bradley tried to convince the Crown that the information he had provided to the police was all a misunderstanding.

Bradley was released from the Edmonton Remand Centre and scheduled to testify the next day. But as expected, he fled the scene again. Consequently, a mistrial was declared and a warrant was issued for Bradley's arrest.

While that case illustrates the frustration the Crown experienced in attempting to prosecute Roszko, the following matter demonstrates the serpentine procedures Roszko would follow to avoid paying a minor speeding ticket.

The trial for Roszko's speeding ticket commenced on March 11, 1994. After requesting numerous adjournments, Roszko was forced to come to trial on November 24, 1994. Although he applied for yet another adjournment, he was denied. When he was convicted at trial, he appealed. A new trial was granted on the basis that the judge erred in not granting Roszko's recent adjournment request.

The retrial for the speeding ticket took place on October 10, 1996, at which time James was found guilty. He appealed that verdict but was unsuccessful and had to pay the fine.

But he had kept the matter before the courts for nineteen months before this relatively minor issue was resolved.

In March 1994, he was charged with one count of breaching a condition of recognizance, for which he was acquitted, and two counts of obstructing justice, which were discharged.

Up to this date, by using one stratagem or another, Roszko had gotten off lightly for his crimes.

But on March 29, 1994, he was about to meet his Waterloo.

On that date, a trial commenced wherein he was charged with one count of sexual assault and one count of sexual touching.

Evidence presented during the trial revealed that from January 1983 until December 1989, Roszko had sexually assaulted

"Edward" on multiple occasions. These assaults began when the victim was eleven years old and James Roszko was thirty.

The assaults included Roszko having Edward fondle James's penis as well as Roszko masturbating the victim. These acts took place approximately once a week and progressed in intensity until Roszko began performing fellatio on the victim. On one occasion the accused attempted anal intercourse with the victim but failed because Edward resisted.

The victim did not report these sexual assaults to the police until March 26, 1994, when he was twenty-two years old.

The trial commenced on Sept. 28, 1995, and resulted in James being convicted and sentenced to five years in the penitentiary.

But Roszko successfully appealed that trial and a new trial began on April 12, 2000, where he was found guilty again, but received a lesser sentence of two and a half years in prison. He then appealed that conviction but his appeal was dismissed.

Although his nominal two-and-a-half-year sentence did not seem to fit his horrible crimes, at least Roszko's sexual deviance had finally been exposed. And the community had the satisfaction of knowing he would be kept off the streets for a couple of years.

However, even during the years that these trials were taking place, Roszko continued to commit other crimes. On January 1, 1995, he was charged with assaulting Edward with pepper spray, possession of a prohibited weapon (the pepper spray), causing a disturbance, and one count of breach of recognizance. This all came about at a New Year's Eve party while Roszko was out on appeal for his sexual assault charges. James went looking for Edward, found him in a bar, and sprayed him in the face.

This charge resulted in a stay of proceedings because Edward told the police he would not attend court and testify against the accused.

In April 1999, Roszko was charged for applying for a second social insurance number. He was acquitted on the grounds that the Crown did not prove James was the actual person who had signed the illicit application.

In September 1999, while Roszko was awaiting his second trial for the sex crimes, he was charged with aggravated assault on "Gregory," plus assault with a weapon on Gregory, and assault with a weapon on "Harold," and pointing a firearm at Gregory and Harold.

In this matter, these two boys had gone to Roszko's farm to vandalize his property. Roszko was awakened by his dogs' barking and by an alarm sounding on his Quonset hut. He grabbed a 12-gauge shotgun and went out and caught Harold near his barn. He tied Harold's hands together and forced him to call out to Gregory to surrender.

After Gregory gave himself up, Roszko threatened them with his shotgun and made them walk towards his house. On the way, he fired a warning shot in the air to frighten them and make them obey his orders.

A second shot superficially hit Gregory on his face and his left arm. As a result of the injury, James offered to drive Gregory to the hospital. But when they all got into Roszko's truck, it soon became evident that James wasn't heading for the hospital. He was driving farther onto his own property.

Alarmed by this, the two boys overpowered James and took his shotgun away. Then they gave Roszko a beating, threw him out of his truck, retrieved their own vehicle, and drove to the hospital.

The results of the preliminary inquiry into this matter ordered Roszko to stand trial.

But he was not convicted, because when the trial convened on Oct. 16, 2003, the Crown case was compromised by the fact that both Gregory and Harold had lied during the preliminary inquiry by testifying that they had gone on Roszko's property to steal gas. In truth they went there to vandalize his property and break some of his windows. Consequently, their entire testimony was tainted, and the Crown's case against Roszko was acquitted.

The last charge registered against Roszko was dated December 29, 2004. It involved the two counts of mischief that Cpl. Jim Martin had charged against him for using a spike belt to damage the tires of the meter reader and the census taker who ventured onto his property. Roszko was scheduled to appear in court to face these charges on April 28, 2005.

Some people in the Mayerthorpe area thought Roszko's long and varied criminal career should have qualified him to be classified as a dangerous offender. And in fact, at the time of his conviction for the sexual crimes, Alberta Justice flagged his file for consideration as a potential dangerous offender.

However, they concluded that proceeding with such an application against Roszko was not a possibility because his criminal history did not meet the Criminal Code of Canada criteria to support dangerous offender status.

While Roszko was in the penitentiary, a psychiatric profile stated that he refused to accept responsibility for his crimes and was preoccupied with legal proceedings. Furthermore, it revealed that he spurned all attempts at treatment. This made him serve two-thirds of his sentence rather than his being released earlier on parole. Even after his release, he was sent back for refusing to accept treatment and for failing to co-operate with his parole officer.

However, over and above Roszko's lengthy record of criminal charges and his many court appearances, there are even more damaging rumours about his unlawful behaviour. In distinct and separate cases, three young men from the Whitecourt–Barrhead area who went to the police about James Roszko ended up dead. In each of these cases, the police had reason to suspect that Roszko might have been criminally involved.

The most suspicious of the three cases involved a mixed-blood, bespectacled, teenager named Dale Mindus who lived in Whitecourt. After visiting Roszko's farm and working with him there, Dale had become an "acquaintance" of Jimmy Roszko's. However, several months later, when Dale attempted to sever his relationship with Jimmy, Roszko became very angry and began to stalk the young man.

Although Mindus moved in with his sister Tracy and her husband, Cash MacMillan, in Whitecourt, Roszko kept pestering him and threatening the MacMillans at their house.

Macmillan, at six feet two inches and 220 pounds, is a big, handsome, strong man who is built like a pro football linebacker. Over the years, he developed and maintained his great body shape by working on physically demanding jobs in the nearby oil fields.

In an interview on CBC's *Fifth Estate*, Cash MacMillan told the host, Linden MacIntyre: "He (Roszko) started appearing around our house, phoning the house. Somehow he had got our phone number. Dale was staying with us at the time.

"He started coming around quite often, just parking in front of the house and making it apparent . . . just letting us know he's here . . . 'I'm here' . . . 'I'm always here,' or whatever. He was trying to intimidate, I guess.

"And the only one he really intimidated was Dale . . . and especially my wife. My wife was pregnant and he came . . . he started coming around more often when I wasn't there. I was never there when he came.

"When Dale wasn't there, he came a few times, and then when Dale went to work . . . we were all gone . . . then he really started coming around and it was just Tracy there. So I don't know if he was looking for Dale or if he was watching Tracy. I'm not sure."

Later in the interview, MacMillan told Linden MacIntyre: "Well, I started to worry about my family, because I thought when I'm there, there's no problem. He's not going to get past me. But when I'm away, I don't know, I feared for my family. So that's when I involved the RCMP, hoping they would take over and stop this."

The Mounties responded. They came over and asked Cash to tell them precisely what Roszko was doing.

MacMillan told them Roszko was hanging around, parked either at the front of his house or in the back. The police told Cash that Roszko was parking on public property, and there was little they could do about it.

Cash told Linden MacIntyre: "So then . . . he showed up in my backyard . . . looking at my wife as she was washing the dishes. She looked out the window and he was right there."

Linden MacIntyre: "In the yard?"

Cash: "Yes . . . looking up into the kitchen window. So as soon as they made eye contact, he left, and she phoned me and she phoned the police. They would do nothing. They would have nothing to do with it."

Finally, in February 1998, Tracy called Cash in his shop at work and told him that Roszko was at the house again. It was around eleven-thirty a.m. She said she was vacuuming and looked out the window and he was out there. She said he was "freaking her out."

Cash left the shop immediately and headed home with Dale in Dale's truck. When they arrived at the house, Roszko spotted them and took off in his truck.

This time, Cash was determined to put an end to Roszko's nonsense. He'd had enough of his pestering his wife and Dale, so he chased after him—at a very high rate of speed.

As they roared through town, Roszko turned into an alley that runs behind some of the downtown restaurants. Cash stayed right with him and finally pushed his truck to the side and made him skid to a stop in front of a telephone pole.

Then Cash ran over, pulled Roszko out of his truck, and dealt with him—as Linden Macintyre says—in "the old-fashioned way." Cash pounded him into the ground.

Predictably, Jimmy Roszko went to the police and laid assault charges against MacMillan. Cash welcomed the charges because he felt that Roszko had been harassing his wife and his brother-in-law far too long. Furthermore, Cash believed he had been provoked into dealing with Roszko physically. And Dale Mindus, who was there and saw the physical confrontation, would testify as a witness against Roszko.

It appeared that all the parties involved looked forward to the case's going to court.

But prior to the trial, Dale Mindus received a phone call from Jimmy Roszko. Roszko asked him, "What are you going to say in court?"

"The truth. I'm going to tell the truth."

"You'll never live that long," Roszko replied and hung up.

Days later, Dale Mindus was found dead at the bottom of a stairwell in a basement apartment in Whitecourt. He had alcohol in his blood and died from a severe wound on his head. The cause of death was attributed to his falling down the stairs head first and smashing his head against a brick wall at the bottom of the staircase.

The case looked suspicious to the Crown and the police but no charges were laid against anyone in the case. The authorities conceded that Jimmy Roszko had both the motive and the means to commit such a crime, but, without proof, they could do nothing.

Linden MacIntyre, his producer, Scott Anderson, and a CBC crew went to the death scene and filmed it.

Linden says, "It looked very suspicious to me. There were only six stairs, they were carpeted, and there was no brick wall at the bottom of them. And there was very little blood spatter at the scene.

"The boy's injuries were not consistent with the recorded explanation of his death which indicated that his head was bashed in. I think Dale Mindus was battered with a blunt object at some other place, dragged to that apartment, and dumped at the bottom of those stairs."

But the authorities maintain that there is absolutely no proof of this.

To this day, Cash MacMillan, his wife, Tracy, and many other residents of the area are convinced that James Roszko had something to do with the murder of Dale Mindus.

Whether or not this is true, the Mindus case in 1998, above all others, makes it patently clear that James Roszko's capacity for violence, paranoia, and hatred of authority was immense.

By all accounts, he truly was a disaster waiting to happen.

3 | The Mounties

TWO RCMP DETACHMENTS — one from Mayerthorpe, the other from Whitecourt — are integrally involved in James Roszko's lethal assault on the police.

The Mayerthorpe Detachment of nine members was under the command of Sgt. Brian Pinder. He was originally from Saskatchewan and was the longest-serving member in the precinct. Sergeant Pinder had previously worked at the Whitecourt Detachment, as well as other postings throughout Alberta.

Corporal Jim Martin was second in command at Mayerthorpe, but a great deal of the Roszko incident involves him because Sgt. Pinder was on holiday leave when this tragedy first began. Martin had fifteen years' experience with the RCMP in Alberta. After graduating from Depot in 1990, he served at Spruce Grove, west of Edmonton. Then, in 2001, when he was promoted to corporal, he was assigned to Mayerthorpe.

And it wasn't long before he became the go-to guy at the detachment.

He says, "Mayerthorpe was my first command, and we had a lot of junior members looking for answers. Sometimes they'd come out to my place and we'd go over a file together sitting outside at a picnic table.

"I told them if they had a problem, they could call me at any hour. Sometimes when they had a tough call to make, they'd phone and ask me to come along, especially if it was a domestic at a troubled home. More than once, a member called at two or three in the morning and I'd tell them to come over and pick me up.

"On one of my two-week holidays I made the mistake of staying home and ended up working ten of my fourteen days off."

The members at Mayerthorpe learned to appreciate Jim Martin. He was their mentor, a terrific boss, and an effective leader who would never ask them to do anything that he wouldn't do himself.

By 2005, Jim Martin was the beating heart of the Mayerthorpe Detachment, as well as a vital part of the local community.

He and his wife, Melanie, and their eleven-year-old daughter, Haley, lived on a farm south of Mayerthorpe. The Martins used to throw detachment parties at their farm every summer or whenever a new member arrived or an experienced member was transferred out.

"The members would all pitch in and we'd buy a bunch of steaks and throw them on the barbecue. Everyone would bring a potluck dish, and after we ate, we'd play bocce ball or lawn darts. Then we'd sit around a bonfire and tell stories. It was a good way for the spouses to meet each other."

Jim was also a dynamic member of the Mayerthorpe community. He would either initiate activities or contribute his support to anything that would help integrate the Mounties with the local residents. His reputation around town was held in the highest regard.

Rev. Arnold Lotholz of Mayerthorpe's Pentecostal Assembly told the author, "Jim Martin is a really good guy. He's very outgoing and totally involved in our community."

The other person who was a primary witness to all phases of the Roszko tragedy is Margaret Thibault. Margaret was fifty-three years old when the Roszko incident began, and although she was not a police officer, she worked out of the detachment office as the Coordinator of Victims' Services. In this capacity she provided support for victims and witnesses of crime from the areas around Mayerthorpe and Whitecourt.

Margaret, her husband, Frank, and their children, Tony and Sheylan, had moved to Mayerthorpe in 1978. Frank was in management in the forest industry and Margaret took a job as a reporter with the *Mayerthorpe Freelancer*, a weekly newspaper with a circulation of 2,500 readers. She became the editor of the paper in 1987 and then moved to Victims' Services in 1994. Her varied career gave her intimate knowledge of the local residents and allowed her to become very involved in community activities.

The eleven years she worked out of the detachment office brought her into close contact with all the Mounties. Most of them thought of her as their den mother and went to see her for help and advice.

Members of the Mayerthorpe Detachment 2004 fundraiser. Back row, L to R: Sgt. Brian Pinder, Constables Al Starman, Clayton Seguin, Julie Letal, Peter Schiemann, Leo Johnston. Front row, L to R: Cst. Joe Sangster, Connor Price, Cpl. Jim Martin

Peter Schiemann with his mother, Beth, Christmas 2001.

In March 2005, the Mayerthorpe Detachment was comprised of the following members: Pinder, Martin, and in descending order of seniority, Constables Joe Sangster, Al Starman, Clayton Seguin, Leo Johnston, Julie Letal, Cindie Dennis, and Brock Myrol.

Corporal Jeff Whipple had an office in the Mayerthorpe building, but was not part of that detachment. He was in charge of Traffic Services (highway patrol) for a long stretch of Highway #43 and a section of Highway #32 that ran from Swan Hills almost to Edson. Whipple, forty-five, was born and raised in Saint John, New Brunswick, and had served twenty-three years as a Mountie in various locations throughout Alberta.

Peter Schiemann arrived at Mayerthorpe in November 2000. He was originally assigned to general duties, but in the fall of 2004 was transferred to Traffic Services under Cpl. Whipple. Peter was from Stony Plain near Edmonton and soon became one of the most popular members in Mayerthorpe. The son of Don Schiemann, a Lutheran minister, Peter was a graduate of Concordia College in Edmonton, where he pursued many interests. He played the violin, sang in the school choir, was a proficient scuba diver, and had even given skydiving a try.

In college, Peter had been a decent student, but when he went to the RCMP Training Academy (Depot) in Regina, he loved it so much he excelled—in both the classroom and in all other phases of his training. Peter was particularly good on the firing range, where he earned his marksmanship badges for pistol and rifle shooting. He relished his assignment to Mayerthorpe because it was less than an hour from his home in Stony Plain. So it was an easy drive for him to stop in and see his mom and dad and have dinner with them and his brother, Michael, and younger sister, Julia.

Schiemann's boss, Jeff Whipple, says, "Peter was a very motivated individual who had definitely found his calling in the Force. He was a lot of fun to be with and had a tremendous work ethic. He had a great future ahead of him and I had no doubt that someday I would be working for him."

Whipple remembers that Peter was extremely close with Cst. Armand Liborion, who had been with Traffic Services, but was recently seconded to provide computer training on a new information system that was being introduced all across the province.

Armand was like a father figure to everyone in the Mayerthorpe Detachment, but he was particularly close with Peter, who spoke to him constantly to ask his advice and get his opinions.

Margaret Thibault really liked Peter. "He was a sweet and gentle person who was very dedicated to everything he did. He had a strong religious faith that he never foisted on anyone. He was helpful and loyal to his friends, but more than anything else, he was an excellent police officer."

Cindie Dennis was just twenty years old when she arrived at Mayerthorpe in July 2003 to become the junior member of the detachment. She and Peter quickly became best of friends.

"Peter was always sweet and kind to everyone. We had such a fun relationship. We went out for dinner a few times and on one occasion went to a bar in Edmonton. But it was generally better to go to a member's home. It was simpler . . . we knew who was on or off shift.

"We attended lots of detachment parties at Joe and Heather Sangster's place and out on Jim Martin's farm.

"Peter was a big part of my life."

Their closest friends in Mayerthorpe were Heather Dills and Troy Heystek. Heather was the steno at the detachment and Troy

Cindie and Peter wearing their
mountain-climbing gear,
August 2004.

Peter and Cindie after climbing
Thunder Mountain in southern
Alberta, August 2004.

was a paramedic with the ambulance service who was waiting to be accepted into the Mounties. When Heather and Troy were married in 2003, Peter was Troy's best man and Clayton Seguin was one of his groomsmen.

Cindie says, "I was new to town but was invited to their wedding and the reception that was held on a ranch south of town."

In August 2004, Cindie and Peter went on a three-week holiday to her grandparents' ranch near Lundbreck in southern Alberta. Cindie's mom, Shelly Ann, was an outfielder on a local softball team and invited Peter and Cindie to play a few games with the team in one of its tournaments.

Cindie and Peter went bike riding and scuba diving in the Old Man River with her dad, Val. At one time, Val had been an electrician but he joined the RCMP when he was fifty years old.

Then Peter, Cindie, and her mom and dad went on a motor trip through Logan Pass in the mountains on a scenic route known as "The Road to the Sun."

"We went down to Waterton, all through Montana, and partway into Glacial National Park . . . on a one-day circle drive in my dad's car."

Back at the ranch, they rode her grandparents' horses.

Cindie remembers, "At first, Peter was scared silly. He looked very uncomfortable on his big horse. But after a couple of hours, he really got good at it. He loved riding fast, and I couldn't get him to stop.

"As he was riding, he was picking Saskatoon berries . . . they're like blueberries . . . the bears eat them. Peter was picking them off the tall berry trees and eating them as he rode.

"On our way back to Mayerthorpe, we stopped and had a meal with Peter's parents, Don and Beth, and told them all about our trip. Julia Schiemann, my sister Bonnie, and Lincoln Nedjelski, a member from Meadow Lake, Saskatchewan, were there too."

Cindie says that she and Peter used to argue about all kinds of silly things.

"We teased each other a lot. One time he told me he could make better sweet and sour meatballs than I could. So we had a contest. His tasted pretty good. But I suspected something wasn't right. Then I saw a package in the garbage and realized they were from the M and M meat shop. I confronted him about that and he had to admit it.

"Peter used to tell me, 'If I can't find a wife, you're my backup.'"

"I told him, 'You can forget that, buddy.'"

Another of Peter's close friends was Andria Gogan, who was the paramedic supervisor with Mayerthorpe's Associated Ambulance Service. It covered the County of Lac Ste. Anne. Andria was in charge of two full-time ambulances, two paramedics, and five emergency technicians.

When Peter first came to Mayerthorpe, he rented a three-bedroom duplex in town and shared it with a Mountie named Chris Pittman, who was Andria's boyfriend. When Pittman was transferred to Montreal, Andria and Peter remained close friends.

Andria loved to cook and often had some of the Mounties and her emergency medical technicians over for dinner.

"It was all very informal. Peter was a single guy and I would call him up and say, 'C'mon over.' Jim Martin would come to my place too, when he didn't have time to get home to his ranch out of town.

"There were usually five or six at my place for Easter or Thanksgiving. We had turkey dinners at Christmas on several occasions. On one of Peter's birthdays I made him a cake and we had a little party.

"If I wasn't cooking, we'd order Chinese food from the restaurant 'on the hill' at Sangudo. And there were lots of breakfasts together at the Lariat Restaurant in town."

Andria says that the Mayerthorpe detachment was a very close, tight-knit group.

"They stuck together big time . . . and most of them were really nice.

"But Peter was really special. He was very religious. And he was very kind. But he was a Mountie 'through and through.' He could be very assertive when the situation called for it. I saw that on calls he made on the highway where I was involved."

In the summer of 2003, Andria, Chris Pittman, and Peter took a car trip to her mother's house in Vancouver and then went for a long drive down the coast of Oregon.

Peter loved to drive. His passion was cars. He kept a little notebook where he recorded the make and model of every car he ever owned. And he was very comfortable behind the wheel of his police cruiser, especially at high speeds.

Margaret Thibault says, "Peter was lovely with his family. I remember one day when he brought his grandmother Elizabeth to the detachment and showed her around. And there was a time in his third year when he took his father on a 'ride along' to demonstrate the type of work he did on one of his shifts."

Cindie Dennis claims, "Peter was going nowhere but up. He laid more drug charges than the whole detachment combined. It came easy to him. All of the charges he laid came from stopping cars on the highway. He had a nose for drugs . . . for picking out a vehicle and finding stuff."

The next Mountie to arrive at the Mayerthorpe Detachment after Peter Schiemann was Leo Johnston. Leo and his identical twin brother, Lee, were born in 1972 on a farm near Lac La Biche, Alberta. In 1992, when they were twenty, they both applied to join the Edmonton City Police.

Lee says, "We did just about everything together."

But their applications were denied and they were told to reapply when they were older.

Then they both started racing motorcycles. When they turned pro, they began to race for money prizes in Calgary, Phoenix, Minnesota, and the Canadian National Series in Ontario, Quebec, and Nova Scotia.

But Lee quit racing to become a Mountie and entered Depot in March 1997.

One week before Lee was due to graduate, Leo was involved in a serious racing accident in Calgary, where he sustained severe head injuries, a collapsed lung, and multiple broken bones. It took him three years to fully recover.

During that period, he began dating Kelly Barsness, a dental assistant from Sherwood Park. Kelly had been working as an auxiliary member of the RCMP. She, too, had been involved in a boating accident on Lake Okanagan, where she suffered a severe head injury that led to long-lasting memory loss.

Leo entered Depot in October 2000 and did well there, especially in the physical requirements, where his athletic ability gave him a decided edge. When he was assigned to Mayerthorpe, Kelly moved there to be with him. And the first person Leo met at the detachment was Peter Schiemann. When Peter discovered that Leo and Kelly didn't have a place to live, he invited them to stay with him. Leo accepted Peter's kind offer and he and Kelly stayed in Peter's duplex for the next five weeks. During this time, the three of them became very close friends. Then Peter bought a house and moved out. Soon after that, Leo and Kelly, too, bought a house.

As time went by, Leo and Kelly met other couples.

Kelly says, "Two of our closest friends in the detachment were Joe and Heather Sangster, who lived close by."

Joe Sangster was a Maritimer. He was a little younger than Leo, but he had a lot more police experience. He had served twelve years with the Brandon Police, two years in Calgary, and then joined the RCMP. Leo admired Joe's passion for police work and his willingness to tackle the hard issues.

Margaret Thibault says, "Joe was a firecracker . . . a go-getter who would take on any file with enthusiasm. He was very intent on cleaning up the streets and making them safe for people to use."

Depending on who was working what shift, Leo and Kelly spent a lot of time with the Sangsters, sharing dinners and barbecues or watching DVD movies.

And the friendship between Leo and Peter remained strong, too. The bond between them stemmed from the fact that they shared the same wholesome values and practised a common, sensible approach to police work.

All three of them—Leo, Peter, and Joe—loved being part of the Mayerthorpe community. They participated with other members from the detachment in a fundraiser that Jim Martin, Joe Sangster, and Margaret Thibault organized for a local boy named Connor Price who was suffering from the same type of cancer as Terry Fox.

For the fundraiser, all of the Mounties shaved their heads. And with the help of the media and the participation of Alberta Premier Ralph Klein, the detachment raised $20,000. This money helped the family with their expenses, particularly their travel costs for getting back and forth from their home in Sangudo to Connor's medical appointments in Edmonton.

Leo was a big man, weighing in at 200 pounds.

Margaret says, "Leo was a very strong guy and a very good policeman. But he loved to laugh and kid around. He told the corniest jokes. He would tell one and then say, 'Do you get it?' And we'd all say, 'Yes, we got it, but it's not funny. Get some better jokes, Leo.'

"He was like a big kid. He was forever saying 'Wow!' for the least reason or at the slightest little surprise.

"But he also said to me, 'Margaret, I don't know why anyone would complain about police work. This is the best job in the world. I love this job.'"

When Cindie Dennis arrived at Mayerthorpe, Leo was her trainer. For the first two months, they rode together in the same cruiser. For the next four months, she was on her own but remained under Leo's wing.

She says, "Kelly wouldn't go to bed until Leo came home. She stayed up if he was out somewhere or working on shift.

"Sometimes Kelly would bring him a double chocolate chip muffin as a special snack and he'd go over the top thanking her. His reaction was amazing.

"Other times we'd stop at his place for a glass of milk or a bowl of soup. That gave Kelly and I a chance to visit.

"I remember they had two big black dogs they treated like babies."

Kelly still has both dogs. "They're both Black Labs crossed with Chow. Belle belonged to Andria Gogan and she had to give her up when she moved. We got Hershey from a home outside of town."

Ex-mayor Albert Schalm was the Johnstons' next-door neighbour. He remembers the dogs when Leo was building them a house in the backyard. But mostly he recalls Leo. "He was very nice with my kids. They were impressed with his uniform but he was so natural and friendly with them. They loved talking to him. Kelly was friendly with our children, too. They really liked her.

"And Leo was just so honest. One time, he borrowed my power saw and damaged its carbide-tip blade. So he bought me another one. Leo's philosophy was if he broke something he had borrowed, it had to be returned in a better condition than when he took it."

Cindie Dennis says, "Leo was very smart, but he suffered a bit from loss of his long-term memory. Consequently, he made meticulous, intricate notes. Leo had more notebooks than any of us. We'd go on a call and he'd start writing. Then, when I thought we were finished, he'd still be writing. I'd say, 'Let's go, Leo.' But he wouldn't budge. He'd just keep making notes.

"It could be irritating, but it sure prepared me well, especially with my interview skills and for my police exams."

Cindie continues, "He was always so cheery. When he came in every morning, he would greet everybody he met and always used their names. He'd say, 'Good morning, Cindie . . . or Patty . . . or Julie.'

"And he had pet names for lots of people. He called Brian Pinder and Jim Martin 'Boss Man.' He'd come in and say, 'Good morning, Boss Man' . . . and they never seemed to mind."

Leo was particularly effective working with the Native young people on the Alexis First Nations Reserve. He seemed to have the magic touch of being able to talk to the kids on their own level.

Leo and Kelly Johnston on their wedding day, November 13, 2004.

Leo and Kelly were married on November 13, 2004 and planned to take their honeymoon the following summer.

Andria Gogan declares, "As a couple, those two were the best two people in the world. They were absolutely meant to be together . . . perfect for each other. I know it's corny, but they were like two peas in a pod."

Brock Myrol, twenty-nine, the newest member of the Mayerthorpe Detachment, arrived in town on February 11, 2005. He was born in Outlook, Saskatchewan, and raised in Red Deer, Alberta.

Brock took a circuitous route to becoming a Mountie. He had been a security guard at Zellers for ten years. During his off-hours, he attended Red Deer College, taking courses in biology and anthropology.

He also had become extremely accomplished in almost every form of martial art. His skills in jiu jitsu, mui tai kickboxing, grappling, wrestling, and karate were at a very high level. In 2002, he was awarded a black belt in shoot wrestling (mixed martial arts). The shelves in his room at home were lined with trophies he had won at a number of major martial arts championship tournaments.

Brock also did a lot of travelling. On various trips, he toured the U.S. and visited Fiji and Australia.

In 2001, he was accepted into the Edmonton City Police Force but severely damaged a cartilage in his knee doing martial arts, which prevented him from passing the Edmonton Police physical. A year

Brock Myrol and Anjila Steeves at the Edmonton Airport, the day after getting engaged, December 2004.

later, he began dating Anjila Steeves, a full-time arts student from Red Deer who was studying anthropology and had plans of becoming an artist. They very quickly fell in love and began living together.

Around this same time, Brock initiated his application process to join the RCMP. After a two-month sojourn as a certified field guide in South Africa's Kruger National Park, he returned to Red Deer and one year later was accepted into the RCMP. He began his training in Regina in August 2004.

Like Peter Schiemann and Leo Johnston before him, Brock was extremely successful at Depot. He was held in such high regard by his troop mates that they elected him valedictorian at their graduation ceremony.

Before he completed his training, he proposed marriage to Anjila, and they planned to be wed at the end of September 2005.

Anjie says, "We were so much in love. Brock would say to me, 'I can't wait for you to be my wife. I'm so ready for you to be my wife.'

"When he was at Depot, I kept some framed photos of him and some of his trophies in a special place. But when we moved to Mayerthorpe, I had to take them down. I told Brock, 'Well, I guess I can finally take down your shrine.'"

Immediately after Brock's graduation, he and Anjie rented a truck and hauled their furniture and other possessions to Mayerthorpe. They had previously made arrangements to rent a three-bedroom back-split on 47th Street across from Margaret and Frank Thibault. They moved in three days before Brock was slated to report for duty on Valentine's Day, 2005.

Clayton Seguin, who was assigned as Brock's trainer, was there to help them unload their stuff the day they arrived in town. Four other detachment members came by to welcome them to Mayerthorpe.

Anjie remembers, "Clayton Seguin came over and helped us. It was very nice of him . . . and all of them . . . to make us feel so welcome. Inside the house there were boxes and cartons all over the place. We didn't know where to begin."

What's more, on their first night in Mayerthorpe, Margaret Thibault had other plans for Brock and Anjila. For the past two years, she and Jim Martin had run a fundraiser for Victim's Services at the Diamond Centre, Mayerthorpe's community hall. Their idea was to have a special event to replace the defunct annual Firemen's Ball — one where the members and the town's residents could come together and relate in a positive way.

The theme of the evening was a fifties night known as "The Soda Shop," where people dressed in fifties attire and danced to the jive tunes of that era. All the local Mounties dressed in their red serge uniforms and turned out to serve sodas to the three hundred people who usually attended the affair.

Margaret went over to Brock's house and told him, "Never mind unloading your stuff. You're going to help us tonight. Put on your red serge and come out and meet everybody in town at the Diamond Centre."

When Anjila asked what she should wear, Margaret replied, "Just put on some blue jeans and a blouse. It's a fifties night. Everyone knows you just moved into town."

The evening proved to be an excellent way for Brock and Anjie to start their new life in Mayerthorpe. But it still took them some time to get settled in.

Anjie says, "We didn't have a lot of friends in Mayerthorpe because we just moved there. Margaret Thibault and her husband, Frank, were very nice to us. They were wonderful.

"Brock told me, 'If you ever need anything or someone to talk to, go across the street and see Margaret.'

"Brock and I did a lot of things together. He was my best friend.

"I remember one night I woke up in a panic. I was having a dream and I couldn't find him in the dream. But then I was relieved to hear him in the shower."

Cindie Dennis says, "Brock was so in love with Anjie. He was so proud of her. He talked to me a lot about how some people just go out and get married. He said, 'But I waited for the perfect person. The person I love.'"

Eventually, Brock got to know every member of the detachment. The two he seemed most comfortable with were Peter Schiemann and Leo Johnston. On a few occasions, Brock took them to the gym and gave them instruction on martial arts techniques.

Anjie recalls, "He really developed major bonds with Leo and Peter. They became very close friends."

When Brock went to work, Anjila never really worried about the danger he might face. She says, "He was phenomenal in every way . . . in his training, his physical conditioning, and in his dealing with people.

"He had so many life experiences and life skills. He had great intuition, great compassion for people. He was a communicator. He would never use force unless it was absolutely necessary. On top of that, he was a marksman. Why would I worry about Brock?"

In the short time that Brock was at Mayerthorpe, he became so deeply involved in his police work that Anjila rarely saw him. "He just had a passion to work. A lot of it was voluntary overtime where he was just really excited to go out there and do police work."

Brock spent most of his time on the job shadowing Clayton Seguin.

Anjie remembers, "Clayton was great with Brock . . . and with me, too. They spent a lot of time together in a cruiser . . . almost every day."

Clayton, at twenty-six, was three years younger than Brock and had been at Mayerthorpe for only three years.

Margaret Thibault says, "Clayton used to take a lot of kidding about his age. He was a good-hearted guy . . . very positive and friendly. He was very active in sports . . . coached hockey, worked with the kids in school, and was a chaperone and facilitator for Grade 8 students in a summer program called COOL camp. He and Jim Martin played on the local hockey team."

Like Jim Martin, Clayton was very active in the community. He and his wife, Amanda, really enjoyed living in Mayerthorpe. "Amanda and I were married in 2001. And before I graduated from Depot in September, 2002, they told me I was going to Mayerthorpe.

"I had no clue where it was and had to look it up on a map. Even then, it was hard to find. But in the end it turned out to be a blessing in disguise.

"For a joke, I told Amanda, 'We're going to Nova Scotia.'

"'Are you serious?'

"Yeah, I'm just kidding. We're going to Mayerthorpe.

"'Where is it?'

"North of Edmonton.

"'OK, let's do it.'"

Clayton continues, "In week eighteen of my twenty-two weeks of training, we went there for a visit.

"My first impression was, 'Oh my God, what have I got myself into?'

"It was small. There were a couple of paved roads, but most were gravel. It looked like a town that wasn't finished.

"But we grew to love it. I could not have asked for a better place. The people in the community are second to none. I have never felt more welcome anywhere in my life."

Kelly Johnston agrees with Clayton. "Everybody seemed to know us. I didn't know hardly anyone, but when I walked down the street everybody waved and said 'Hi.' It is just a beautiful place to live.

"At the same time, Mayerthorpe people would leave us alone. Leo and I were very private with our lives. Every minute that he wasn't at work, we liked to spend together . . . just the two of us. We treasured that. So we were really glad to be left alone."

Clayton and Amanda Seguin soon became an integral part of a very tight police family that lived in the same neighbourhood. They bought a house in town that backed on Peter Schiemann's place and was only a half block away from Leo and Kelly Johnston. Joe and Heather Sangster and their daughters, Laura and Megan, lived only few minutes away. Julie Letal, another Mayerthorpe member who had previously served with the Alexis First Nations Police, lived in a house that was about sixty kilometres out of town, but when it burned down, she came and stayed with the Seguins for four months.

The other Mountie who played a principal role in the Mayerthorpe catastrophe was Tony Gordon. At home he was always called Anthony, but at work he was Tony.

Tony was from the Whitecourt Detachment. At the time of the incident, Whitecourt was a town of 8,500 located about forty kilometres northwest of Mayerthorpe, on Highway #43 at the confluence of the MacLeod and Athabasca rivers.

Whitecourt was a thriving community with all the amenities of a big city. People from other rural communities came there to shop. It had a busy downtown area with a lot of small but flourishing businesses. It also had a twenty-five-bed hospital, three high schools, a Canadian Tire, a Walmart, a Boston Pizza, a Tim Hortons, and a movie theatre.

The average age of its residents was twenty-eight years; many of them were employed in the local lumber or pulp and paper industries or in the lucrative jobs in the oil fields to the north.

The detachment building at Whitecourt was built in 1991 to accommodate a staff of eleven members. It includes offices, change rooms, a workout area, and an eight-room cellblock.

The NCO commanding was Staff Sergeant Tom Pickard, who was assisted by the Operations NCO, Sgt. Blaine Rahier. Most of the Whitecourt members were young and many of them were single. These included Constables Jeff Feist, Charlotte Sorensen, Dale Bereza, Bobby Kuehn, Des Sandboe, Beth Hoskin, Trevor Josok, and Rolland White.

Other members serving at Whitecourt were Cpl. Chris Short and Constables Line Rolland, Jim Drolet, Daniel Bouwmeester, and Barry Baskerville. Baskerville was Tony Gordon's closest friend.

Des Sandboe, Trevor Josok, and Rolland White worked the traffic detail under Cpl. Whipple. When Peter Schiemann was transferred to traffic duties, he and Rollie White became very close. They would phone or text each other every day.

But it was Constable Anthony Gordon who, by fate, was thrust into the vortex of this tragedy.

At six feet four inches and 230 pounds, Anthony Gordon was the one of biggest Mounties in both the Whitecourt and Mayerthorpe detachments.

After graduating from high school, he tried a number of different jobs — cabinetmaking, driving a tow truck, and managing a Swiss Chalet restaurant. But none of these jobs were what he was looking for.

What he really wanted to do was become a Mountie. To give himself a reasonable chance of passing their qualifying tests, he enrolled at Red Deer College and took a course for a year, particularly to upgrade his facility with English.

In June 2000, he met Kim Gamracy, a registered nurse, and it wasn't long before they fell in love. But Anthony still wanted to become a Mountie. Kim says, "That was his goal from the moment I met him." And she encouraged him to pursue that dream.

In May 2002, Anthony entered Depot. And he absolutely blossomed there. His troop mates elected him "right marker," an honorary position of leadership with his thirty-two-man troop.

He took his responsibilities very seriously and earned high marks in all of his courses. His future with the Royal Canadian Mounted Police seemed very bright and promising.

Even under the pressure of his courses in Regina, he and Kim decided to get married while he was attending Depot. Anthony flew home to Red Deer for a weekend in August, and they were married. Then it was back to Depot to finish his training program.

After graduating in October, Anthony was assigned to Whitecourt. When Anthony, Kim, and their son, Spencer, arrived in town, they rented a two-bedroom apartment and settled in very nicely. Kim immediately got a job nursing at the Whitecourt Hospital. Not long after their arrival, they submitted the down payment to have a new house built.

As a rookie, Tony spent his first six months with his trainer, learning the ropes and getting a feel for the community. Because

Kim and Anthony Gordon at his graduation from Depot, October 15, 2002.

Whitecourt was a town where young workers made good money, there were lots of alcohol- and drug-related problems, B and E's, petty crimes, and bar fights.

Because of Tony's size and his trim physical condition, no one ever challenged him to a fight. And this suited Anthony very nicely because that was not the way he wanted to carry out his police work. Tony was known and liked for his gentleness, his honesty, and his integrity.

Although he didn't work at the same detachment as Peter Schiemann and Leo Johnston, he had met Peter and had played golf with Leo. And it is interesting how similar the three of them were in their personalities and character.

Off the job, he and Kim got to know the other members and their families at parties, barbecues, golf tournaments, ski weekends, and Detachment Christmas dinners. Tony and Kim often were the hosts for those Detachment dinners and other celebrations. Kim says, "I'd cook a big turkey for Christmas or Thanksgiving, and everyone would come over. The last big party at our house was in February 2005."

Anthony was a sports fanatic. He played hockey and baseball and especially loved playing golf. He water-skied and played squash and was an extremely competent black diamond downhill skier. Kim says, "He would attempt to do anything that was challenging or new."

He loved camping by tent in Jasper National Park and had been there fifteen times in the last five years. On one occasion, the Gordons went camping with thirty people.

In the summer of 2003, Anthony, Kim, and Spencer spent ten days of his holidays camping in a tent in the mountains at Kananaskis. But Kim says, "Anthony's biggest accomplishment was being a dad. He used to sit and stare at our son, Spencer, with such love and pride. Even my ninety-one-year-old grandmother remarked about that to me."

When Kim was working nights and Anthony wanted to hang out with the other members to watch a hockey or football game, Anthony used to bring Spencer with him. And everybody loved his being there—including Spencer.

In October 2004, Anthony was delighted to find out that Kim was expecting again. In February 2005, she had an ultrasound revealing that their second child would be another boy.

Anthony was off work on holidays for eight straight days before his encounter with James Roszko. During those days, he spent a lot of time with three year-old Spencer, helped a friend move, and meticulously packed items from their apartment for his family's move to their new house, which was almost ready.

Then during the last weekend in February 2005, he went on a ski weekend to Banff with twelve of his Mountie friends. From what he told Kim, they had a wonderful time.

It's clear that Anthony Gordon and his three star-crossed colleagues all enjoyed wonderful lives and careers. Unfortunately, fate was lurking to intervene against them.

Young policewoman Cindie Dennis may have best expressed the unpredictability of a police officer's destiny. "In life, you can never tell what will happen—especially in the police force. You can do what those guys did a thousand times and nothing ever happens. But then . . ."

4 | Hennessey and Cheeseman

WHEN ROSZKO FLED his farm, he was filled with rage. He strongly suspected that the bailiffs would call the police, and there was a reasonable chance that they would go into his Quonset and discover what was going on in there.

But he couldn't afford to stick around and watch his place, because the police would probably come after him and help the bailiffs repossess his truck. He had to find a place to hide his truck until the situation quieted down. Then he could make his next move, depending on whether or not the authorities discovered the contents of his barn.

He knew his mother could clearly see his Quonset from the back window of her trailer. He would phone her and she could tell him everything that was happening on his property.

Right after the bailiffs arrived, Roszko phoned his aunt, Ann Chayka, who lived in Cherhill, some thirty-eight kilometres (twenty-three miles) away. He was trying to find his mother, but his aunt didn't know where she was.

Around four p.m., after he fled his farm, Roszko phoned his aunt again, sounding somewhat anxious and disturbed. He indicated there was a distressing situation occurring at his farm. Not long after that, he phoned his sister Josephine Ruel to rage about the authorities' harassing him again. He had always felt close to Josephine. She seemed to understand him more than the others.

Roszko must have either driven by his farm or possibly stopped at his mother's place to see that the police were now at his farm. His mother lived on the next Range Road, and he could have seen his Quonset and his farmyard from her trailer.

Roszko angrily told Josephine what was going on at his farm. She tried to calm his anger, but wasn't very successful.

Josephine says, "He said there were police everywhere. I wish I could have said something that could have made a difference. Maybe this [incident] wouldn't have happened."

As enraged as he was, he realized the police would be on the lookout for his truck, and he had to hide it somewhere. The first place he thought of was his aunt Ann's place near Cherhill. He wouldn't ask her directly, but if he could get in touch with his mother, he knew she would ask on his behalf.

However, there was a chance that his aunt might say no, so he definitely needed a backup plan.

Another place that came to mind belonged to a guy he knew named Shawn Hennessey who worked in Barrhead but had told him he owned a few acres in the country.

In the past few years, Roszko had come to realize that he had worn out his welcome in the Mayerthorpe area. He had no friends there and very few acquaintances he could trust or rely on. So he had turned away from Mayerthorpe and started hanging out in Barrhead, a community of 4,600 some forty-five minutes east of Mayerthorpe.

Barrhead was another small farm town north of Edmonton. Typically, it had a low-lying profile. The tallest buildings did not exceed two storeys in height — with the exception, of course, of its antiquated grain elevator. But it had a thriving main street with one traffic light and not one big-box store to be seen anywhere.

Unlike Mayerthorpe, Barrhead had a movie theatre that changed its feature presentation once a week and a twenty-four-hour IGA grocery store. It also had a Chev, Ford, and Dodge dealership and a couple of places where farmers could buy or trade a new tractor or other farm machinery. There was a busy industrial area by the fire station, a hospital, a red brick RCMP detachment office, and three schools that taught the children at various levels of education.

There was also a good-sized tire store there called Kal Tire that Roszko liked to frequent. They sold and repaired all kinds of tires — for cars, trucks, tractors, loaders, graders, skidders.

Roszko did business with them for his vehicles and liked to hang around there. From time to time, he would go into town and spend time talking to some of the guys in the shop.

One of those guys was a twenty-five-year-old driver named Shawn Hennessey, who had become one of the few people in Roszko's life that he seemed to genuinely like and trust. They didn't hang around together or anything like that, but Roszko got to know him at Kal Tire and had him come out to his farm to install a stereo in his Camaro. Eventually their relationship included Shawn's selling some of Roszko's marijuana to the local youths.

There is some dispute as to how much he sold. By Shawn's own admission he did it "numerous times." Shawn's father, Barry, says it happened very infrequently where, on three occasions when he was younger, Shawn sold small amounts to some of the boys in town.

Barry Hennessey was originally from Newfoundland. He had been a commercial deep-sea diver who toiled as an underwater oil patch worker in Aberdeen, Scotland, and South America. In his younger days, he had even worked on commission, diving down to the wreck of the *SS Republic*, which sank in 800 feet of water in 1903 off Nantucket with a treasure on board.

After he married, Barry looked for work in Calgary and Halifax, and finally settled in Barrhead.

Shawn was born in Calgary, but his formative years were spent in Barrhead, where he became an athletic, outdoorsy type who loved fishing, hunting, and boating with his grandfather John Hennessey. Shawn, like his father before him, was particularly talented when he was working with his hands. He could fix any kind of mechanical device or electrical equipment.

His mom, Sandy, says Shawn was "shy and timid" as a young boy. He was a sensitive kid. On one occasion, Sandy had to go and speak to one of Shawn's teachers and ask her not to speak to him too harshly.

His dad says that in high school Shawn was a "pretty good" student who always passed successfully from one grade to another and had no difficulty in graduating from high school.

In his off-hours, Shawn loved riding snowmobiles and driving vehicles of any kind. On one occasion he drove a car in a local Demolition Derby.

He was a talented athlete who loved playing all sports, but took a particular interest in boxing. After joining the Brotherhood Boxing Club, he soon began competing in Golden Gloves Tournaments as a junior welterweight, where he won several awards.

In 1999, Shawn was selected as Northern Alberta's Athlete of the Year.

Shawn and Christine Hennessey, June 6, 2008.
(Rick MacWilliam/*Edmonton Journal*)

As a young man, he was employed at local furniture and hardware stores and when he got older, left town to work at high-paying jobs on the big oil rigs in northern Alberta.

In 2003, he married his high-school girlfriend Christine Cheeseman.

They had their reception at a local hotel and most of the guests at the party claimed they were "a couple of great kids." Others thought they were "a dream couple."

After they had two daughters together, Shawn resigned his lucrative job in the oil fields and took a job in town at Kal Tire to be closer to his wife and kids. His primary job was driving a service truck, but Shawn was hoping to eventually become an assistant manager.

Shawn was well-liked in the community. Many people in town thought of him as "a nice quiet, dedicated family man."

Shawn, Christine, and their girls lived in a huge house on seven acres out in the country north of Barrhead. The home had belonged to Christine's mother, but Shawn and his dad had assumed the mortgage a few years ago.

"It's a beautiful house," Barry says. "It has over 3,000 square feet with four fireplaces in it."

Christine's younger brother, Dennis, lived in a bedroom in the basement.

Both Christine and Dennis Cheeseman had tough early lives. A drunk driver killed their father when Dennis was only two years old and the accident had crushed their mother so badly she never seemed quite the same again. Although she remarried, her new husband and Dennis didn't have much of a relationship, and Christine played a major role in raising him.

Although Dennis was four years younger than Shawn, when Christine started dating Shawn, the two men became friends.

Dennis Cheesman, June 6, 2008.
(Canadian Press)

Christine says, "Shawn is Dennis's hero. Shawn kind of became his dad, a male figure in his life he never had before."

While Shawn is well built and athletic looking, Dennis is slightly pudgy and appears to be less agile.

Dennis lived his entire life in Barrhead and seldom went anywhere. He was an introverted boy who spent a lot of his time alone building models and reading comic books.

One of his employers said, "He was reliable. He was hard-working. He was quite quiet. We didn't know a lot about his life outside of work. Dennis is a lovely guy but he hasn't been around much. He hasn't seen much of life and consequently he's kind of uncultured and has had few life experiences."

Christine, who loves him dearly, admits, "He is shy and naïve."

A local woman who knows him says, "He was very shy, very quiet . . . kind of an innocent kid."

Dennis knew James Roszko. He worked at his farm one time in the spring digging holes to plant some saplings. Dennis never said much about that experience, but he never went back to work there again.

School was not something Dennis really enjoyed. He was a polite and co-operative student who was well liked by his teachers, but he dropped out of high school when he was sixteen.

A year and half later, in 2001, he took a job at Sepallo Foods in Barrhead and eventually became a team leader in the plant.

Sepallo is a company that processes wheat grass and other health products, and makes health food capsules.

Dennis worked there as a spray dryer, operating equipment that processes grass products from liquid into powder.

One of his managers says, "He was moving his way up to a supervisor's position."

Sepallo and two other health food companies listed in Barrhead are partly owned or operated by a man named Brad McNish.

McNish was once a sergeant with the Calgary Police. But after developing Crohn's Disease, he began to practise organic farming and ultimately discovered the healing properties of greens like barley and wheat grass.

He left the police force, graduated in Agribusiness from the Harvard Business School, and eventually became a principal in the three Barrhead health food companies: Sepallo Foods, Stand Six, and Natural Farmworks.

A passage from his Stand Six Web site states: "From humble beginnings of growing a few acres of green barley and wheat grass then harvesting and processing it by hand to becoming one of the largest producers of inorganic greens in North America has been an eventful and fun journey."

The text continues: "With our large state of the art manufacturing facility, my own farms, and a team of bright people working with me, Stand Six was born."

McNish doesn't live in Barrhead. There are rumours that he owns a 2,500-acre farm in the area, but whether he lives there or not is unknown. There are also reports that he has returned to the Calgary Police service as a constable.

One prominent Barrhead resident says, "He came to Barrhead in 2001. I understand he is a very nice guy. But very few people in town know him. He is not one to give up any information at all."

Barry Hennessey worked for Sepallo Foods as a maintenance man and says the company appears to be in trouble. He says it has laid off workers and has fewer employees now than when Dennis Cheeseman worked there.

Barry claims he is owed a significant amount of back wages by Sepallo and plans to initiate a lawsuit against the company to get his money.

The only reason that Brad McNish is mentioned at this point is that he will eventually play a very significant role in this story.

Both Shawn and Dennis knew about Roszko's scurrilous reputation and both of them feared his propensity for violence.

Shawn was probably less frightened because he could handle Roszko physically while Dennis probably could not. But both of them knew he had access to weapons and seemed prepared to use them. So both of them were wary of what he might do if he were angered or pushed too far.

As the afternoon of March 2 wore on, James Roszko was becoming desperate. His aunt was refusing to co-operate, and he needed Shawn Hennessey to let him park his truck in his secluded yard at his country house.

The record of Roszko's cell phone calls indicate that between 3:34 p.m. and 4:37 p.m., he phoned Kal Tire. He was told that Shawn was out on a service call.

After that, Roszko made numerous calls to a "bag" phone that was registered with Kal Tire but assigned to Shawn when he was on the road making service calls.

Roszko also made several calls to Shawn's residence.

He finally got through when Shawn was fixing a tractor tire at a farm north of Barrhead. Roszko explained that the police were swarming all over his farm and he didn't want to lose his truck. He asked Shawn to let him leave it at his place.

Shawn told him no, he didn't want him to do that. Although he didn't tell Roszko this, he must have thought that if Jimmy

Roszko was in trouble for the dope growing in his Quonset, he didn't want to be tied to him in any way.

Even when Roszko persisted, Shawn made it clear that the answer was no. He wanted Jimmy to find another place to hide his truck.

So Roszko called Kal Tire again and found out from one of the guys working there exactly where Shawn lived.

At 5:24 p.m., Shawn used his "bag" phone to call Christine at home. He told her that Roszko had been calling him. He said, "Roszko wants to hide his truck on our property."

Christine says, "Shawn said he was trying to tell him no, but the phones kept cutting in and out."

Just then, Roszko took it upon himself to show up at the Hennesseys' house when Christine and her two daughters were at home alone.

"Shawn was telling me if Roszko shows up at the house to make sure that I tell him he can't leave the truck there. And I was standing in the kitchen and said, 'Well you know what—somebody's here.'"

Shawn asked, "What kind of vehicle is it?"

"It's a truck."

"What kind?"

"I don't know . . . it's a white one."

"Well, that's him. Okay, let me talk to him."

"I just stood there and waited for Roszko to come to my door. Then I handed him the phone and said, 'Shawn wants to talk to you.'

"And then I walked away."

The two men spoke briefly on the phone. The gist of their conversation was like before. Roszko pressed Shawn to let him park his truck on his property but Shawn held his ground, telling him he could not do that. So Roszko went away.

At 8:00 p.m., Ann Chayka received a call from Stephanie Fifield. During their conversation, Chayka advised Stephanie that Jimmy had called again looking for her. Stephanie then told her that she could see a lot of activity at Jimmy's place. She said there were a number of police cars there and others had come and gone.

After Roszko left, Shawn Hennessey went looking for Dennis Cheeseman. He knew that Dennis had gone over to Jessie Zasiedko's house to help him move. And that's where he found him.

Shawn took Dennis aside and told him he needed his help because there were RCMP officers at Roszko's farm and the police were looking for Jimmy's truck. Shawn said he was concerned because Roszko was insisting that he be allowed to park his pickup at Shawn's place. He told Dennis they needed to help Roszko because he (Shawn) might be connected to Roszko's grow-op that was being investigated.

Dennis knew about Roszko's marijuana grow operation but he was not involved in any way with it. Nevertheless, he understood why Shawn was concerned and promised he would get home as soon as he could.

Roszko's mother continued to watch James's residence throughout the night. She could see vehicles driving in and out and assumed that they were police vehicles based on what she had seen in the daylight. She also saw the lights go on in Jimmy's trailer.

Between 8:13 p.m. and 11:55 p.m., Roszko made five phone calls to his mother's place. From the first of those calls, he was aware that the police were there in significant numbers checking out his Quonset and his trailer. When he learned that a tow truck had arrived, he knew he was done for.

His desperation was evident in one of his later calls when he told his mother that he had made out his will and said she should pray for him.

That seems to be the point where he made up his mind that all was lost and he was ready to die before they caught him and sent him back to jail.

Up until then, his mind had been in an escape mode. He had planned to hide his truck and play for time — somehow find a place to stay where the cops couldn't find him and then decide what he was going to do next.

Maybe he could get to Edmonton or Calgary and hide in the tangled maze of their crowded streets. Or run out of Alberta and avoid being detected in the anonymity of a big city in Saskatchewan or British Columbia. Maybe he could get someone to smuggle him across the border into the U.S., where he could play it smart and evade the American police.

Although his thoughts would have been scrambled, his plans vague and imprecise—and most likely impossible—they were focused on escape.

But now—from what he told his mother—he was prepared to stay and fight. And ready to die in the process.

And once his mind was converted to this more aggressive attack mode, he would have started to conceive his suicidal plan. He was going to sneak back to his farm, surprise the Mounties that were there and kill as many of them as he possibly could . . . knowing full well he, too, would be killed in the violent encounter.

At 10:30 p.m., Stephanie Fifield called Ann Chayka asking her to let Jimmy park his pickup truck on her property. Chayka did not comply with her request.

After watching her driveway for a while, Ann Chayka phoned Stephanie to let her know that Jimmy had not shown up at her place with his truck and she was going to retire for the night.

Shawn had driven straight home after speaking to Dennis at Jessie Zasiedko's house. He and Christine had just gone to bed when Roszko pulled up in his truck at their house.

Christine says, "I was laying in bed with my husband and I saw headlights."

Shawn hopped out of bed and said, "I'll be right back." He wasn't terribly concerned. He says, "I didn't think anything of it."

But when he answered the door, Roszko was standing there with a 9mm Beretta pistol in plain view, tucked into the front of his waistband.

From this point on in the story, there are some actions by the principals that are in dispute. Some people contend that Roszko threatened Shawn by holding the Beretta to Hennessey's head or his chin. Other evidence indicates the gun remained in Roszko's waistband throughout the entire conversation between them.

Roszko knew that Shawn was in possession of a high-powered .300 Winchester Magnum rifle. The rifle had been given to Shawn by his grandfather John Hennessey. And Roszko had borrowed it one time previously to hunt a bear that was being a nuisance on his farm property.

As the two men were talking about the Winchester, Dennis Cheeseman pulled into the yard and came into the house. When he entered, he found Roszko and Shawn sitting at the kitchen table. Dennis knew his sister was home and seeing she had chosen to remain in the bedroom with her children, it was obvious she was avoiding Roszko.

Court evidence states that it was clear to all present that Roszko was enraged at the police and made comments to the effect that he intended to return to his property and burn down the Quonset that contained the illegal marijuana grow and chop shop operation.

In an interview on *Fifth Estate*, Shawn says it was Roszko's plan to use the Winchester to blow up the gas tanks that were in his yard and thereby burn down the Quonset and all the incriminating evidence inside it.

There is a possibility this might have worked, but it is very doubtful. The fuel tanks in Roszko's yard were located about thirty yards from the Quonset, and it is difficult to comprehend how he could imagine that exploding them would somehow ignite the Quonset. Furthermore, the Quonset is a steel structure, and it's equally difficult to understand how anyone or anything could burn it to the ground.

And all three of them knew the place was crawling with police. For Roszko to start shooting at gas tanks would have brought an immediate return of gunfire. Besides that, if Roszko had managed to start a fire by puncturing the fuel tanks, the police would have immediately called firefighters to contain the blaze. And the fire trucks would have been at the farm in a matter of minutes.

If it was Roszko's idea to burn down the Quonset, it was a misconstrued plan that was assuredly doomed to failure.

But it is understandable that Shawn would want the Quonset burnt down. If that were to happen, all the evidence that might incriminate his involvement with the marijuana grow would be gone.

No matter, Roszko demanded he be given the Winchester. Shawn went and got it and before he handed it over, wiped it down. Some interpret this action as an indication that Shawn didn't want his fingerprints on it. Others think it was just a matter of Shawn wiping off the dust and dirt that had accumulated on the gun with its lack of use. Shawn also gave Roszko a box of ammunition to use with the rifle.

And Cheeseman took it upon himself to go downstairs and retrieve a white pillowcase and a pair of gloves. Dennis put on the gloves and inserted the Winchester rifle into the pillowcase. This was supposedly done for ease of transporting it.

Then Roszko demanded that Shawn follow him to his aunt's place in Cherhill. His plan was to hide his truck there and then have Shawn drive him back to a place near his mother's home on Range Road 80.

Feeling he had little choice, Shawn agreed to do it and asked Dennis to come along for support and comfort.

Whether Roszko's demand was clearly and menacingly enforced by his threat of using his gun is debatable. However, whether he pointed the gun or he didn't, it does appear that he alluded to it in some fashion and, in so doing, intimidated them into accompanying him on his travels that night.

The much bigger issue is whether or not Hennessey and Cheeseman knew that an armed confrontation with the police was a real possibility and concomitantly realized the situation was clearly heading for very serious, violent, trouble.

In any case, the three of them went out to their vehicles. Roszko got into his pickup; Shawn and Dennis climbed into Hennessey's Dodge Neon. Roszko led the way, and Shawn followed as they headed south for Ann Chayka's house in Cherhill.

When they arrived at her place, Roszko pulled into her driveway. Hennessey pulled over on the side of the highway and waited while Roszko parked deeper in the yard.

While Roszko was out of the car, Shawn and Dennis discussed taking off and leaving Roszko to his own devices. But their fear of Roszko's violence and his vindictive thirst for revenge overweighed their longing to flee.

So they waited.

How different their lives might be today if they had acted on their inclination to run.

It wasn't very long before Roszko appeared on the highway carrying the Winchester and the ammunition with the Beretta tucked into the front of his waistband.

Roszko ordered Dennis to get into the back seat. Then he put the Winchester, wrapped in its pillowcase, on the floor of the back seat beside Dennis. Then he climbed into the passenger seat and told Shawn to drive.

Traversing the country roads, they headed for Roszko's mother's place.

The court papers state that Cheeseman said that during the trip he and Shawn remained quiet and did not converse with Roszko. Meanwhile, Roszko was ranting and complaining about the RCMP and threatening to get even with them. Roszko indicated he was going to burn down the Quonset. Cheeseman described Roszko's ravings as "devil talk."

Barry Hennessey differs with this. He says his son told him that en route Roszko was pensive and withdrawn. And what little he had to say was so quiet that, Dennis, sitting in the back seat of the noisy old Dodge Neon, didn't hear.

When they got close to Roszko's road, Roszko made Shawn drive past it to Range Road 80, where his mother lived. Then he directed Hennessey to drive past his mother's driveway. Shawn says they were about one hundred yards from her driveway when he let Roszko out.

"You could see the end of her driveway," is the way Shawn describes the location.

Court documents state that Shawn and Dennis could see the lights from police cars on James Roszko's property. Shawn disagrees, claiming he only saw the lights of one police cruiser. The disparity in these two statements is dealt with later in chapter nine.

When Roszko got out of Hennessey's car, he pulled socks on over the boots he was wearing. This was done to muffle his footsteps in the snow as he approached the Quonset. He then pulled the Winchester off the floor of the back seat. Armed with the rifle, his Beretta, and a box of .300-calibre bullets, he left them and started heading towards the police at his Quonset.

According to court documents, the time was estimated to be between one a.m. and three a.m. Barry says his son told him he thought it was between one a.m. and two a.m.

As soon as Roszko got out of the car, Shawn and Dennis departed and drove directly home. Along the way, Cheeseman suggested that they should call the police and warn them about Roszko. Shawn discouraged this idea. He felt if they did that and Roszko were to then evade the police, he would end up coming after them intent on revenge.

So in those early morning hours of March 3, 2005, these two men watched an enraged, heavily armed James Roszko leave them. He went with socks over his shoes to muffle his approach on a number of unsuspecting policemen who were performing their duty at a crime scene filled with marijuana plants and stolen vehicles.

And their only reason for not warning the police was their fear of a possible reprisal by this lunatic.

The scenario that unfolded that early morning brings up a number of interesting issues.

First of all, when Roszko was found later, he had in his possession the following items:

1. TheWinchester rifle
2. The Beretta handgun
3. A pair of socks
4. A semi-automatic assault Heckler-Koch rifle
5. A white sheet that he used for camouflage
6. A can of bear spray
7. A plastic bottle of water

When he left Hennessey and Cheeseman on the road that fateful morning he had items one to three with him. Where did he get items four to seven?

Jim Guiry, a Professional Engineer who worked for several years as a land surveyor, was made familiar with a drawing of the three-quarter section of land on which James Roszko lived. Because a section of land equals one square mile, it measures 1,760 yards by 1,760 yards. Thus, the length of a diagonal across this area can be geometrically calculated rather accurately.

Guiry estimates the overland distance from the place on Range Road 80, where Roszko got out of Hennessey's car, to his Quonset hut on Range Road 75 is slightly more than one mile.

An average healthy person walking steadily can travel three miles in an hour. Even if Roszko crawled, crept, and slithered his way from brush patch to brush patch, he should have been able to cover the distance in two hours.

Shawn Hennessey claims they left Roszko off on Range Road 80 between one and two o'clock in the morning. Using Shawn's latest estimated time, Roszko would have about five and a half hours before the sun rose that morning at approximately seven-twenty a.m.

This means Roszko had approximately three and a half hours to spare to get himself to the Quonset before sunrise.

Where did he spend those hours? Huddled out in the field with the wind blowing and the temperature near zero?

Where did he get the white sheet to help him sneak up on the police without being detected?

Where did he get the bear spray and the bottle of water?

Wouldn't he have been hungry? It seems the only bit of food he had all day was a bowl of soup at Shawn Hennessey's place.

As one investigative reporter has commented, "He would have had many needs during the course of that long night."

Later that morning, just before dawn, Dennis Cheeseman left for his job at Sepallo Foods in Barrhead.

Sometime between seven a.m. and eight a.m., Shawn Hennessey showed up for a Kal Tire meeting at the Mayfield Inn in Edmonton.

When Ann Chayka woke up in Cherhill, she saw that Jimmy, against her wishes, had parked his white pickup truck at the far end of her driveway.

As the new day began, no one across the broad expanse of beautiful Alberta could have suspected that this would soon turn out to be one of the ugliest days in the history of the province.

5 | Thursday Morning

IT WAS CLOSE TO TWO in the morning when Julie Letal, Clayton Seguin, and Brock Myrol were released from their duties and left the Quonset hut.

And in all likelihood, James Roszko watched them leave. He had a good view of his barn from Range Road 80. From there, he dashed from one stand of brush to another. When he came to open areas, he crawled and crept his way uphill among the dips and hollows of the fields, carefully working his way towards his Quonset hut. He would have seen several uniformed Mounties get in the cars and drive away, but would not have been able to identify them.

It seems clear what his intentions were. He was scorned and laughed at by a lot of people in the area. Some of his own family had turned against him. Now he was going to lose his truck. That's why the bailiffs had come. But worst of all, as soon as the cops got into his barn and saw the marijuana plants, he knew they were going to send him back to prison for trafficking. And the chop shop would be added on top of that.

He was afraid he would be going to jail for a long stretch this time. He hated it there. And he hated the police.

In his twisted mind, it was all the Mounties' fault. They had harassed him for years over every little thing . . . speeding tickets, no seat belt, tinted windows on his truck. He'd always wanted to get back at them . . . give some of their own grief right back. This was his time to do it. It was now or never. He had nothing more to lose. He was going to kill as many of them as he could.

All he had to do was get close to them without being seen. But even if the police spotted him, he was ready for them. Even if they came out after him, he had Hennessey's Winchester rifle loaded and ready. And if they got close to him and tried to jump him, he had the Beretta in his waistband.

It was a long way from the Range Road to his Quonset, but he could cover that distance easily. There was a half moon to guide him, and he knew the terrain very well. And the weather was in his favour. During the day, the temperature had approached double digits and it would barely dip below zero overnight.

For the first part of the trek, he could run and walk upright and never be seen. As he got closer, there were large patches of poplar and willow bush that would hide him. When he darted from one patch to the other, he would have to be more careful. And when he got closer to the Quonset, he knew there were two big patches of brush that would help conceal him.

He would have to creep and crawl from the last stand of brush to the Quonset, but that was a long way off, and he was confident he could do that without being seen.

For now, he had to keep walking and crawling to make sure he arrived at his Quonset before daylight.

When Brock Myrol got home, it was close to two-thirty a.m. Anjila was waiting for him at the door and was relieved to see him.

"God, I can't stand the smell," he said, referring to the skunky odour from Roszko's Quonset hut that clung to his clothes. "I have to take a shower right away."

"Was the guy there that owns the place?"

"No, he was gone . . . early in the afternoon."

"Do you think he's coming back?"

"No," Brock said with conviction. "He has no reason to."

Then he was off to take his shower and get some sleep.

Out at Roszko's farm, Cpl. Jim Martin had put in a phone call to Sgt. Tom Pickard, the NCO in command of the Whitecourt Detachment. The purpose of his call was to explain to Tom that his Mayerthorpe members were exhausted and to ask Tom if he would send one of his constables out to guard the evidence in the Quonset overnight.

Pickard said he would be glad to help and would make the necessary arrangements. He had Cst. Barry Baskerville phone Cst. Tony Gordon at home.

Baskerville told Tony that the Mayerthorpe Detachment needed assistance with a surveillance project on a farm near

Rochfort Bridge. He asked Tony if he would be willing to work some overtime on his last day off.

Tony, who was always willing to work, agreed to come in and do it.

Baskerville told him to get dressed and come to the detachment office and get further instructions about the surveillance job. He could also pick up a cruiser to drive out there.

Tony put on his police gear and, before he left the apartment, looked in on Kim. Seeing that she was sleeping, Anthony flashed the overhead light on and off a few times.

Kim opened her eyes and saw him standing in silhouette, outlined by the hall light behind him.

"What's going on?" she asked, half asleep.

"I'm going out to do surveillance on a place."

"Okay," Kim replied.

"See you in eight hours," Anthony said.

"Okay."

Anthony put on his bulletproof vest, quietly left the house, and headed for the Whitecourt Detachment.

The image of his silhouette at the door still lingers in Kim's imagination to this day.

Leo and Kelly Johnston had a similar experience.

Leo had come to bed after midnight because he had been chatting with his brother Lee in Surrey, British Columbia, for a half hour or so on their MSN Messenger computer service. This was something they did every day—either by phone or on their computers.

Lee recalls, "We didn't talk about anything special . . . just brother talk . . . like we did all the time."

Just before three o'clock Thursday morning on March 3, Leo was awakened by a phone call from the detachment office that gave him some detailed instructions about leaving immediately to carry out a surveillance assignment at a farm out in the county near Rochfort Bridge. A member was going to bring over the detachment pickup so that Leo could take the truck and "go sit on this shed for the night."

Leo clearly understood the details of the assignment: He was to drive out to a farm owned by James Roszko on Range Road 75, secure the scene, and make sure nobody touched or altered the evidence in Roszko's Quonset hut. He was told that two members from the Edmonton Auto Theft Unit would be out to search the farm around nine a.m.

Leo was also advised he would be joined on this surveillance job by Tony Gordon, a member who was heading out there from the Whitecourt Detachment.

That suited Leo fine. He knew Tony pretty well and looked forward to seeing him again.

Leo got dressed quickly and prepared to leave the house.

Before he went out the door, Kelly gave him a kiss and said to him, "I love you, handsome. Be safe."

"I love you, beautiful," Leo replied. "I'll see you when I get home."

And with those few final words, he was off into the night.

It was about three-thirty a.m. when Leo Johnston and Tony Gordon got to the farm. By then, only Jim Martin and Cindie Dennis were still on the property.

Leo was to replace Cindie for the overnight security watch. He was armed with his 9mm service pistol and had a loaded detachment .308 calibre rifle in his vehicle. Tony was also armed and had a loaded detachment 12-gauge shotgun in his cruiser. Both were wearing their soft body armour and their full RCMP uniforms.

Jim Martin greeted them and gave them a brief summary of what had been found on the property. He told them that Roszko had fled the scene yesterday afternoon, and, although there had been a couple of sightings of him on the nearby roads, as yet he hadn't been apprehended.

He repeated the information that the Auto Theft specialists from Edmonton would be out first thing in the morning to go over the articles in the Quonset. And Brock Myrol would be out to relieve them at that time, too.

Before Jim left, he told both Leo and Tony to position their vehicles in such a way that they could observe the site in all directions.

"Right now, I'm bushed. I'm going home to get a couple of hours' sleep. I'll see you guys tomorrow morning."

After Martin left, Cindie stayed only a few minutes longer. She was the last member to leave the crime scene that early morning.

Martin got home around four o'clock and kept his PC at his house because he figured he would be going straight back to Roszko's place around nine in the morning.

Meanwhile, Tony and Leo took up their posts on the farm. They parked their vehicles on the southeast side of the Quonset hut in such a manner that they were able to see both the front doors of the barn and Roszko's trailer, which was about eighty yards to the south.

Their responsibility was to make sure no one entered the Quonset hut and touched anything inside. In this type of surveillance work, they had been trained to maintain the scene and regularly walk the perimeter.

As they walked around the outside of the Quonset, they would have checked both outside the hut and inside the large, open door at the front of the Quonset.

Kelly Johnston says, "I have no doubt that Leo was diligent and focused on that assignment. When Leo went to work, he went to work. He always had his game face on."

Tony Gordon was equally diligent and careful in performing his police duties.

It was a matter of professional pride for the two of them.

Both Leo and Tony were aware that this was going to be a long night. One thing they could be thankful for was the fact that it wasn't horribly cold. Although the temperature hovered around zero, the wind was moderate, which helped make their time out in the open more tolerable. They knew the weather could have been an awful lot worse.

There was a light on inside the Quonset, but outside the building the night was pitch black, with little reflection from the snow in the fields. At that particular time, the land was only lightly covered with a thin layer of snow that mostly gathered in the dips and hollows. On the crest of the hills there was hardly any snow at all.

Radio checks were made with the two members throughout their shift. Occasionally, as the morning wore on, Leo Johnston radioed the telecom centre and let them know that all was quiet at the scene.

An aerial view of Roszko's farm. Notice the patches of brush and bush and the windbreaks he could have used for cover as he approached the Quonset. (RCMP)

It is fair to assume that some of the time, the two Mounties sat together in a cruiser, and some of the time they got out and moved around, checking inside and outside the building with their flashlights.

But from the time they had arrived on the scene, Roszko was working his way towards them over the frozen fields from the southwest of his farmstead. And as he got closer, he would have been watching carefully, trying to determine how many police were there, looking for any movement he could detect from the light going on and off inside the police cruiser or from the beams of their flashlights as they moved around his property.

Although the path of his final advance is unknown, an examination of his property would seem to indicate he probably approached the Quonset from the rear (the west).

This would mean that the only open space he had to cross was between the last patch of brush to the west and the windbreak behind his Quonset. From there, he could have used the building itself to shield his movement.

In any case, as he continued to move furtively towards his building, he would have been aware that he needed to get into the best possible position before dawn.

When the first glimmer of daylight began to show itself in the east at about seven-twenty, Leo and Tony must have been glad to see the dawn replace the darkness and ease the tension of their lonely vigil.

Around that same time, Brock Myrol was getting up again, because he was eager to get out to the crime scene by nine.

Before he left the house, he came into the bedroom to snuggle a little bit with Anjila. But with his full gun belt, his cuffs, and his vest, it was awkward for them to hug.

"This isn't working, Brock," she whispered.

Brock agreed, and they kidded a little bit about some cartoons that Anjila had been watching the night before.

As Brock began to leave, Anjila said, "When are you going to be home?"

"I'm off at seven, but I don't know when I'll be home."

He blew Anjila a final kiss, and she whispered, "I love you."

And he was gone again to meet Clayton Seguin so they could walk over to the detachment office together.

At 8:00 a.m., Cst. Steve Vigor left his home in an unmarked Yukon Suburban to pick up his partner, Garret Hoogestraat, in Sherwood Park, an eastern suburb of Edmonton. They were the two specialists with the Auto Theft Unit who were assigned to attend Roszko's farm and investigate the stolen vehicles and stolen auto parts that were found on his property.

The other two members of this unit were Cpl. Murray Savage and Cst. Chris Laubman. The unit's mandate was to investigate the role and function of organized crime in the realm of stolen vehicles. Over the years, stealing cars and trucks had developed into a highly structured and extremely lucrative criminal enterprise that drained millions of dollars from the Canadian economy.

The focus of the Auto Theft Section was on the major players in the stolen car game. The unit didn't get involved with single automotive thefts or go after joyriding teenagers who stole cars for weekend thrills. They were after the organized network of thieves who made the big money in this illegal venture.

Steve Vigor and Garret Hoogestraat were both accomplished policemen whose individual talents and interests made them effective partners.

Corporal Steve Vigor, the Mountie who shot James Roszko. (RCMP)

Constable Garrett Hoogestraat, the Mountie who shielded Steve Vigor from Roszko's lethal guns. (RCMP)

Vigor, fifty-two, had twenty-six years' experience as a Mountie. At five-nine and 175 pounds, he was a slightly built man who wore glasses and looked more like a librarian than the daring policeman he was—one who would eventually be honoured for his bravery by the Governor General of Canada.

Steve graduated from Depot in 1979 and then served in Alberta detachments at Fort McMurray, Fort Chipewan, Jasper, and Sherwood Park. Most recently, he was posted to the Auto Theft Section at Edmonton Headquarters.

Vigor had always harboured an interest in becoming a member of the "K" Division (Alberta) Emergency Response Team. And in May 1992, his potential in this capacity was recognized when he was invited to join them as a probationary "striker." Six months later, he was sent to Ottawa to take the RCMP's special ERT training course, which he passed with flying colours.

The five-week ERT course is a physically demanding process offered at the RCMP college in Ottawa. Candidates in the course spend a lot of time on the shooting range firing high-powered weapons. This is Steve's forté. He is an excellent shot, rated as an RCMP marksman.

Participants in the course also spend time practising their skills in sniper training, fighting in the gym in close-quarter bouts, and driving on the roadways at Depot making high-risk vehicle stops.

When Vigor became a bona fide member of Edmonton's ERT, he soon learned the hazardous work they do creates a special bond among its members.

"I can't tell you how much being an ERT member means to me. The bond among us is very strong. The realization that these guys are willing to put their life on the line for you is overpowering. And, of course, you're going to do the same for them. Their dedication is second to none. When that ERT pager goes off, everybody turns up ready to go."

In his twelve-plus years with the ERT unit, Steve had participated in his fair share of dangerous assignments. The most perilous occurred in February 2004, when he was involved in a tragic case at Spruce Grove, Alberta, a western suburb of Edmonton. In that incident, one of the RCMP's best dog masters, Jim Galloway, was shot and killed by a violent and emotionally unstable man named Martin Ostopovich.

Ostopovich, who was known to the police as a troubled personality, had shot the windows out of his neighbour's car and then holed up in his house most of the day with some high-powered weapons. He had also contacted the media claiming he was going to kill "some cops."

The Edmonton ERT was called in to handle the situation, and as soon as they came on the scene, Ostopovich declared to them over the phone he was going to get into his pickup truck with his guns and leave the area. The police advised him he could not do that.

When Ostopovich came out of the house armed with two high-powered rifles and climbed into his vehicle, the ERT made their move. Steve Vigor and two other ERT members rushed Ostopovich's truck on foot while Jim Galloway rammed his GMC Suburban into his vehicle. The idea was for Galloway to tip Ostopovich's truck over. But because of the snow on the street, the pickup didn't roll over, it just slid sideways.

And, after the collision, as Galloway tried to run for cover, Ostopovich shot him in the back at close range. That's when Vigor and the two other ERT members charged Ostopovich's pickup, opened fire, and shot him dead.

In that case, it is of interest to note that Steve Vigor will never be told whether or not it was the shots he fired that killed Martin Ostopovich. That's because it is ERT policy not to divulge this information to anyone, particularly the ERT members who participated in a fatal incident.

Garret Hoogestraat's police experience is quite different from Steve Vigor's, but equally interesting. At six feet and 195 pounds, Garret Hoogestraat was a bigger man than Vigor and eight years younger. The great interest in his life has always been automobiles. Ever since he was a youngster, Garret loved working with them and learning about them. As a teenager he took an apprenticeship in diesel mechanics.

During his fourteen-year police career he served in detachments of varying sizes. His first five years were spent at a small rural unit in Two Hills in northern Alberta. Then he was transferred to Sherwood Park, where he served for six years with its huge sixty-five-member contingent. From there, his application was accepted for him to join the Auto Theft Section at Edmonton Headquarters. And for the last three years this particular type of work had become his passion.

Like his partner, Vigor, Hoogestraat also serves on a dangerous specialty crew. In 2004 he became a part-time member of the Explosives Disposal Unit, which also works out of Edmonton Headquarters. By all accounts, this is the most delicate and dangerous specialty there is in police work.

And so it's obvious that although these men are quite different in their personalities and their interests, the common trait they share is their intrepid daring.

But that was a quality that didn't seem to be required as they prepared to go to work at James Roszko's farm.

When Vigor picked Hoogestraat up that Thursday morning, they both figured that they were going out on another routine call to assist a detachment with a search warrant.

As Vigor says, "As far I could tell, it was just another case of checking out a small part of a bigger picture."

They didn't even have an address for the search site. But they knew it was near Mayerthorpe, so Vigor headed west on Highway #16 and then north on Highway #43.

Along the way, Garret got on his cell phone and called the Mayerthorpe Detachment for more specific directions. From what they told him, he figured the drive would take about two hours.

"But we aren't going to make it going this slow," he said to Vigor. "My grandmother drives faster than you do."

"We're doing the speed limit. That's good enough for me."

They both smiled. They'd had this conversation before.

Steve says, "I remember it was a beautiful day . . . bright sunshine . . . temperature around zero. Actually it was a lovely drive."

About this same time in Mayerthorpe, Clayton Seguin and Brock Myrol were in uniform walking toward the detachment office.

Clayton was Brock's trainer, which meant the two of them would work closely together for the first two months that Brock was on the job. That worked out well because they lived only two blocks from each other.

Clayton says, "We met outside my place just after eight o'clock and we were both kind of drowsy because we'd got to bed so late."

As they walked along, Clayton remembers he said to Brock, "This is just like being on foot patrol . . . like we're walking a beat together."

Just after they got to the office, Peter Schiemann came in. He was dressed in civvies — a dark jacket, blue jeans, and running shoes. Peter told them he was going into Edmonton to buy some camera equipment for the interdiction crew. The reason he was wearing civilian clothes was because detachment policy dictated that no member should wear his or her uniform while shopping.

Jim Martin was up at 8:30 a.m. He had a quick shower and a cup of coffee and was out of the house by nine. "I wanted to get in there early and see who was there . . . get some manpower and head out to Roszko's."

He got to the detachment just after nine o'clock and the first thing he did was contact Leo Johnston out at the Roszko's farm.

"How's everything going out there?" he asked.

"Everything's quiet," Leo replied.

"Any sightings of Roszko yet?"

"No. We haven't seen him. We haven't seen anybody."

"Auto Theft said they were leaving around eight this morning. They're going directly out there."

"They should be here soon, then."

"Right. I'll be out there right away, too."

"Okay, we'll see you then."

Then Martin phoned the detachments at Barrhead and Evansburg and let them know what was happening in the Roszko investigation.

That morning, Brock Myrol had been assigned to go back out to Roszko's farm, and Clayton was supposed to drive him out there. But Clayton had to attend a trial with Julie Letal on the Alexis Reserve, a Nakota Sioux reservation located on Lac Ste. Anne 45 kilometres southeast of Mayerthorpe. Alexis is a modest-size reservation with a population of less than 900 Natives. Some of the reservations in Alberta are ten times that size.

For Clayton Seguin, it was very important that he attend this trial, because the case involved a man who had pointed a rifle in his face during a domestic dispute. Consequently, Clayton's testimony was crucial.

"Peter," Clayton said, "I've got this trial on the Alexis reserve. Do you mind taking Brock out to Roszko's place?"

Peter didn't mind at all. It wouldn't be far out of his way.

Clayton presented their altered plan to Jim Martin, and that was fine with him.

It was just an insignificant little change of plans that happen all the time among colleagues, but for both Peter Schiemann and Clayton Seguin, the consequences of that change would soon prove to be monumental.

As Seguin and Letal were preparing to leave for their trial, Peter and Brock approached Jim Martin about feeding Roszko's dogs some sedated meat to keep them docile for the day.

"Sure," Jim responded. "That's a good idea. Go ahead."

So Peter and Brock left to buy some meat.

Coincidentally, it was at that time that Cpl. Jeff Whipple was on the phone to Roszko's mother, Stephanie Fifield, about the dogs.

Jeff says, "I phoned her at her home and told her we were having trouble with his two dogs. I asked her if she would come over to his property and take the dogs away . . . take them over to her place."

Stephanie said no. She claimed they were vicious animals and she didn't want anything to do with them.

Jeff continued, "Well, do you know anybody who can come over there and look after these dogs . . . a neighbour, a friend, a member of your family?"

Her answer was still no.

Jeff remembers, "She wasn't angry or anything. She just wasn't helpful at all. She didn't want to get involved.

"So on that basis, it was a good thing that Peter and Brock were going to sedate those dogs with the meat. If those two dogs ever got loose, they could have been a real handful."

At 9:05 a.m., Jim Martin radioed Leo Johnston and Tony Gordon at the farm. They advised there had not been any sightings of Roszko during their shift.

Martin was just about to go out the door when the office manager, Pat Lakeman, called Jim back. She advised him that the Green Team needed some information off the search warrant.

So Martin came back in and phoned Lorne Adamitz in Edmonton and spoke to him for about twenty minutes about the warrant.

By this time, Peter Schiemann and Brock Myrol had bought the meat and were now pulling up to the local veterinary clinic on 42nd Avenue. They went inside and explained to Dr. John Kyle that they wanted a sedative they could inject into the meat to calm Roszko's savage beasts.

Kyle remembers their visit to his clinic and the request they made to him.

"I knew Peter Schiemann. He was a real nice guy. But I knew Leo Johnston and Kelly better, because I tended to their black lab when he had a lesion on his tail.

"I also knew Roszko's dogs. They were vicious. One time I had to go out there and pull some porcupine quills out of their faces. And the only way I could work on them was to put them to sleep.

"I know James Roszko had a bad reputation around town, but he was all right with me. That's because he used to have a herd of cattle . . . maybe fifty head or more, and I serviced them . . . so he needed me.

"Anyway, they wanted to sedate the dogs, so I gave them a sedative in a syringe so they could inject it into the meat.

"Then they were on their way."

There is a slight quiver in the doctor's voice as he adds, "That's the last time I saw those guys."

Out at the farm, Leo and Tony were waiting to be relieved. As the clock reached 9:25 a.m., they knew that a bunch of their members would be out there soon. Jim Martin and Brock Myrol were on their way, and the Auto Theft guys from Edmonton would be there soon, too.

They were unaware that sometime during the night or early morning, Roszko had managed to sneak by them and get into the Quonset hut.

Thinking about it in retrospect, that would not have been a difficult thing for him to do. As he got closer, he could see most of the moves they made.

In the dark, he would have been able to see flashes of them when they went past the lighted open end of the Quonset. He could detect their movements around the yard from the beam of their flashlights or tell when they were in their vehicles by the lights going on and off inside their PCs.

Conversely, in the dark, he would have been almost impossible to see. The patches of brush would have concealed him completely. When he crossed an open space, he had a white sheet to camouflage him. And, when necessary, with the sheet over him he could lie low and hide in the irregular depressions in the open field. As he got very close to the Quonset, the socks he had pulled over his shoes would have muffled the sound of his feet crunching in the snow.

And, of course, when daylight came, he could see every movement they made.

As Roszko advanced closer to the Quonset, there were lots of places for him to hide: behind his trailer south of his barn, behind the pine windbreak to the west of the trailer, behind the tall wooden windbreak at the back of the Quonset, or behind the evergreen hedge at the back of his steel barn. And he could use the huge bulk of the Quonset hut to his advantage. When Leo and Tony were on one side of the structure, he could be hiding on the other.

No matter when he crept into the Quonset or how he managed to do it, by the time Peter Schiemann and Brock Myrol arrived that Thursday morning, Roszko was in there, hiding.

Furthermore, he was waiting with the Heckler and Koch semi-automatic assault rifle in his hands.

Did he have that gun hidden somewhere in the Quonset and retrieve it from its hiding place when he crept in? Or did he keep that gun somewhere else and retrieve it before he ever got to the Quonset?

We will probably never know the answer to those two questions.

What we do know is that James Roszko did not have the Heckler and Koch rifle with him when Shawn Hennessey let him off some seven hours earlier on Range Road 80.

At 9:30 a.m., Schiemann and Myrol pulled into Roszko's yard and parked their car beside Leo's and Tony's vehicles at the southeast end of the Quonset hut.

After a brief exchange of hellos, Peter told Leo and Tony he had brought some sedated meat to give to the dogs.

The two curs were still trapped in the old granary shed at the west end of the Quonset. Part of the roof on the shed had some boards missing and it was through that gap that they intended to feed the meat to the animals.

They got a ladder, propped it up against the shed, and threw the meat down to the two snarling beasts below who tore into the flesh like ravenous predators.

Out on Highway#18, Vigor and Hoogestraat were having a little trouble finding Range Road 75.

"We missed the sign and drove a little ways past it before Garret told me to stop and back up."

When they got squared around, it was a short trip down the Range Road to Roszko's lane.

While the four Mounties were tending to the dogs, Roszko had taken up a position in the Quonset behind some large white plastic casks that had been used to water the marijuana plants. These casks were just inside the southeast corner of the hut a few feet inside the human door.

The four at the dog shed had just finished feeding the dogs when Vigor and Hoogestraat pulled into Roszko's laneway. Steve could see all four standing beside the old shed as he steered his way through the yard towards them. He ended up parking his Yukon parallel to the Quonset at its southwest corner. The dog's granary shed was only a few yards away.

Hoogestraat climbed out of the vehicle and went behind it to get his coveralls out of the back section. Vigor remained behind the wheel making some investigation notes. His first annotation indicated their arrival time was 9:56 a.m.

As Hoogestraat was pulling on his coveralls, the four Mounties left the dogs and came towards him. Hoogestraat chatted briefly with all of them, but the one he knew best was Tony Gordon. They had worked on a previous project together. Garret asked him about the crime scene. He wanted to know how big the property was and asked for a layout of the search site.

Tony pointed out the property lines and told him the main search area was in the Quonset, but there was a piece of a vehicle under a blue tarp behind the steel hut.

Garret walked with Tony about halfway along the length of the Quonset and had every intention of going inside the building with the other four, but at the last minute changed his mind.

"I have to go back and get a couple of tools," Garret said to Tony. "I'll be with you shortly."

And with that the two parted. Tony joined the other three as they headed for the front of the hut; Garret went back to the Yukon to get his tools.

In reflection, Hoogestraat says, "I guess that was the luckiest decision of my life."

As the four disappeared around the corner of the hut, Garret was gathering a scraper and a couple of other tools from the back of the Yukon. Steve was still behind the wheel, writing.

Garret says, "Then I heard two loud cracking sounds like metal hitting on metal."

Steve says, "Initially, I didn't realize what the loud bangs were. It sounded like someone had hit the inside of the Quonset wall with something heavy. Then, in a very brief period of time following those two bangs, there was a series of more bangs . . . between twelve and fifteen that I recollect. And I heard someone screaming in pain."

When Vigor and Hoogestraat heard the multiple bangs, they both realized the sounds were gunshots. They immediately began to run the length of the building toward the big main door.

On the run, Vigor pulled out his weapon and when he got about halfway along the building, he yelled, "Garret, get back to the car and call in backup. We probably have officers down. "

Hoogestraat turned and ran back to the Yukon Suburban, grabbed his cell phone, and dialed 911. When he got Edmonton telecom, he yelled, "Officer down! Officer down! Request backup. Shots fired. Officer down!"

As Vigor ran past the three police vehicles (Gordon's, Johnston's, and Schiemann's) parked at the east end of the Quonset, he saw a small man emerge from the building with some articles in his hands.

"A male suspect exited the Quonset hut. He was about thirty-five feet away. He was carrying a long-barrelled weapon in his hands, a semi-automatic rifle. There was another long-barrelled weapon over his shoulder.

"He turned and had a surprised look on his face. He obviously didn't think there were more officers outside."

No words were exchanged between them.

"I had never seen James Roszko before, but somehow I knew it was him."

6 | Officer Down!

AS SOON AS TOM PICKARD at Whitecourt Detachment heard the alert "Officer Down! Officer Down!" he determined that the location of the problem was at Roszko's farm. Then he contacted Superintendent Marty Cheliak, the commander of the RCMP's Western Alberta District. At that time, Cheliak was on an assignment in Grande Prairie, Alberta. When he received Pickard's alert, he, in turn, immediately phoned Assistant Commissioner Bill Sweeney, the commanding officer of "K" Division, to advise him of the situation. Sweeney notified Chief Superintendent Rod Knecht, the officer in charge of Criminal Operations.

Throughout the morning—as Cheliak sped for Rochfort Bridge—he received constant updates from Pickard and passed them on to Sweeney and Knecht in Edmonton.

It would be one p.m. before Cheliak arrived at the command post on Range Road 75. "By then," he says, "I suspected the worst. My heart so badly wanted those four members to be alive, but my mind told me that . . . that it probably wasn't so."

When Clayton Seguin heard the first call of "Officer Down!" on his radio, he was in the courtroom on the Alexis Reserve waiting to testify.

"My radio was on, but out there the reception is terrible. So I was getting a lot of static and bits and pieces of what the dispatcher was saying."

But it very quickly became clear to Clayton that there was a major incident occurring where one of their members had been shot.

"I yelled to Julie Letal that we had to get out of there and get going."

They ran out of the building and jumped in their PC. By then they knew the location was Roszko's farm. Seguin drove as fast as he could to get there.

Rev. Arnold Lotholz, the minister of the Pentecostal Assembly Church, is an electrical contractor. In 2005, he also held the position of being the Director of Emergency Management for the Mayerthorpe community.

"It was my responsibility to lead the town and help them get through times of crisis and disaster."

On that Thursday morning, he was doing some electrical work at the Mayerthorpe Detachment office.

"Around ten a.m., I noticed the members moving about rather quickly, and pretty soon they had all vacated the building. Then I saw Margaret Thibault, the Victims' Service Coordinator, preparing to leave the building. She was the one who told me there was an officer down.

"And at that moment my role changed."

The first thing that Arnold did was to call his church prayer line, a network that's used to get people praying for various causes. Then, because he knew that all of Mayerthorpe's volunteer fire brigade would respond to the Officer Down emergency, he phoned the Lac Ste. Anne county office and asked Jeremy Wagner to have his firefighting unit cover for the town's brigade.

Then he declared a Level Two emergency for the town of Mayerthorpe.

Pastor Wendell Wiebe, the chaplain of Mayerthorpe's volunteer fire brigade, was in the shower when he heard his pager go off. When he checked it, the pager indicated an alert that there was an "officer down" near Rochfort Bridge.

"Because the fire hall was so far away, I ran over to the Uptown Auto Garage whose owner, Tom Eichhorn, was also the town's deputy fire chief. He drove me over to the fire hall and we climbed aboard the rescue vehicle and headed for Range Road 75.

Dr. Kyle, the veterinarian, didn't hear a radio call or any other alert but, when he saw an ambulance and several police cars go roaring past his clinic, he knew that something serious had happened somewhere.

The mayor of Mayerthorpe, Albert Schalm, was working at his "day job" on a huge cattle farm south of town. His boss owned five and a half sections of land—well over three thousand acres.

And every year in early spring, Albert was busy helping 400 new calves come into the world.

Normally Albert would have had the radio on in his pickup truck or in the barn, but this particular morning he didn't. Sometime between ten and eleven, his wife, Janet, phoned him and said, "There's an incident happening with the RCMP. There's a possibility that one officer has been shot."

Albert was very concerned about the situation, but decided to stay working at the farm until he received more definite news.

Later in the morning, he phoned the town office, and the secretary, Candi Graumann, told him a lot of media were milling about the town hall asking the staff for answers about the RCMP incident. Arnold told her he was on his way home for lunch and would check into the office for an update.

The incident was beginning to sound serious to him.

In fact, it was very serious.

Reconstruction of the crime scene told a grim tale of what had happened that morning inside the Quonset hut.

Schiemann, Myrol, Gordon, and Johnston had rounded the southeast corner of the Quonset together. Brock Myrol went inside and headed towards the back where the two makeshift marijuana sheds were located. Schiemann and Johnston followed Myrol inside and went about halfway into the building. Anthony Gordon remained outside standing in the middle of the big doors.

Inside the hut, Roszko waited until he thought the time was right and then opened fire with his semi-automatic weapon. The Heckler and Koch rifle spit out large-calibre bullets with the same rapidity as a machine gun.

His first target was Tony Gordon, whom he killed with two shots to the torso. Then he fired repeatedly at Johnston and Schiemann. Peter was unarmed and defenceless. Leo got his gun out and fired one round that ricocheted off the butt plate of the Beretta pistol in Roszko's waistband. Tragically, that was the only shot he got off. The slide on Leo's gun got caught in his clothing and failed to properly eject the shell casing of the first bullet he fired. Consequently, his gun jammed.

Both he and Peter were felled by multiple wounds to the upper body.

The three Mounties were killed within a matter of seconds.

While Roszko was firing at them, Brock Myrol made a valiant attempt to get out the back human door, but it was locked from the outside. When he realized this, he tried to lunge for cover behind the frame of one of the marijuana sheds. As he was diving, Roszko hit him with a shot to the head. He also had a superficial gunshot wound that grazed his left hip.

It is estimated that the total elapsed time for the murder of these four men was less than fifteen seconds.

Roszko's semi-automatic rifle held a clip of twenty rounds. Nineteen spent shell casings were found scattered inside the Quonset hut.

Then, after killing the four young policemen, Roszko went outside to take a look around.

As he emerged from the building, he immediately saw Steve Vigor moving towards him with his gun drawn.

Steve says, "I could tell he was surprised to see me. But he recovered very quickly. In a split second, he raised his automatic weapon and fired two shots in my direction."

One of the shots missed Vigor by inches, shattering the mirror of the police car beside him. The other shot blew out the window of the cruiser.

"When a situation like this arises, your senses seem to shut down and adrenalin and instinct take over. You concentrate on the target. It's all a blur to me now but I know I didn't hear the shots from his gun. But I saw the flashes from its muzzle.

"By instinct I went into a crouch and got off two two-handed shots. I thought I hit him but I couldn't be sure. I saw him stumble back into the Quonset hut."

Hoogestraat says, "It all happened so fast that I didn't even see the gunfight between Steve and Roszko. Steve thought he'd hit him, but he wasn't sure, because Roszko went back inside on his own steam."

Later they learned that Vigor had hit him in the hand and in the thigh.

When Roszko went back inside the Quonset, Vigor called for Hoogestraat to drive their large Yukon vehicle to the east end of

Leo Johnston,
photo taken April 2001.

Brock Myrol,
photo taken February 1, 2005.

Anthony Gordon,
photo taken October 2002.

Peter Schiemann,
photo taken November 22, 2000.

the building so they could use it as cover in a location where they could keep a watch on the Quonset's front door.

"I maintained cover on the entranceway to the Quonset so no one could go in or out. Then Garret slowly backed up the vehicle to my position and I backed myself up so that I was behind the rear corner of the passenger side."

While Hoogestraat continued to back the vehicle up, Vigor used it as a shield, walking in a crouch behind it. They kept moving back until they reached a sand pile outside the hut. From here, they were in a position to have the best possible view of the two front doors of the building.

Steve says, "Garret was unbelievable through all this. He put himself at such risk backing that Yukon up. And he was so thorough, calling for backup and talking to Control."

After Hoogestraat used his cell phone to make the initial call to 911, he switched over to the radio to make further communication with telecom control. He also listened to the radio traffic as Control directed other members to the scene.

While Garret was crouched down on the floor of the Yukon working the radio, Steve kept an intense watch on the front doors of the building.

It was dark inside the Quonset.

"I couldn't see Roszko inside the Quonset, but I could see a fallen officer at the entrance. There was a boot and the lower right leg . . . from the knee down . . . of one officer that could be seen to the south of the main entrance, inside the Quonset. That's all you could see."

There were no movements, no sounds in the Quonset, with the eerie exception of the voices being broadcast over the radios that the fallen Mounties had on them inside the building. These were the frantic calls of members at various locations calling back and forth as they made their way to the scene.

When Hoogestraat heard the members' voices being broadcast inside the Quonset, he realized that Roszko could hear them, too. So he used the radio to try and talk to the fallen members and to establish some kind of rapport with Roszko himself.

Vigor says, "We decided that we would call over the radio to try and get the officers' radios to work so that if anybody was alive we would get them to press the mike buttons . . . talk to us . . . anything. And we were hoping to get Mr. Roszko to give up."

Using his radio, Garret called to the members inside, "If any of you can hear me in there, key your mike."

He repeated this several times but there was no response — just silence.

He alternated these calls with pleas to Roszko: "We can see a member down. Let us come in so we can help him."

Roszko's semi-automatic Heckler and Koch assault rifle. (RCMP)

Roszko's 9mm Beretta pistol and Hennessey's .303 Winchester rifle. (RCMP)

The effect of Hoogestraat's voice emanating from the radios and echoing throughout the Quonset was chilling.

Moments later, he tried again: "We've got officers down in there. We want to get them out. Give yourself up and let us come in and get our officers out."

But Garret says, "We got no response whatsoever. No clicking of the mikes. No nothing."

Vigor became more and more disturbed with the lack of response. He recalls the emotions that swept over him. "I had such feelings of helplessness. I suspected the worst. I felt this was not going to be a rescue attempt. This was going to be a recovery."

What Vigor and Hoogestraat didn't realize was that Roszko was dead.

After Vigor shot him twice outside the Quonset, Roszko had stumbled back inside and hidden among the debris. As he sat there in pain, he must have quickly assessed his wounds. The hit he had taken to his hand from Vigor was debilitating, but not lethal. Leo Johnston's shot that hit the butt plate of Roszko's pistol had fragmented and superficially scarred his face.

But the bullet wound in his upper leg was serious. It was bleeding badly and his thighbone had been shattered. He couldn't bear to move his leg, let alone stand on it. Unable to get around, Roszko was virtually defenceless. He must have thought it was just a matter of time before the Mounties rushed in and killed him or captured him.

And he was determined not to go back to jail. After he assessed his wounds, it only took him a few seconds to decide to kill himself. From a sitting position, he raised his assault rifle and pointed it at his chest. Then he pulled the trigger.

But Vigor and Hoogestraat hadn't heard the suicide shot and didn't know he was dead.

Consequently, they assumed that Roszko was lying in wait with his powerful weapon and would kill anyone who entered the hut.

Vigor called Edmonton requesting the ERT team. Hoogestraat called for an Explosive Disposal Unit Remote Mobile Investigator—a robot.

In Edmonton, the RCMP dispatcher raised two ERT crews—one from Red Deer and one from Edmonton. A police service dog, a STARS air ambulance, and an Edmonton Air-1 police helicopter were deployed to the scene. A request went out to close the airspace over Roszko's farm area.

Canadian Forces Base Edmonton was contacted for military assistance. The garrison dispatched two armoured personnel carriers, an armoured ambulance, and twenty military personnel to the scene.

Meanwhile, people were starting to gather on a hill on Range Road 80 that is located directly across from the rear of Roszko's Quonset.

Dianne Romeo says, "Some people in the area have police scanners and when they heard what was going on, they came out to see what was happening. The police stopped them from going down Jimmy Roszko's road, so they came over to ours.

"There's a big hill just south of our property, and dozens of people started to gather there . . . including newspaper reporters and a TV van. There must have been at least twenty people sitting on the hill.

"And a helicopter circled overhead all day.

"I watched from our back deck. We can see Jimmy's yard from there. I heard the gunshots and everything. I heard the last shot, too . . . where Jimmy killed himself."

Earlier that morning, Cindie Dennis had just finished breakfast when her mother phoned.

Cindie says, "My mom said that my grandmother had called and told her there was a problem with the police in Mayerthorpe. She asked if I was okay.

"I said that I was fine and I didn't know what she was talking about.

"As soon as I got off the phone, I called the detachment office. Margaret Thibault answered and said I should come in to the office and she would explain everything to me when I got there. At first, I thought there might have been a problem at the Alexis Reserve."

Cindie jumped into her truck and when she got out on the highway, she spotted the Edmonton ERT van heading towards Mayerthorpe.

"I followed it into town. That's when I learned the problem was at James Roszko's farm."

When she went into the detachment, she saw that Margaret Thibault was tied up on the phone. All of the Mayerthorpe members were gone, but there were a lot of Mounties from other detachments in the office, and some over at the Legion hall across the street.

It wasn't very long before the detachment was swarming with out-of-town personnel.

"There must have been thirty of them—a tactical squad, members from the Major Crimes Unit, members from Grande Prairie, Whitecourt, and Edson, and a number of inspectors and superintendents from Edmonton.

"There was very little talking. They were all very busy . . . very intense."

One of the officers assigned Cindie the job of pulling files on James Roszko.

"I was digging into everything we had in the archives about him and his previous history with the RCMP."

It was Cst. Rollie White of the Whitecourt Traffic Unit who gave her the most information. He said he'd heard that Peter and Brock were out at Roszko's place with Leo and Tony Gordon.

"Rollie told me there was a problem in Roszko's Quonset hut. The four members had gone inside and weren't responding to their radios. He said, 'It didn't look good.' One of the members was down. They could see his legs protruding out the Quonset doorway.

"The members in the office weren't saying much, but there was an urgency in their manner that made it obvious that something very serious was happening."

By the time Jim Martin left the Mayerthorpe Detachment office and got in his cruiser, it was after ten a.m. He was almost out on Highway #18 when he heard the call on the radio: "Officer Down! Officer Down!"

At first Jim didn't know who it was on the radio. He responded, "Who is this?"

The voice said, "It's Constable Hoogestraat from Edmonton Auto Theft. We're at the search warrant site. Shots fired. We have an officer down."

"When I heard that, I stomped on it."

He radioed Jeff Whipple and told him there was an officer down at Roszko's place.

"Multiple gun shots fired!"

Jeff had already heard the call at the detachment. He had thrown on his coat and was hurrying out the door.

Jeff says, "My regular car was being repaired, so they gave me a replacement car . . . a used Ford Taurus. It was unmarked . . . had no roof lights or siren . . . but that didn't matter. I drove that car faster than it had ever gone before."

Not far ahead of him, Jim Martin was racing his cruiser at top speed towards Roszko's farm. When Jim turned north on Range Road 75, he saw a car coming towards him. A woman was driving.

"I had no idea who she was, but she could have been fleeing the scene. So I stopped her and searched her vehicle. She didn't know what was going on. She was on her way to work and was totally oblivious of the situation at Roszko's farm."

As Jim was dealing with the woman, Jeff Whipple drove up beside him and rolled down his window.

"Where's Roszko's place?" he asked Martin.

"Just up the hill on the left."

Whipple gunned his car straight ahead.

As he roared away, the confused woman in the car must have been wondering what was going on. But she didn't ask.

Martin released her immediately and sent her on her way.

When he got to the top of the hill, he radioed Hoogestraat and asked him, "Where were the shots fired?"

Garret replied, "At the Quonset."

Jim thought he meant someone was shooting at the Quonset from the tree line near Roszko's trailer. But then, as he pulled into the yard, he spotted Hoogestraat and Vigor crouched down behind their Suburban.

It was then that Hoogestraat radioed Jim, "The shooter is in the Quonset."

"When I heard that, I made a beeline towards their position in front of the building. From there, I contacted our guys as they arrived and instructed them so we would cover off the area as best we could."

Meanwhile, other RCMP members were rushing to the scene from all directions. A bunch of them were taking a course in White-court, and when they heard the alarm, they all headed for the scene without weapons and wearing their civilian clothes.

As Clayton Seguin and Julie Letal raced from the Alexis Reserve, they tried to find out as much as they could about the crisis. They phoned other members and listened to the busy radio traffic that was calling for ambulances and members from several detachments to respond to the scene.

In all the confusion, they tried to piece things together. Both of them were crying.

From what they could tell, at least one officer was down. But who was it? And were there more than one? How many were involved? Were they hurt—or worse?

"And we knew there was only one .308 rifle in the detachment. So we definitely needed more firepower at the scene to contain the shooter."

As they roared along the road, they used their cell phone to contact other members and see if they could get some rifles.

Clayton recalls, "Our basic message was, 'Get guns and get there.'"

They called Al Starman and Joe Sangster at their homes. At first, both men had a hard time believing such a disaster was really happening.

"I could hear the disbelief in their voices," Clayton says, "But when they heard the quiver in my voice, and then heard me crying, they knew it was no joke."

Starman said he could get a couple of rifles and told them he was on his way. He called several of his farmer friends who had hunting rifles. All of them promised to drop off their rifles and some ammunition with the police at the crime scene.

Sangster was a crossbow hunter. He didn't have access to any rifles but said he would leave for Roszko's place immediately.

Clayton continued to drive as fast as could . . . almost recklessly.

"We got there in fifteen minutes . . . right after Jim Martin and Jeff Whipple had arrived."

Clayton remembers, "As soon as I jumped out of the car, the first horrible thing I saw was a member's leg . . . the yellow stripe on his pant leg . . . it was sticking out of the main door of the Quonset.

"Julie and I were assigned to cover the back of the building. We went around and crouched down behind a fence post with our guns drawn. Our job was containment. Others were assigned to cover each of the four corners . . . to make sure the shooter didn't get out and run away.

"We didn't know where Roszko was. Maybe he already got out by the back door. It was so quiet out there. It was eerie. We kept hoping that some of our guys were hiding, keeping quiet so they wouldn't be detected.

"Then we heard gunfire in the distance. It was really kind of alarming, but we soon learned it was our guys testing rifles out on the range road."

Jeff Whipple was the first member to arrive on the scene. As he drove through the second gate into Roszko's compound, he saw Vigor and Hoogestraat hunched down behind their Yukon with their guns drawn and aimed at the Quonset.

Jeff jumped out of his unmarked Taurus and ran towards them. Vigor and Hoogestraat quickly advised him of what had happened so far and warned him that the gunman was inside the Quonset and well armed.

Hoogestraat kept calling into the Quonset trying to get a response but there was none.

Whipple kept darting back and forth trying to get a better angle of vision,

He says, "I saw a member down in the doorway and I wanted to go in there."

But Vigor would not allow it.

"I couldn't let him go in there," he says. "Everything was against us. It was dark in there. He [Roszko] knew the interior of the building. He had high-powered rifles and wouldn't have hesitated to shoot anybody trying to get in there. Roszko was looking out into the bright light. We would have been silhouetted in the driveway. It would have been a suicide attempt."

Moments later, Jim Martin arrived and ran to join the other three Mounties behind the Yukon. Vigor apprised him of the situation.

All the while, Jeff kept saying he wanted to charge into the Quonset. But Martin sided with Vigor and ordered Whipple not to try that.

"It would have been suicidal," Jim says.

Whipple is not so sure. He says, "My biggest regret is that I didn't go in there. I should have gone in. Everyone tells me there was no use . . . that I couldn't save them. But we'll never know that for sure. We can only presume that was the case. I should have gone in."

When Staff Sgt. Tom Pickard arrived from Whitecourt, he set up a command post on Range Road 75 and took charge of the operation. He, too, issued an order that no one was to try and enter the Quonset.

So they waited.

And, as the four of them hunkered down behind the truck in front of the Quonset, the situation became more and more unsettling.

It was eerie. They could hear the radios continue to echo inside but could not detect another sound from anyone.

Nevertheless, they had to assume that Roszko was still alive in there.

Martin says, "I thought he'd used a ladder and had positioned himself on the high ground on the platform above the marijuana sheds."

As more members from Mayerthorpe and Whitecourt Detachments arrived, they, too, wanted permission to charge the Quonset and rescue their friends.

Vigor says, "I had to put a stop to that. It was one of the hardest decisions I ever had to make but I had to do it.

"Some of the younger members weren't happy with my decision. They were very emotional about it. And I understood their feelings. They worked with these men . . . they loved them. But it wasn't wise to go in there . . . our position was not good . . . I just couldn't let it happen."

Jim Martin knew that Vigor was right. Steve was an ERT member who understood dangerous situations and was trained to handle them. And Jim was in total agreement with him that they should not go in.

"Every fibre in my body wanted to go in there, but that was our emotions trying to overrule our thinking. But still . . . waiting for the ERT to arrive was the longest minutes of my life. I felt so useless . . . and we continued to get no response from the Quonset."

As they waited, Steve Vigor described the type of guns that Roszko had in his possession to use against them.

Jim Martin remembers being very impressed with Vigor's accuracy. Steve had only seen Roszko for a flash, yet he could describe the assault rifle with its scope, the Beretta pistol in Roszko's waistband, the Winchester rifle over his shoulder.

For forty-five minutes, they continued to call to Roszko. But then all the radios completely went silent and stopped echoing any calls.

Still there was no reason to assume that Roszko was dead. Especially since Steve Vigor didn't think he'd hit him.

By this time, Brian Pinder and Tom Pickard had set up a command post on the range road. They took charge of the outer perimeter surrounding the farm. Jim Martin was in charge of the inner perimeter adjacent to Roszko's barn.

Out on Highway #18, Wendell Wiebe and his firefighters were directing traffic, making sure no unauthorized vehicles proceeded up Range Road 75. They were also making sure that people weren't stopping and gawking on the highway and thereby congesting the flow of traffic, which would prevent the arrival of essential police and military personnel at the crime scene.

While Wendell was sitting in the fire truck, Tom Eichhorn, the deputy fire chief, approached him and said, "There's a need for your chaplain services with the police at the Legion hall. You need to go back right now."

Without hesitation, Wendell complied with Tom's suggestion and was driven back to Mayerthorpe.

In town, the news of trouble at Roszko's farm had spread like wildfire. Everyone seemed to have their radios on and their televisions, too. People gathered in shops and stores to speculate on what was happening. Items of information were gradually transmitted to the public—initially to the local area, but then across the province; the military was being called in, a light armoured vehicle called a Coyote was on its way from Edmonton, and the Mounties were bringing in the bomb squad with a robot.

Rev. Lotholz knew the situation had to be very bad when he saw the Mountie Detachment from Grande Prairie come into town and take over the policing responsibilities in Mayerthorpe.

At 12:05, the Edmonton ERT team arrived on the scene and was deployed around the Quonset. Fifteen minutes later, the Explosives Disposal Unit pulled up on the range road with a motorized robot in their caravan. From that time forward, their truck was used as the command post. A helicopter from the Edmonton Police Services began circling overhead ready to help out in any way it could.

Not long after this, the RCMP contacted the Edmonton garrison and asked them to recall their military vehicles and personnel.

At 12:40 p.m., the EDU deployed their robot inside the Quonset. Its video camera relayed pictures back to a monitor in the command truck. The first tragic image on the screen was a picture of Cst. Anthony Gordon lying motionless near the entrance.

Then Constables Schiemann and Johnston were located near the centre of the Quonset.

There were no signs of life among the three Mounties.

Constable Myrol was not seen by the robot.

The machine turned and showed Roszko lying on his back. He appeared to be dead. His Beretta was still tucked into the waistband of his pants. Lying to the right of him was the .300 Winchester Magnum. His semi-automatic .308 Heckler and Koch assault rifle was between his legs.

He was wearing two pairs of pants and five layers of tops and jackets, as well as black socks that covered his boots. The socks are an old hunter's trick that allows someone to muffle his footsteps in the snow so he can sneak up on his prey.

It was later determined that neither the Beretta nor the Winchester had been fired in the Quonset hut.

In the command truck, the bomb disposal controller decided that, just in case Roszko wasn't dead, he would use the arm of the robot to hold the shooter down and keep him away from his weapons.

The ERT team was then deployed and entered the Quonset. Members moved the weapons away from Roszko, rolled him over, and handcuffed him. Not far from him, the police found the white bedsheet he used for cover plus a bottle of water and a container of Bear Spray.

Other members went deeper into the building looking for Brock Myrol. They found him near the rear door, which was padlocked from the outside.

Two of the officers were carried out of the building in the vain hope that they might be resuscitated.

It was no use. All four RCMP members were dead.

Jim Martin was in a daze. He could not believe it. Even though he feared the worst, for a while he had retained some small hope that at least one of them might be alive. But in time, even that expectation had diminished.

"After watching the Quonset for an hour, I had a bad feeling that they all might be dead. We should have heard *something* . . . but we didn't."

"But when you actually see them . . . it's awful . . . it's like losing a member of your own family . . . Peter and Leo were really good friends of mine."

As stunned and pained as Jim Martin felt, he knew their first responsibility was to notify the next of kin.

In tragic situations like this, there is a concern at all levels of the RCMP that the wives and parents of the slain members be notified of their deaths in a personal, dignified manner, as opposed to their hearing the news from the media.

Martin radioed this concern to Sgt. Pinder and Staff Sgt. Pickard in the command truck. And they both agreed. Pinder asked Martin to come out to the caravan and said that he and Jim would proceed into town together.

Pickard would assume the grim task of officially identifying the members' bodies. It was an act of agony that still haunts him.

Early on Thursday afternoon, Kim Gordon, Kelly Johnston, and Anjila Steeves had begun receiving calls from friends and relatives who had heard disturbing rumours about RCMP members having been shot near Mayerthorpe.

As the day wore on, representatives from the Mayerthorpe detachment came to see Kim and Anjila personally and confirmed the fact that they had lost radio contact with Tony and Brock. They asked the two women to come with them to the Mayerthorpe Detachment office.

Kelly Johnston was at home and she did not like what she was hearing from friends and neighbours. She had made two phone calls to the detachment office but couldn't get any kind of satisfactory explanation as to what was going on.

After Kelly's second call, Margaret Thibault of Victims' Services came over to the house and asked Kelly to accompany her to the detachment office. When Kelly got there, one of the members told her that a few hours had passed since they'd last had radio contact with Leo.

The three women were gathered in a room together but no one was telling them very much about the situation. They were advised that the four men had gone into a Quonset hut on an investigation and there had been no communication with them for quite a while. They were also advised that a motorized robot was being sent in to the Quonset to survey the site.

Upon hearing that information, Anjila and Kim were horribly upset and began crying. Kelly, who was equally disturbed, kept a brave face and tried to comfort the other two.

Their apprehension heightened as several members of the media began to gather in front of the detachment office. Eventually the media numbers grew to such a size that the three women were hurried out the back door of the detachment office and escorted to the fire hall nearby.

Now, isolated from the distracting activity of the excited media, their wait was quieter, but more intense and no less apprehensive.

Meanwhile, Jim Martin and Brian Pinder were on their way to the fire hall carrying the unbearable burden of being the messengers of death. They would be telling these women the worst news they would ever receive in their lives. What made it all the more devastating was the fact that the three women were so young and had shared such precious little time with their mates.

"That was the worst day of my life," says Jim Martin.

Kim and Anjila and Kelly had waited in the lunchroom of the fire hall in anguish until mid-afternoon.

Then Sgt. Pinder and Cpl. Martin came in accompanied by two other members.

Martin says, "Sgt. Pinder did all of the talking . . . and it was a very tough thing for him to do."

All the women stood around Pinder to hear what he had to say.

Kelly Johnston didn't seem to be correctly interpreting his words. When Pinder told her he was so sorry that Leo was gone, Kelly asked, "Gone where?"

Kim Gordon says she should have known what he was going to say by the look on his face.

"His face was pasty white and there were tears in his eyes. I don't know what he said. All I can remember is his last word — 'dead.'"

Anjila did hear him say, "All four officers are dead."

She didn't believe it. "No, he's not. It's not right. Just let me see him. I know he's all right."

The three women's grief was overwhelming, their pain inconsolable.

After that, Jim Martin went over to the detachment to tell the members in the office the terrible news.

Cindie Dennis says, "Later in the afternoon, Julie Letal and Clayton Seguin came in. They looked awful. And they were soaking wet from lying in the snow out there.

"Then Jim Martin came in and told us, 'They're gone. They're all gone.' He could barely speak. But I knew what he meant and I felt sick. It was horrible."

Peter Schiemann's father, Don, was in Winnipeg at a church conference. His daughter Julia phoned him because she had heard that police officers in Alberta had been shot. Don tried to alleviate her fears and said he would look into the matter and get back to her.

While listening to the radio, he heard even more alarming news that the shootings had taken place near Mayerthorpe. And that four officers were not responding to radio contact. Don Schiemann's worst fears were realized at the Winnipeg airport when he was about to board his plane home to Edmonton.

Superintendent Marty Cheliak contacted him and told him that Peter was dead. He apologized for giving Don such dreadful news over the phone but explained that he wanted to tell him personally before he heard the news via the media.

Don, who was heartbroken, then phoned his wife and told her and his two children the awful news. He says, "It was the worst thing I've ever done in my entire life."

Wendell Wiebe was in the lounge at the Legion hall. He says, "There were about six Mounties in the room watching TV. Some of them were crying."

Wendell thought he wasn't doing much good there. He'd heard that the firefighters were gathered in the basement of the hospital, so he decided to go over there. He wasn't there long when the fire chief, Randy Schroeder, came in and announced that he had just learned that all four RCMP officers had been killed.

Wiebe says, "It was one of those overwhelming catastrophes that are beyond understanding. It was simply too much to grasp. I remember I had the feeling I was floating through it . . . like it was a dream."

After Mayor Albert Schalm finished his lunch, he decided to go to the town office and stay there for the rest of the day. All afternoon he was either on the phone or dealing with the media face to face. He had refrained from calling the RCMP detachment for information because they had enough on their plate without him interfering. So Albert had to pick up his information in bits and pieces from whatever source he could find.

What seemed to be confirmed was that the RCMP was involved in an investigation and hours ago had lost radio contact with four of their members on the site.

But then some time after two p.m., a media person came in and said to Albert, "Haven't you heard? Four of them have been shot . . . and killed."

"It was such a shock," Albert says. "It's a good thing I was sitting down at the time. I just couldn't believe it. And then I started to think, who were they? I knew almost all of them, so I wondered who it was that had been killed."

Before long, Albert and everyone else in town knew their names.

Earlier that day, Andria Gogan, who had married and was now Andria Reid, was driving her car to her house in Spring Grove. The road conditions were good, and everything seemed normal until she saw three police cars go racing by her. They appeared to be heading towards Mayerthorpe.

When Andria got home, she asked her husband, Rachied, if he knew what was going on with all the police activity on the highway.

Because Andria was pregnant, he didn't want to tell her what he'd heard on the radio, so he said very little.

Andria wasn't satisfied with that and phoned her friend Karen Killen in Mayerthorpe.

Karen told her, "Something major is happening . . . a shooting, I think. I don't know what's going on, but I think it's bad."

On hearing that, Andria immediately got back in her car and headed for Mayerthorpe to be with Kelly Johnston. On the way, she heard on the radio that the STARS helicopter ambulance had transported two Mounties to Edmonton.

Andria says, "So I thought to myself . . . well, that doesn't sound too bad. Maybe they were just wounded."

She continues, "Because I couldn't get Kelly on the phone, I decided to drive over to the Mayerthorpe hospital. As soon as I got in the door, I saw Tanya Kendall, a paramedic, walking in the hall. She was bawling her eyes out.

"I asked her what was wrong . . . what was the matter?"

She was sobbing and mumbled, "They're all dead."

"Who is dead?"

Tanya couldn't reply.

"Tell me who is dead."

"Peter, Leo, Brock, and Anthony Gordon."

"I was in shock. I had to sit down. That was the worst thing . . . the saddest news I had ever received in all my life."

Cindie Dennis says, "After Jim Martin informed us of our friends' deaths, we all sat around in shock . . . sobbing and crying. I do remember looking outside and seeing all the media gathered around the building . . . TV satellite trucks, guys carrying television cameras, others with notebooks and tape recorders.

"They gathered up Julie and Clayton and me . . . I can't remember who else . . . and told us we had to get out of there.

"They rushed us out the back door and piled us in the green Victims' Services van and took us all over to Joe Sangster's house. Almost everybody from the Mayerthorpe and Whitecourt detachments . . . and their families . . . were there.

"Everyone was terribly upset . . . people were trying to talk to each other, but it was difficult, because most of us were bawling.

"I finally got myself together and called my parents on their cell phone. They were already in the car on their way to

An aerial view of the crime scene taken on March 3, 2005. Notice the dog's shed at the rear of the Quonset and the distance of the fuel tank (behind the three steel grain bins) from the Quonset. (*Mayerthorpe Freelancer*)

Mayerthorpe. They had left right after my mom phoned me in the morning. It's a six-hour drive from their place in Pincher Creek, and now they weren't that far away.

"After that, I sat around with the others watching television. The incident was all over the provincial news . . . every channel."

And soon that frightful news began to spread all across the country.

Banner newspaper headlines announced the awful truth: *Four Mounties Slain in Alberta*. National radio and television programming was interrupted to convey the dreadful news to an astonished nation.

And ever since that terrible Thursday in March 2005, the most notorious mass murder in the history of the Royal Canadian Mounted Police would be forever tied to tiny, unpretentious Mayerthorpe.

7 | Devastation

THE DEATH OF THE FOUR young Mounties sent the towns of Mayerthorpe and Whitecourt into shock. Everyone in those communities knew at least one of the policemen; lots of people knew all of them.

Agonizing townsfolk recalled to themselves or to others the last time they had seen or spoken to one of the dead policemen. They remembered when they said hello to kindly Peter Schiemann or when they waved to friendly Leo Johnston. Brock Myrol was new to town and not as well known, but lots of people could remember the handsome young policeman who had just moved into town with his beautiful fiancée.

Big and tall Anthony Gordon was well known and highly respected in the region, but was especially familiar in the community in Whitecourt, where he worked and lived with his wife, Kim, and their little boy.

Any mention of the officers' names caused people to lower their eyes and shake their heads in pain and dismay.

These four were not just good policemen, they were the very best type of wholesome young men that Canada can produce. Each of them was bright, fit, athletic, handsome, personable, alert, curious, considerate, and extremely capable. As police officers their potential was tremendous.

And now, in one appalling act of madness, they were gone.

On Friday, March 4, both Shawn Hennessey and Dennis Cheeseman had gone to work. When Cheeseman heard about the murders, it was about one-thirty p.m. He then left his job at Sepallo Foods, saying he had a family emergency. In fact, he was almost physically ill when he learned what had happened after they dropped Roszko off the night before.

Shawn remained at the Kal Tire meeting in Edmonton for most of the day. He heard what had happened at Roszko's farm while he was listening to the car radio on his way home. The news was extremely disturbing to him.

Shawn's wife, Christine, was at home washing the dishes and listening to an Edmonton radio station when she heard reports that four Mounties were feared dead near Mayerthorpe.

Christine says, "They were saying that they didn't know about the safety of four RCMP officers, they weren't responsive. And I was just like. 'Oh no, that's really sad. I wonder what's going on.'

"Then all of a sudden I heard the name [Roszko] and I was just . . . my heart sank. I was like, 'No, no way.'"

Christine remembers what Shawn said when he arrived home that day around four-thirty p.m.

"He said, 'Oh, my God,' and he couldn't even talk. He just went blank. The look on his face, I knew something terrible had happened. And I just sat there. He just sat there for a long time. He didn't say anything.

"He just said after a while, 'Are you okay?' and I said, 'I don't know.'"

Then Shawn told Christine that Roszko had showed up at their house the night before when they were in bed. He said that Roszko was carrying a handgun and demanded help.

He said, "[Roszko] came here with a gun, Christine, and I was so scared."

Christine remembers that while he was speaking, he was pale with fear.

Meanwhile, people were showing up at the Mayerthorpe and Whitecourt detachments in droves. Men and women, children, even some entire families, began placing flowers and cards in front of the detachment offices. Among the cards were long, handwritten notes poignantly expressing each bearer's sorrow and sadness. The common themes among the messages were words of thanks and appreciation, and promises that the four dead Mounties would not be forgotten.

The media, with the first hint of a developing story, had started to arrive in Mayerthorpe before noon. By two o'clock, they had inundated the town and were rushing madly about trying to get a unique angle or scoop on the tragedy.

Pastor Wendell Wiebe says the media were terrible.

"They were intrusive and unbelievably insensitive. Their manner lacked any sense of professionalism.

"There was such a competition among them. Everybody wanted an edge to get the inside story.

"I remember one of our firefighters being chased by a reporter who wanted to know: 'Did you see the bodies? Did you see the blood?'

"People in our town are naturally cautious, but the media's approach made them even more so.

"Their glaring intrusion and insensitive behaviour made me angry. I wanted them to leave our town and not come back."

John Kyle, the vet, says, "They never bothered me . . . but I was working inside. There were lots of them in town . . . parked in front of the police station and interviewing people on the street."

Rev. Arnold Lotholz says, "It was my experience that the media were generally well-behaved . . . but I was mostly inside the Legion hall away from all the chaos outdoors. However, I do remember the phones never stopped ringing."

Arnold helped to set up the Legion as a command post and spent most of his day inside the building, hooking up phones and computers with high-speed Internet. He also brought in food for everyone in the hall and arranged accommodation for the police who were coming into town to help.

So many townspeople had called the Co-op and ordered trays of food be sent to the Legion that they had much more food there than they needed.

Lotholz remembers, "I had to phone the Co-op and tell them not to send over any more food."

The most difficult sight for Lotholz to deal with was when the Mayerthorpe police officers—one after another—started returning from the crime scene where they knew all hope was lost for their four colleagues and good friends.

Lotholz says, "Around two o'clock some of the detachment officers began straggling in . . . all of them ashen and downtrodden. They didn't speak . . . they kept a stunned silence."

Seeing them in such pain shook him badly.

For the widows and the families of the dead, the first few days were a blur. Relatives came, friends dropped in, the phones rang and rang but someone else answered, food was sent over, flowers arrived, cards were read, words were spoken, nothing much registered. There was no consolation for their grief. The minutes dragged by with an aching numbness. One hour spilled into another . . . then another . . . ever so slowly. The only reprieve was sleep . . . when it came. The dark of night was welcome, but did not always provide relief from their pain.

On Thursday night near Barrhead, Shawn Hennessey and his mother discussed the fact that the Winchester rifle Roszko had taken on his murderous rampage was registered to Shawn's grandfather, John Hennessey. Fearing the rifle would be traced to John and eventually Shawn, they called for a family meeting.

The gathering included Shawn, Dennis, Shawn's father, Barry, and his mother, Sandy. They discussed the fact that the rifle would invariably be traced back to John and it wouldn't be long before the RCMP would come knocking and ask about it.

Barry claims they went along with John Hennessey's idea to concoct a "story" as follows: John had always possessed the rifle; he had never given it to Shawn; the rifle had been stolen out of John Hennessey's welding truck several weeks prior to the time of the murders.

Everyone at the meeting agreed to stick to this story when the police came calling.

Over in Mayerthorpe, a deluge of media was descending on the town.

Mayor Albert Schalm says, "The media scrum at my office lasted all day and went well into the evening."

At one point, a call came from a government secretary in Ottawa asking where he would be at 7:00 p.m. Albert told her, and at 7:00 sharp he received a phone call from Prime Minister Paul Martin.

"The gist of his message was that he wanted to send condolences to the people of Mayerthorpe on behalf of the country. He asked me to relay his message to our community."

Albert left his office late, but even when he got home, the phone kept ringing.

At 12:45 a.m. he received a call from the BBC in London, England, asking for a live interview.

"The British radio host was very nice. He didn't seem to understand the time difference between England and Western Canada. He told me that the Canadian Mounties are known all over the world."

Other phone calls came in from radio stations across the country. Several were from Toronto. One of those calls came in from a producer at 3:45 a.m. trying to set up a 6:00 a.m. live interview.

In retrospect, Albert says he really can't complain. "When I was dealing with the national and international media, they treated me very well," he says. "As a matter of fact, they were very considerate . . . awesome, I would say. And I appreciated that."

For five or six days after the tragedy, Albert was so busy with the daily deluge of phone calls and interviews, he decided to take "a bit of a leave" from his farm job. "I asked my boss, Harvey Hagman, if I could have the mornings off . . . and he was good enough to accommodate me. He didn't replace me, he just agreed that I could take the mornings off. Sometimes I wonder how he got along without someone, because that was our busiest time of year. And you had to be alert and careful.

"Every half hour, we used to drive through the herd on a sleigh or a pickup truck and when we spotted a new calf, we'd lift it up and put it on the sled or on the tailgate of the truck. Then we'd drive slowly to the calving barn and the calf's mother would follow right behind us . . . always followed right behind."

That Friday night, RCMP Superintendent Marty Cheliak announced that Roszko's white pickup truck had been located near Cherhill by Alberta's Rural Crime Watch organization.

The media immediately began to wonder how Roszko had

managed to travel the twenty-some miles from Cherhill to his farm on Range Road 75. And this question soon became the main topic of discussion and speculation among just about everyone in the county, if not the country.

Christine Hennessey's reaction to this news item was that it now seemed that people were wanting to blame someone for helping Roszko.

As the media continued to scour the area for a new angle on the story, they did respect the RCMP members' privacy and stayed away from them.

And that was a godsend, because all of the Mayerthorpe and Whitecourt Mounties, from the youngest to the oldest, were suffering from deep shock. Some of them had seen the bodies of their dead friends, and as one member recalls, "Their injuries were horrific."

Many of the members endured horrible flashbacks of the incident. Most of them had recurring nightmares. Almost all of them would eventually be diagnosed with post-traumatic stress disorder.

Each of them was offered immediate leave, and they were replaced at their posts by members from other nearby detachments who came in and served on a rotational basis.

Jeff Whipple says, "I remember those first few days, but it's all pretty hazy. I would go in to work one day. The next day I would feel awful and I'd stay home. Then I'd go back in. Then another day, I'd see the psychologist. I was in, off, back in, off . . . everything seemed like a complete blur. And this went on for months after the incident."

Cindie Dennis's parents stayed with her at her house near Sangudo for a few days. They cared for their young daughter and comforted her, tenderly aware that she had suffered such a terrible blow so early in her police career.

Cindie remembers: "Even in those first few days, I realized how much I was going to miss them. They were all such fun to be with. I didn't know Tony Gordon, but I heard so many nice things about him. But the three I knew . . . Peter and Leo and Brock . . . everyone just loved them. And now I was going to their funerals."

Sergeant Bob Meredith, the staff relations representative responsible for the Mayerthorpe Detachment, had rushed to town within an hour of the shootings. He remembers how the RCMP called in three psychologists as well as a dozen peer counsellors to assist the members and the families of the slain Mounties. All of these people in pain were urged to talk about their feelings and seek professional help if they felt they needed it.

The RCMP has a comprehensive member assistance program, but it is up to each individual to ask for help. For the Mounties to insist on their members' accepting this assistance would make it appear as if they were having this support forced upon them.

Members were also free to seek medical professionals on their own or seek help from the federal occupational health centres operated by Veteran Affairs.

Within the course of the first week, a special meeting called a "Critical Incident Debriefing" was held to go over the specific details of the Mayerthorpe incident from beginning to end. Because the trauma of the experience was still so fresh and painful for the Mayerthorpe and Whitecourt members, their attendance at this meeting was not mandatory.

On March 12, an open letter to the public signed by Sgt. Brian Pinder and Staff Sgt. Tom Pickard, the respective Detachment Commanders for Mayerthorpe and Whitecourt, read as follows:

> On behalf of the members, staff, and their families of both Mayerthorpe and Whitecourt Detachments we would like to express our gratitude to the people of our communities, our province, and our country for the overwhelming support we have received.
>
> The deaths of our four friends and colleagues has been a tragedy beyond comprehension and we as a family needed some days to be together in private grief. However, we need the communities we serve to know that their outpouring of support, love, prayers, hugs, flowers, and caring has touched all our hearts, the hearts of our families, and the families of Constable Peter Schiemann, Constable Leo Johnston, Constable Brock Myrol, and Constable Anthony Gordon. You have eased a burden that could not have been borne without your support. For that we are eternally grateful.
>
> We are proud of our communities, proud to live in them,

and proud to serve and protect them. We are still here and please know that we will see you soon.

There is no doubt that the local members and the families of the deceased Mounties suffered most from the horror of the multiple murders, but the residents of the communities were deeply affected, too.

"It was like a bomb went off," says Margaret Thibault. "There wasn't time for anger. It was too big . . . you'd look into the eyes of your friends and neighbours and the shock was reflected back at you.

"There was a solemn quiet among us . . . like after a great storm passes or after an explosion happens or a bomb goes off. What is there to say? People were still sorting things out . . . digging deep inside themselves for their strength.

"The quiet came from a combination of shock and denial. You cannot accept something this huge in one moment."

John Kyle agrees. "I was working in the clinic and someone came in and told me. I couldn't believe it. I had seen two of those guys just this morning when they picked up the meat. I was stunned.

"When I went out later, it was very subdued, very quiet in town. Everyone was shocked and saddened. It was like they didn't know what to say."

"It was all-consuming, " Margaret says. "The pain was visible . . . palpable in peoples' body language. Just to breathe was a challenge at first.

"Nobody was running around wild or screaming. We stayed close to home and remained calm. We visited each other's houses, shared food together, and tried to sort things out through the rubble of our hearts and minds."

Residents reached out to each other in quiet conversations, away from the prying eyes and ears of reporters.

Albert Schalm says, "You could talk to your neighbour, or virtually anyone in town, without feeling like you were intruding. It was just people leaning on each other, venting their feelings.

"There was some anger, but it was hard to know where to direct it. People would say, 'Why did this happen? Who can we blame?' But at this point the only person you could blame was

James Roszko, and he was dead."

Margaret Thibault remembers, "There was lots of hugging, and people were touching other people on the shoulder to assure each other we weren't living in a nightmare.

"It took a while before tears came. We had to shift gears and get back to some sort of normalcy first."

To get away from it, some people got out of town.

Margaret and some of her friends went to her cabin on the lake.

And then the funerals began.

The first of these was for Peter Schiemann.

On the eve of his funeral, Queen Elizabeth II sent a message to Alberta Lieutenant-Governor Norman Kwong.

It read: "Prince Philip and I were shocked to learn of the deaths of the four Royal Canadian Mounted Police officers in Alberta. Please convey to the families of those killed our sincerest condolences on their terrible loss. Our thoughts and prayers are with them at this most difficult time."

Peter's funeral was held on Tuesday, March 8, in St. Matthew Lutheran Church at Stony Plain west of Edmonton.

A Greyhound-type bus was chartered to transport detachment personnel to the church. This included uniformed officers, civilian employees, their husbands, wives, and a few of the members' parents.

Many local citizens drove down in car pools.

The service was preceded by a procession of tartan-clad pipers leading a large contingent of police officers to the church.

Inside, 1,400 mourners filled the pews while another 600 watched the service on closed-circuit television in two gymnasiums at Memorial Composite High School. Among them were 800 police officers who had come from far and wide.

During the service, Peter's coffin was draped with a Canadian flag on which lay his Stetson and his holster and gun.

The congregation heard Peter's heartbroken younger sister Julia say, "He was a son and a brother whose love for his family was evident at all times."

Peter's older brother Michael could barely refrain from

sobbing as he concluded his comments by declaring to Peter, "I'll leave you with five words: I'll talk to you later."

Dr. Ralph Mayan assured the Schiemann family that they were not alone in their grief, because millions mourned with them. He recalled that Peter had attempted to assuage his father's fear of the dangers of police work by telling him, "If something should happen, you won't need to worry. I'll be with Jesus in heaven."

Dr. Mayan said that Peter even joked to his sister that he wanted to be buried with a bag of potato chips and a flashlight because it would be dark and he'd get hungry. And Peter's family planned to honour his request.

Peter's father, Don Schiemann, a Lutheran pastor, told reporters his son saw his job as a vocation that God had drawn him toward. His advice was: "Don't ever pass up an opportunity to tell your child that you love them.

"I know with all my heart that God will bring some good out of the death of these men. And the first good that I know of is that Peter is in heaven."

The churches in Mayerthorpe played a significant role in helping the community get through this most difficult time. Forgiveness was a theme that was emphasized throughout the week in all of the churches.

Ed Broadway, a minister at the Whitecourt Baptist Church, said the Roszko family needed some consideration and understanding in this tragic situation.

He said, "They have gone to the police and expressed their apologies. They have been very forthright. They are seeking some comfort just like the rest of the people."

At Sunday mass at St. Agnes Roman Catholic Church, the priest asked his parishioners to pray for James Roszko and consider the circumstances that led to his downfall and caused this incident.

Rev. Wendell Wiebe began his Sunday service with the words: "Ugliness and sorrow have filled our week. Hope starts today."

Mayerthorpe residents make a point of distinguishing between the man who committed the murders and members of his large extended family. Roszko's relatives are dotted around Mayerthorpe,

Whitecourt, and the surrounding countryside. Twenty-eight of them are listed in the phone directories pertaining to this area.

Colette McKillop, who owns an insurance business and also served as head of the Mayerthorpe and District Chamber of Commerce says, "We protect our own. Just because they are relatives, the community is not going to hold that against them . . . ever."

James Roszko's brother George, an oil field contractor from Whitecourt, says his neighbours and coworkers rallied to his side after the shootings. "They realized this had nothing to do with us."

At an evening service, Pastor George Ridley prayed, "Lord, we also want you to pray for the Roszko family, the family caught in the middle of all this sorrow."

Mayor Albert Schalm said he didn't want anyone to target the Roszko family.

Some of them are stellar citizens. Lil Roszko, the widow of Fred, runs the Case dealership in Mayerthorpe. She is a prominent citizen who is considered to be a great community person.

Margaret Thibault says, "Lil is widely known and appreciated for serving on town committees and helping to raise funds for various causes. She is just a great woman. Everybody respects her."

All of Jimmy Roszko's brothers and sisters are law-abiding citizens who are gainfully employed. Several of them practise trades or professions in the area.

But even James's own family is divided about their feelings for him.

He and his father had been estranged for over nine years. Their relationship was never very good, but it deteriorated even further when Bill found out that James was using marijuana. Bill still believes that drugs were the cause of his son's bizarre behaviour. As James got into one difficulty after another with the law, Bill came to think of him as a "loser." And he told him so.

When Bill, a self-proclaimed devoutly religious man, heard that his son had murdered four policemen, the eighty-year-old man was shattered. He described the massacre as "terribly evil."

"The devil from everlasting hell could not have done what Jim did . . . the way he shot police. I feel very sorry for the families of the policemen. They were trying to stop a situation of bad behaviour, and they got shot."

During an interview with the press about the tragedy, he referred to James as a "wicked devil" whom he believed "is now in hell."

Bill said, "He had an angry streak as far back as I can remember . . . and a lifetime hatred for police.

"I am his father, but he was not my son."

Bill claimed he had not spoken to Jimmy for nine years and made it clear he would not be attending his funeral. "I'll be making a bad sin to have anything to do with it."

In contrast to those sentiments, James's mother, Stephanie, who divorced Bill when James was twelve, grieved the death of her eccentric son. She says, "My son was not the devil."

But she will admit that he did have a fierce temper. "When he gets a grudge against someone, he will be mad at you for the rest of your life. That's the way he is."

It seems Stephanie had always been more tolerant of James. Some say she was unfailingly supportive of him. Others say he could do no wrong in her eyes. She was known to aggressively confront people in defense of her darling Jimmy.

She helped him, too. After he quit his work in the oil fields of the Northwest Territories in the 1980s, Stephanie allowed him to live with her and her third husband at their farm. She even encouraged him to run a small herd of cattle on their land.

Jimmy's now infamous white pickup truck is registered in Stephanie's name. And it is her belief that the whole problem with the bailiff's coming to Jimmy's farm to repossess the truck was caused by the automotive agency.

She maintains that Jimmy claimed the tailgate on the truck was dented or defective and he had asked them for a new one. When the dealership wouldn't comply with his demands, Jimmy refused to pay them and, as a consequence, they wanted the truck repossessed.

His sister Josephine, who lives nearby in Whitecourt, seemed to understand him best and was particularly close to him. She spent hours on the phone talking to him, counselling him.

She said, "He wasn't the monster they made him out to be. He had a good heart and he never hurt us in any way."

Roszko's twenty-two year-old niece Deirdre expressed her

love for her uncle: "He often came to our rescue when bills couldn't be paid and there was food to be bought.

"We're not only grieving. We have to deal with the anger of society which makes it even harder."

James Roszko's brother George hadn't seen Jimmy in the past fifteen years. He says, "Jim was trouble. Who knows what was rolling around inside his head? Whatever it was, it had nothing to do with the rest of us.

"He was just a sick little man who did a sick, awful deed. He should have been deemed a dangerous offender and locked away years ago."

John Roszko is a finishing carpenter and the father of an Edmonton police officer. John was not enamoured with his younger brother James.

After hearing of his lethal rampage against the police, he lamented, "Sadly, I cannot find it in me to grieve for my brother.

"He was never much of a brother to most of us. I don't know . . . it would be like mourning a stranger. Somehow I feel a sense of relief that he is no longer with us."

John wrote condolence letters to the families of the four constables murdered by his brother. He wanted them to know: "We're going to apply all our efforts to see that something good comes of all this."

John went to the National Memorial in Edmonton to honour the fallen four and said that he wanted to attend their funerals but was concerned that he would not be able to "contain his emotions."

It is John's opinion that his brother did not conceive and carry out his daring and devious plan on the spur of the moment. John maintains that James had been planning to exact his vengeance on the RCMP for years because he believed the police had been persecuting him. "This was something he was thrashing around for many, many years."

John also feels there was likely no way that the police could have prevented the slaughter. He said that the four officers didn't have a chance against his brother because it was "*on his property*"—a little phrase that speaks volumes.

In choosing these words, John implies that James was familiar with the fields around his farm and knew the best way to approach his Quonset hut unnoticed. John's choice of expression means that James was acquainted with every nook and cranny in his steel Quonset hut, he knew the entrances and passageways, and he was acutely aware of every item strewn on the floor throughout the place.

His implication is that James could stealthily approach and enter his Quonset hut and move about inside it without the police's being aware of his presence. And that appears to be precisely what occurred.

Roszko's funeral was held on Thursday night, March 10, at Park Memorial Funeral Home in Mayerthorpe. Several of his family members were present at the small, unpublicized, thirty-minute service. James's father did not attend. His sister Josephine Ruel stayed her loyal course, remembering some nice things about her infamous brother who had forever linked the family name to a national atrocity. Roszko's remains were cremated and the disposition of his ashes is unknown.

That same Thursday morning, an extraordinary memorial service was held in Edmonton to honour the four fallen Mounties. In its magnitude and solemn pageantry, it was one of the most remarkable ceremonies ever witnessed in Canada.

Melanie Grower, a spokesperson from the Prime Minister's Office, offered an explanation as to why the service would have such an impact on the nation: "There are thirty-two million Canadians whose hearts go out to these families."

The entire memorial service from the opening procession to the closing March Past by the RCMP Honour Guard was carried across the country on network television. Millions of Canadians from the western Arctic to eastern Newfoundland tuned in to watch with fascination as the drama of the ritual played out.

An elderly Ontario man who watched the proceedings from start to finish remarked, "It was a day when the whole country mourned."

First came the magnificent procession—so long and large that the marchers had to muster at several locations in the valley beside the North Saskatchewan River. With precision, these various

RCMP horses and riders lead the procession of 10,000 police officers marching to the Butterdome at the University of Alberta for the National Memorial Service in Edmonton, March 10, 2005.
(Epic Photography)

sections merged together into a massive entourage that marched up the hill on 116th Street towards the University of Alberta campus.

Leading the way was the RCMP Regimental Pipes and Drums. Immediately behind them came the four-horse, diamond-patterned Guidon Party, which escorted the RCMP's Guidon, their own unique standard similar to the traditional battle flags of the British Cavalry. Bearing the Colours at the head of the party was Sgt. Major Bill Stewart riding twelve-year-old Kasar, a veteran mount of the Musical Ride flown in from the Rockcliffe stables in Ottawa. Eight more RCMP horses followed the Guidon Party with their riders flying red and white pennons on their lances.

Then came four marching Mounties carrying the fallen members' Stetsons on ceremonial pillows. Next was the one hundred-member Honour Guard comprised exclusively of comrades who had served with the four deceased. Behind them was a rolling sea of red serge—5,000 RCMP members—marching eight abreast in columns that stretched from sidewalk to sidewalk. They were followed by thousands of uniformed police from hundreds of jurisdictions. After them came rows and rows of uniformed public

Headdress bearers enter the Butterdome. L to R: Cpl. Joan Kuyp (for Cst. Peter Schiemann), Cst. Joe Sangster (Leo Johnston), Cst. Beth Hoskin (Anthony Gordon), and Cst. Jason Lapointe (Brock Myrol). Corps Sgt. Major Gene Maeda is behind them. On the horses, L to R: Sgt. Mark Godue, Sgt. Maj. Bill Stewart, S/Sgt. Gerry Sharp. (Epic Photography)

service personnel. In total, the procession of 10,000 marchers measured a full kilometre in length.

When the cortege arrived at the university's Butterdome Pavilion, Sgt. Major Stewart rode Kasar a few strides into the cavernous facility and presented the Guidon to Sgt. Major Robert Gallup, who carried it to the stage while the capacity audience of 15,000 maintained a silent reverence. The service officially began when the Guidon was placed on the head of a ceremonial drum.

The four Mounties' Stetsons were placed on RCMP shabracks (horse blankets) in front of their portraits on stage; the Cadet Choir from Depot Division sang "O Canada"; two ministers extended bilingual greetings to the congregation and gave the call to service.

The two-hour ceremony featured many speakers, none more eloquent than Governor General Adrienne Clarkson and Prime Minister Paul Martin.

The Queen's representative concluded her remarks by addressing the families of the deceased: "To you who suffer, any comfort may seem cold and sympathy somehow remote. But we are here to give what consolation we can; we know that you may

Portraits of the Fallen Four behind the ceremonial drum on the stage at the memorial service. (Epic Photography)

feel no consolation is possible, yet we offer it all the same. We extend all our sympathy, all our strength to those who will always hold constables Gordon, Johnston, Myrol, and Schiemann in a sacred place in their hearts."

Paul Martin's best words captured the sentiments of all Canadians: "To wear the uniform of the RCMP is to dedicate oneself to feats of courage and nobility of purpose. These four young men, alive in the early summer of life, rest now in the serenity of God's embrace. They are mourned by neighbours, and by a nation. Their memory will be eternal. So, too, will be our gratitude."

On behalf of the RCMP, Commissioner Giuliano Zaccardelli proclaimed, "Our way is now lit brighter by the shining memory of these four men who have joined the list of those who have gone before."

Peter Schiemann's father brought tears to many eyes when, at the end of his address, he spoke to his fallen son: "Peter, we will see you in Heaven . . . but we can hardly wait."

Lee Johnston paid homage to his twin brother, Leo, referring to him as "my brother, my best friend, and the most important person in my life."

Constable Barry Baskerville reminded the mourners that his close friend and troop mate Anthony Gordon was just twenty-eight with a wife, Kim, and son, Spencer, and a baby on the way, a child who will never know its father, except through the memories of

Cst. Lee Johnston spends a quiet moment before the portrait of his twin brother, Leo Johnston. (Epic Photography)

others.

In his eulogy for Brock Myrol, Rev. Art Hundeby stated that Brock ". . . always set the bar high and jumped over it. . . [Now] God has carried Brock over the final bar."

Interspersed among the speakers, Ian Tyson offered a powerful rendition of "Four Strong Winds"; Inuk activist and song-writer Susan Aglukark sang "Snowbird"; Aboriginal Tom Jackson accompanied himself on a Native drum singing a poignant version of "Amazing Grace."

Then the house was hushed as a lone bugler, Cst. Owen Rusticus, played the Last Post. When he ended its haunting call, the congregation rose for a minute of silence.

There were prayers for the fallen. Then the Honour Guard exited with a March Past, and the service in Edmonton was ended.

But elsewhere on this day, there were many other memorials attended by thousands in halls and churches across the country from Vancouver to St. Johns.

At Depot Division in Regina, speaker Bob Bourget reminded

the 300 in attendance, "This is indeed the spiritual home of the RCMP here at the Academy. These four cadets have graduated all within the last four years."

In Thorold, Ontario, fifty-two of sixty members from the Hamilton Detachment attended a regional service at St. John's Anglican Church. "There would have been more of us," said Sgt. Mike Campobasso, "but we couldn't abandon ship. Somebody had to stay home and mind the store."

At a sombre service in Winnipeg, RCMP Chief Superintendent Bill Robinson told his grieving members, "They were the best we had to offer, in their youth, vibrancy, and professionalism. We will honour their memory, and we will never forget them."

The magnitude and solemnity of the services held this day across the country were unprecedented in the history of the RCMP.

The following day, private services were held in Alberta for Leo Johnston and Anthony Gordon.

The chartered bus had transported the detachments' personnel to the National Memorial. After the service, the entourage stayed overnight in an Edmonton hotel. Now the bus was moving on to Lac La Biche some 160 kms (ninety-six miles) to the north.

Here, at Leo Johnston's funeral, his widow, Kelly, hugged the honour guard as her husband's casket, covered with a Canadian flag, was carried out of the Evangelical Free Church and was loaded into a hearse.

Earlier that week, Kelly had told the media that she and Leo never even had time to view their wedding pictures nor to go on a honeymoon. "We had a beautiful life each day and we were supposed to have a long and beautiful future together."

Now, as his hearse disappeared in the distance, so too did all of those dreams.

That same day, a service for Anthony Gordon was held at St. Mary's Catholic Church in Red Deer, where his widow, Kim, suffered the same heart-wrenching experience as did Kelly Johnston.

Kim's pain was compounded by the realization that she had not only lost her "gentle giant of a man," but her two-year-old son and the child she was carrying would never know their father's loving care.

It would be June before their second son was born. Kim

named him Anthony after his fallen father.

Because of the 300-km distance between Lac La Biche and Red Deer, it was impossible for the chartered bus entourage to get to Anthony's funeral.

However, after an overnight in Lac La Biche, they got an early start the next morning and set out on the long ride to Brock Myrol's funeral in Red Deer.

The service was held on Saturday, March 12, at the Cross-roads Church on the outskirts of Red Deer and was attended by 2,700 mourners.

Every member of Brock's troop thirteen from Depot Division was at the service, which was quite remarkable, since all of them had just settled into their new postings at various detachments across Canada.

Brock Myrol's mother, Colleen, had previously lashed out at the "liberal-minded justice system" that had allowed James Roszko, a convicted child molester and known threat to police, to remain out of prison.

However, at Brock's final service, her remarks were focused on her son. "Brock was driven as a child, driven as a teen, and in overdrive as an adult."

In sad reflection, she said, "We were supposed to be planning a wedding now, but God changed that for his own reasons."

As Brock's body was loaded into the hearse, his sobbing fiancée, Anjila Steeves, kissed his casket and said goodbye.

That final kiss was the last scene in a tragic national drama that had riveted the country's attention for over a week.

There was, however, one bit of unfinished business for the bus entourage. Many on board wanted to stop at the graveyard where Tony Gordon had been buried the day before.

Before the motor coach got to the cemetery, Jeff Whipple got off and went into a florist's shop, where he bought a huge bunch of assorted flowers.

When the vehicle stopped near Anthony's grave, Jeff distributed the flowers among the group. Then each person took his or her turn laying a flower on top of his freshly turned grave.

Everyone then bowed their heads and had a silent moment

with their own thoughts for their fallen comrade.

"We really needed to do that," Jeff says. "I'm very glad we did."

Back in Mayerthorpe, Rev. Arnold Lotholz, Pastor Wendell Wiebe, Sharon Foster, the minister of the United Church, and father Ray Guimonde of St. Agnes Roman Catholic Church coordinated a memorial service for the community.

It was held in the high school gymnasium with audio feeds into several classrooms and into the nearby Elmer Elson Elementary School. Over 2,000 people attended, and there was extensive media coverage of the program. One of the most touching parts of the service featured the Grade 1 children singing and signing the song, "Love can Build a Bridge."

Two local women, Charlotte Arthur and Colette McKillop, initiated a campaign throughout the town and the surrounding area, where red and white ribbons were distributed inscribed with the words "We Remember." Large ribbons were distributed to businesses so they could hang them in their windows; small ones were for residents to wear on their lapels. The ribbons were free, but many people started to make voluntary donations.

Within days of the murders, there was a lot of talk around town of creating a permanent memorial to the slain Mounties. And Margaret Thibault, who had worked closely with all four constables, agreed to form a committee to pursue such a cause.

Then Haley Martin and Megan Sangster, the eleven-year-old daughters of two Mayerthorpe members, came up with the idea of asking every student across Canada to donate a loonie towards this RCMP memorial. Together with Megan's sister Laura, fourteen, and two local high school students, Katie Mattson and Katherine Lakeman, they launched Kids 4 Cops to help raise money for the cause.

Megan says, "We really loved them and missed them, so we wanted to do something."

And as the reader will determine in chapter eleven, these young women were extremely helpful in making the idea of a memorial become a reality.

But of all the activities that were held to commemorate the

loss of the four Mounties, the one that seemed to have the most immediate impact was a hockey game held in the Mayerthorpe arena.

For the past few years, Jim Martin had organized a charity hockey game between the local Mounties and a team of Mayerthorpe old-timers called the Wranglers. This year's game was scheduled to be played on Monday, March 7, only four days after the tragedy.

Albert Schalm says, "There was some serious soul-searching and many doubts about whether or not the game should take place. But in the end, they decided to go ahead and play.

"That game was possibly the single biggest defining moment that started the healing process for our community.

"The arena was packed to maximum capacity and then some (causing mild grief to the fire commissioner).

"It was such a joy to see our detachment members plus a large contingent of past members smile, have fun, and put aside their own grief . . . even for just a few hours.

"It helped us residents put aside our grief also. It may have been the first time that every resident in attendance was actually rooting for the cops to win—which they did."

Margaret Thibault agrees. "Playing the hockey game was smart. It brought the community and the police together. The community had to see that their police were still there. And the police needed to have the community surround the detachment with their support.

"It also gave the members an opportunity to skate off their anger and their high emotions."

Jim Martin says it seemed to be good for everyone. "Most of our detachment played—me and Clayton Seguin, Al Starman, Joe Sangster, Cindie Dennis, and Julie Letal and a bunch of members from other years."

Albert Schalm says, "Rod Phillips and Morley Scott from the Edmonton Oilers broadcast crew came in and broadcast the game over 630 CHED. The game has been a sellout every year since the tragedy."

Immediately after the murders of the four Mounties were confirmed, the media began asking a number of pertinent questions.

1. Did James Rozsko have an accomplice, unwitting or otherwise?
2. How did James Roszko travel the 38.5 kms (twenty-three miles) from his aunt's farm in Cherhill to his Quonset on Range Road 75?
3. At what time did James Roszko sneak into his Quonset hut?
4. From where and from whom did James Roszko get the heavy black socks he used to muffle the sound of his boots and the white sheet he used as camouflage?

These were the burning questions that were asked over and over by every media source that covered the story.

The RCMP replied that they had started an extensive investigation that would examine these questions thoroughly. And hopefully, in time, they would be able to provide answers to them.

Furthermore, they requested the public's assistance and co-operation with all these matters.

The media buzz and the police pronouncements were of little consolation to Shawn Hennessey and Dennis Cheeseman.

They weren't exactly sure what crime they had committed. They didn't know the degree of their culpability or the legal extent of their complicity in Roszko's actions. What they did know was that they had driven him from Cherhill to Range Road 75 and dropped him off close to the murder scene. And they were the last two people to see Roszko alive.

They also knew that it was just a matter of time before the RCMP would come knocking on their door.

8 | Investigation

IMMEDIATELY AFTER THE RCMP robot confirmed the four Mounties were deceased, Inspector Bob Williams from Edmonton's "K" Division (Alberta) Major Crimes Unit came in with his "Initial Response Team." They locked down the crime scene and secured the entire property in preparation for the investigation of the multiple murders.

Williams, fifty-seven, who was originally from Saskatchewan, was uniquely qualified to lead the Mayerthorpe investigation. He had thirty-seven years with the RCMP, during which he had served as a senior supervisor dealing with homicides, serious criminal investigations, and several high-profile cases across Canada. He also had been the commander of an ERT unit and had experience as a polygraph examiner. In 1999, Williams had taken charge of "K" Division Major Crimes North, a unit that covers the northern section of Alberta from Millet (just south of Leduc) to the border of the Northwest Territories.

Inspe tor Bob Williams. (RCMP)

At 10:35 a.m. on March 3, he was called to Chief Superintendent Rod Knecht's office at Edmonton Headquarters. Knecht told him that something significant was occurring at Mayerthorpe. "We're not exactly sure what it is just yet. But it sounds serious . . . we might have an officer down. I want you to go out there and take over as site commander."

Anticipating a worst-case scenario, Williams immediately put together a team of eight

Major Crime investigators and instructed them to proceed to Mayerthorpe with dispatch.

His eight team members included:

- Sergeant Terry Kohlhauser, forty, who had seventeen years' experience, seven of them with "K" Division Major Crimes. Williams knew that Kohlhauser's dedication and determination would make a great contribution to a thorough investigation.
- Corporal Valerie Lahaie, a twelve-year veteran of the RCMP, an experienced file coordinator who was assigned to manage, sort, and prioritize the vast quantity of materials that would be sent in by the field investigators
- Sergeant Dennis Travanut, forty-seven, with twenty-eight years' experience in Alberta and selected as a highly motivated and tenacious investigator
- Corporal Kevin Quail, forty, an experienced major crime investigator, assigned the role as the crime scene coordinator
- Corporal Ron Campbell, forty-seven, a focused and meticulous homicide investigator who had served all of his twenty-eight-year career in Alberta
- Sergeant Jerry Dunn, a seasoned veteran who had spent thirty-two years with the Force. His expertise was in the area of crime scene and autopsy investigations. He would oversee the autopsies of the four deceased members.
- Constable Garry Lotoski, forty-four, an experienced member of the Edmonton Homicide Unit. One of his primary responsibilities at Mayerthorpe was to serve as the exhibit person at the crime scene.
- Constable Jason Reeve, thirty-three, who had served nine years with the RCMP in a variety of assignments. He would assist with the interviewing and interrogation.

That same morning of March 3, Deputy Commissioner Gary Leoppky, the acting commissioner of the day, called from Ottawa and spoke to the "K" Division commanding officer, Assistant Commissioner Bill Sweeney.

They were both concerned that the situation at Roszko's farm looked ominous. Leoppky wanted to make sure if a major investigation should be required, the RCMP would be ready to proceed in a precise and politically correct manner.

Because of public perception, they agreed there would be a strong need for independent oversight of the Mayerthorpe investigation, one that presented a clear understanding that "K" Division was not examining the incident on its own. To satisfy this requirement, the man they chose to bring in was Chief Superintendent Al MacIntyre, an experienced homicide investigator who was in charge of the Major Crimes Section of "E" Division (British Columbia).

MacIntyre, who was fifty-three years old and originally from Sault Ste. Marie, Ontario, had twenty-four years' experience in homicide. In 1983, he helped convict two brutal thrill killers in Alberta. He had also led the homicide task force that solved the murders of the nine strikebreakers at the Giant Gold Mine in Yellow-knife in 1992. MacIntyre had been alerted to the Mayerthorpe situation since its onset and was stunned when he learned that the four young members had been murdered at the farm site.

Chief Superintendent Al MacIntyre.
(RCMP)

At 12:20 p.m. on March 3, MacIntyre received a phone call from Deputy Commissioner Gary Leoppky, who asked him to be the lead investigator in the Mayerthorpe case. Leoppky tasked him to pull a team together immediately and bring it to Alberta to lead the investigation. MacIntyre accepted the assignment and advised Leoppky that he and his team would be at the crime scene by the following morning.

About half an hour before that, Inspector Bob Williams,

driving alone from Edmonton, had arrived at the Mayerthorpe Detachment office. As he was parking his car beside the building, Superintendent Brian McLeod and his Edmonton ERT members began arriving, car after car, in the parking lot. Shortly after that, Superintendent Brian Simpson and his Red Deer ERT crew started to pull in. Within minutes about twenty-five heavily armed ERT members in their camouflage uniforms were mustering in the parking lot.

The first thing Williams did was to acquire an office for himself in the detachment. From there, he immediately connected with the Division's Emergency Operating Centre, with which he stayed in contact throughout the day.

Williams says, "We still didn't know precisely what was happening out at Roszko's farm, but I remember thinking things weren't looking very good."

When the robot went in and determined the worst, ERT commander Brian McLeod phoned Williams with the bad news. "We have four members down and one suspect down."

Williams says, "That was close to three p.m. And at that point I knew my Major Crimes Unit would be responsible for a principal role in the homicide investigation.

"And with the sheer size of the operation . . . the number of investigators that would ultimately be involved in the case, I knew the Mayerthorpe Detachment building would not suffice as a command centre.

"When I first drove into town, I had noticed the Royal Canadian Legion building across from the detachment. Now, I thought that would be a facility that could serve us very well."

Williams remembers, "The people in charge of the Legion were most willing to accommodate us. They were more than supportive. They let us use the entire main floor of the building."

To secure the crime scene and start processing evidence, Williams named Sgt. Jerry Dunn as supervisor of the investigation. Corporal Kevin Quail and Cst. Garry Lotoski were given the responsibility of gathering evidence exhibits, logging and tagging them, and storing them.

The next thing Inspector Williams did was to establish his command triangle. He would be at the top of the triangle, Inspector

James Hardy would be at the second point and serve as the primary investigator, and Constable Valerie Lahaie would assume the third point as file coordinator.

Both the second and third points of the triangle were immense jobs.

Hardy would coordinate and supervise every aspect of the investigation. He would be responsible for the speed, flow, and direction of the process, deciding what was to be done, the order in which things were to be done, and who would do them.

Lahaie was responsible for managing the administrative aspect of the investigation. This entailed all the electronic files and all the paperwork generated by the investigation. Every task and each bit of information had to be logged and filed including evidence exhibits, interviews, interrogations, autopsy results, forensic reports, items for disclosure, media releases, etc.

"I knew this was going to be a massive file," Williams says, "and I needed the best possible people in those two positions. Both Inspector Hardy and Constable Lahaie had extensive experience and both of them were extremely capable in their respective areas. Lahaie was well-trained. She was meticulous with paperwork and with the gathering and retrieval of electronic information."

Williams remembers, "I knew the investigation was going to be a big job . . . an enormous undertaking . . . but we had the very best people in place and we were given tremendous support. Anything we needed, we got."

Throughout that first day, the technical specialists from the "Informatics" Branch were busy installing multiple phone lines and setting up a myriad of computer stations and their requisite power connections.

That evening, Al MacIntyre and his selected crew from "E" Division caught a Westjet flight to Edmonton. His special team was comprised of six members, each of them amply experienced and extremely capable.

Inspector Don Adam, in his early fifties, was known for his criminal investigative ability and his comfort in the interview and interrogation room. He was also a no-nonsense, industrious police manager who was good at keeping other investigators focused and on task.

Staff Sergeant Brenden Fitzpatrick, in his early forties, was a smart, energetic policeman held in high regard for being a tenacious, hard-working criminal investigator.

Sergeant Bruce Hulan, in his early fifties, was a well-known, well-liked, seasoned criminal investigator with a reputation for being thoughtful, thorough, and dogged in his determination.

Corporals Paul McCarl and Matt Toews were young, aggressive homicide investigators who were tireless workers noted for doing the heavy lifting and hard digging on any case assigned to them.

Sarah Russell was a gifted young civilian member who would share her expertise with Alberta's Constable Lahaie, who was in charge of all electronic data entry, retrieval, and analysis. Sarah had a special skill. Using the RCMP software called "E & R" (evidence and reporting), she had developed a unique ability of being able to convert the evidence of a major crime into a logical format.

The Vancouver team spent the night at an Edmonton hotel; at 6:30 a.m. the next morning, they arrived in Mayerthorpe and reported to the command post in the Legion hall.

Their first meeting that morning was with the police unit that assesses police needs for a particular project. This unit has the authority and the means to rapidly provide essential equipment and resources for the special investigators. These would include such items as police cars, cell phones, laptops, desktop computers, and all other necessary office equipment.

At 8:00 a.m., MacIntyre met with Inspector Bob Williams, and together they united the "K" Division and "E" Division members into working partnerships. This included the command triangle, where MacIntyre and Williams would share command, although MacIntyre, with his higher rank and assigned responsibility, was considered to be in charge.

With their responsibilities clearly defined, each of the investigators staked out a small working area on the long banquet tables that were set up around the Legion hall. The hall itself, as well as a few other small rooms in the building that would be used for interviews, was secured and declared off limits to anyone except authorized police personnel. The RCMP had determined that no member from either the Mayerthorpe or Whitecourt Detachments would be allowed to work on the investigation in any capacity.

Over the course of the investigation, over 200 officers worked in the Legion hall, coming and going as they performed their various assignments and duties.

Al MacIntyre says, "The guidelines I stressed to all of them were pretty straightforward. They had to do it right. They needed to be thorough and careful. There was no sense in rushing.

"There was to be no such thing as an informal statement. They were to get everything on tape . . . on video or digital or audio. And the evidence they collected needed to be clearly articulated . . . clearly unambiguous. It wasn't about what evidence looks like today but what it would be like two or three years down the road . . . when we went to court. The evidence needed to be seized and articulated; the record needed to be clear."

Many of the working members were selected for their special skill sets and had been sent to Mayerthorpe by their various detachments. Some members had asked for permission to leave their home detachments to serve in Mayerthorpe. Others took their holidays and volunteered to serve their time in the Legion hall. Seven members from Calgary were taking an interviewing course in Edmonton. All of them volunteered to come in and help the investigation in Mayerthorpe. Other members came from all over Alberta. Some came from as far away as Nova Scotia or from the proximity of British Columbia. Forensic Identification Specialists were dispatched from Edmonton, Winnipeg, Regina, and Halifax. A forensic firearms team drove in from the Regina Crime Lab to investigate all aspects of the involvement of firearms in the Mayerthorpe crime.

For the next two weeks, the Mounties would use an arsenal of investigative techniques: interrogation, interviews, physical and electronic surveillance, searches, forensic identification, and analysis.

After several briefing meetings on that Friday morning of March 4, Al MacIntyre, Don Adam, and Bob Williams drove out to Roszko's farm. The crime scene was securely contained. A perimeter had been established where the police checked all vehicles coming near the farm. There was absolutely no access to the property from any unauthorized person.

After MacIntyre, Adam, and Williams presented their credentials, they were admitted and received a thorough briefing on the crime scene and the crime itself. Personnel on site familiarized them with all aspects of Roszko's inner compound, his buildings, and the lie of the land on his property.

Elsewhere, the RCMP had set up checkpoints on several roads near Roszko's farm where they stopped cars and asked the drivers and their passengers whether or not they had seen or heard anything regarding the incident.

The crime scene was a busy place. Searches continued unabated. Using infrared and other scanning equipment, police persevered with their attempts to recover evidence. They employed ground radar to determine if there were any signs of disturbance to the land. This was done to see if anything had been buried in the earth or uncovered from it. Techs from Ident (Forensic Identification Section) and the Explosives Disposal Unit swept the farm with metal detectors and sifted dirt inside the Quonset hut looking for shell casings. Oil drums, water casks, and other paraphernalia were removed from inside the Quonset. All of it was examined and stored for future reference. Backhoes were brought in, just in case any digging had to be done.

That evening, back at the command centre, Sgt. Jerry Dunn phoned Al MacIntyre at 6:40 p.m. He had spent the day at the Edmonton Medical Examiner's Facility as a witness to the autopsies of the four murdered Mounties.

MacIntyre recalls, "He described the devastating injuries the .308 calibre bullets had caused. I could hear the sheer upset in his voice as he explained their types of injuries. It was obvious there was clearly no chance of survival for any of them . . . absolutely no chance.

"That was very upsetting to me. The killer was obviously so violently angry. The number of shots he fired was so over the top. I could imagine the hell the members went through . . . the time they had for terror . . . waiting . . . as they went down, one after another. It was very distressing for me to think about that."

Day after day, with MacIntyre and Williams in the lead, the investigative process went on. There were digital photograph screenings, forensic analysis reports, applications for search warrants, development of flow charts, constant overviews, and briefings.

At the outset of the case, one of the first procedures that the police had employed was to apply for five different search warrants.

The first was for Roszko's cell phone records. These indicated that prior to the time of the murders, Roszko had made phone calls to his mother, his sister, his aunt, and to Kal Tire in Barrhead. He had also made several calls to phone numbers that were eventually traced to a man named Shawn Hennessey.

This same Shawn Hennessey was a person who was suspected to be selling marijuana grown on Roszko's farm.

Another of the search warrants addressed the .300 Winchester Magnum rifle and the ammunition for it that was found beside Roszko's body. In short order, the RCMP traced the Winchester hunting rifle to John Hennessey, the grandfather of Shawn Hennessey.

Shawn Hennessey immediately became a person of interest to the police.

When Shawn heard the news of the police massacre late in the afternoon of March 3, he was afraid. "I was absolutely terrified of the involvement I had," he says, "and I didn't know what was going to come out of it."

He says that he decided to "lie low."

His primary concern was that the Winchester rifle he had given to Roszko was registered in his grandfather's name. John Hennessey, his grandfather, had given the rifle to Shawn two years previously when he thought the government planned to eliminate the gun registry requirements.

Shawn and his mother, Sandy, discussed the fact that the rifle was registered to John and that the police would undoubtedly check that out by seeking out the grandfather and questioning him.

Shawn contacted his grandfather and told him that James Roszko had taken the Winchester from Shawn's home the night before the murders and definitely had it on him when he attacked the police. After that conversation, John Hennessey says it was his idea to tell the police that his rifle had been stolen from the back of his welding truck in October 2004. Shawn and his mother and dad agreed that they all would stick to this "story." In so doing, the Hennessey family had all agreed to perpetrate an orchestrated cover-up concerning the Winchester rifle.

On Sunday, March 6, four days after the murders, the RCMP came to John Hennessey's house and asked him about the Winchester rifle. As planned, the old man lied to them. He said he usually kept his rifle behind the seat of his welding truck but he hadn't seen it since October 2004. It was his belief that the rifle had been stolen from his truck.

When a writer from the *Globe and Mail* interviewed John and asked him how it was that Roszko had possession of John's rifle, John told them, "I don't know how he got it."

Shawn told the *Globe and Mail* that he had known Mr. Roszko as a customer at Kal Tire for the previous four years. He said he had visited the property once but he rejected allegations in one of the police search warrants that he was selling marijuana for Mr. Roszko.

This was the first in a series of lies and misrepresentations that Shawn would tell the police and the media.

He said he felt ill when he first heard of the murders and denied any suggestions that he played a role in the killings. "I've never been in a situation like this before," he said. "I've never been accused of such huge things. This is absolutely beyond me."

Yet all throughout the RCMP investigation Shawn Hennessey did not act like he was innocent. Neither did Cheeseman. They lied about where they'd been and what they'd done. They denied assisting Roszko in any way.

Over the duration of many months, the police questioned Shawn Hennessey approximately fifteen times. Sergeant Terry Kohlhauser conducted many of those interviews. Some of the sessions took place at Hennessey's residence; a few occurred at Kal Tire where Shawn worked. One lengthy formal interview took place at the Barrhead Detachment office. Some of Kohlhauser's conversations with Hennessey were informal interviews where the two men stood around and talked to each other.

In all of these interviews, Shawn provided basically the same information each time and refused to admit any involvement in the murders. He constantly lied about his involvement with Roszko on the night before the massacre.

In one affidavit, an officer who interviewed him wrote: "Shawn Hennessey said he knew James Roszko for approximately three to four years. He said he went to Roszko's farm and put a stereo in his Camaro for Roszko during the summer of 2004 and the next time he attended the property he looked at a car his wife wanted to purchase. The third time, he did some yardwork for Roszko."

As for the events leading up to the murders, it was Hennessey's contention that when Roszko came by his place, he insisted that Roszko could not park his truck there. He said Roszko left. He denied having any knowledge of how the rifle ended up at Roszko's place.

But the police weren't buying his denials.

Another police observation read: "Hennessey is a person to which Roszko would turn for assistance."

As time went on, Shawn became more and more testy with the media. When a reporter phoned him, Shawn angrily replied, "I don't want to speak to you people."

To another newsman's question he answered, "That's none of your business."

The police interviewed Shawn's mother and Dennis Cheeseman several times as well. Each and every time, they admitted nothing and maintained the family's concocted "story" with regard to the Winchester rifle.

Hennessey's boss at Kal Tire, Steve Hunter, told the media that he thought Shawn was smeared by the simple fact he knew James Roszko. He told Michelle Collins, a writer for the *Edmonton Journal*, "There's no story with Shawn. It's been almost a year now, and if the police had anything on him, they would have charged him . . . Shawn didn't take his [Roszko's] truck or help him in any way."

Hunter told the *Barrhead Leader* that if Hennessey were guilty of anything, it was his being stupid about with whom he chose to associate. With regard to Shawn's being involved in Roszko's marijuana grow-op, in the *Leader* story Hunter said that Shawn worked at Kal Tire sixty hours a week. This made it almost impossible for him to have any extensive dealings with Roszko.

However, other information contained in one of the RCMP search warrants reveals that the police believed that Shawn Hennessey was involved in a marijuana cultivation and trafficking operation with James Roszko. According to the documents, James Roszko's mother stated to investigators that she believed James grew the marijuana and Shawn Hennessey sold it.

Hennessey steadfastly denied such an allegation to the police.

As the RCMP investigation continued, the residents of Mayerthorpe and surrounding area showed their appreciation for the police by bringing food and goodies to the Legion.

"The local residents were very considerate," says Al MacIntyre. "They brought in casseroles, cakes, cookies, and all kinds of fruits and snacks. I was extremely impressed with their kindness."

The townspeople also started asking a lot of their own questions.

Ever since Roszko's truck had been found at his aunt's place in Sangudo, the public had been wondering how Roszko managed to travel the 38.5 kms from his aunt's place back to his farm. There was widespread speculation that Roszko had an accomplice.

Rev. Arnold Lotholz said, "Even from the get-go, there was always a nagging question about who helped Roszko get away from the site and get back."

Mayor Schalm commented, "Once the smoke cleared, everybody knew that somebody had given Roszko a ride."

One Mayerthorpe resident told the Canadian Press that Mr. Roszko likely didn't get back to his Rochfort Bridge-area farm on his own. "It's something that everyone is wondering. How did he get back to the farm and do the things he did?"

Randy Schroeder, Mayerthorpe's fire chief asked, "How did Roszko get back on the property and why would he do that? Normal criminals flee the scene, they don't return to it. What was he protecting? There wasn't anything there that would have put him away for life. Why would he come back and ambush these guys?"

Other people kept wondering how Roszko did it. How did he manage to ambush and cut down four armed police officers?

Cliff Walde, a retired RCMP sergeant, knew Roszko's property. He said, "It wouldn't have been difficult for someone to sneak back undetected to Roszko's property in the dark. Considering the size of the farm, the back roads in the area, and the cover provided by the nearby brush and rolling hills.

"If you had thirty officers it wouldn't have made any difference . . . you could have still snuck back onto the property. You got to remember you're out in the country. There's no street lights."

Besides the questions there were a lot of rumours, second-guessing, and untruths flying around. Some people claimed that the four Mounties died during two separate time periods. Others thought that the four members were shot outside the Quonset and then dragged back inside by Mr. Roszko.

One man stated, "I don't believe for one second Roszko was inside the hut when he opened fire. It doesn't make any sense. Roszko practised shooting all around his property and he wouldn't take a position in a building where he could be trapped.

"Roszko managed to kill or severely wound all four officers during his opening salvo. He probably started taking them into the Quonset hut so arriving members wouldn't see them."

There were rumours about crosses being on the farm that marked the graves of other dead people buried on Roszko's property.

Media coverage insinuated that the police were "pleading" and "desperate" for information and further suggested that a possible accomplice might be scaring witnesses from coming forward.

Some residents said that charges had already been laid against someone who had aided and abetted James Roszko with the murders.

All of these rumours were unfounded and ranged from being untrue to being absurd.

The media began featuring stories that asked questions about RCMP training and preparation. One published story asked if the RCMP chain of command had adequately prepared the young Mounties to deal with a dangerous subject like Roszko.

Even a former RCMP superintendent, Clyde Kitteringham, who had a thirty-nine-year career with the Force, was quoted in *Time* magazine and the *Toronto Star* about what he considers a crucial lack of protection for the officers who were killed.

"Based on my many, many years of experience in both rural Alberta and elsewhere as an operational police officer," said

Kitteringham, "this was a failure. It was negligent supervision, quite frankly, and I haven't heard anyone tell me different."

Kitteringham said supervisors clearly erred by leaving junior members overnight to keep watch. He said the officers were exposed to an ambush because no one kept tabs on where Roszko was throughout the night, allowing him to sneak back onto the farm without the officers' knowledge.

Corporal Wayne Oakes, the Media Relations Officer for "K" Division, responded to Kitteringham's assessment: "The superintendent does not have all the facts or the points about this investigation. If we sent more people in there, we would have had more people to bury. The armchair quarterbacking is unbelievable. It's inappropriate for any of us to sit back and say anything."

Bill Helland, a retired RCMP staff sergeant from London, Ontario, who had spent much of his career reviewing and assessing operational plans and risk assessments, took exception to Kitteringham and a few other retired members of the Force "who professed to have much more information than anyone else."

Responding to them in the press, he quoted Lucia Benaquisto, a McGill University sociologist, who maintained that the blame game is not always sensible. "It appears to be a way that people look for answers, but too often it's a form of posturing by politicians and public figures to make it look like they are doing something."

Helland questioned why these blame-game people were not prepared to wait until at least a preliminary investigation was complete. "The finger pointing, hand-wringing, and haunting hypothetical 'what ifs' from those who had little first-hand knowledge of what really happened bothered me.

"Are they helpful . . . hardly. Do they represent the vast majority of police officers . . . certainly not. Will they be involved in searching for answers . . . probably not, as they are irrelevant to the investigation. Will they be unhappy if, in the final analysis, their prejudgements are not upheld . . . probably."

Retired Staff Sergeant Carl MacLeod, who had thirty-two years with the RCMP and had commanded the Joint Forces Unit in Hamilton, stated that the overnight deployment of two members at Roszko's Quonset was correct and proper.

MacLeod told the author, "Police forces react and prepare for the most part on intelligence information received on an individual from a variety of sources. For example, if information on Roszko had been to the effect that he had killed or had the potential to kill, then you can be assured that the RCMP involved at the Quonset hut would have been on high alert until the search had been completed or Roszko had been tracked down and arrested."

He emphasized, "This was definitely not a high-alert situation. It would have been different if Roszko had served time for murder or was a suspected killer or even a serious threat to police.

"But that was not the case.

"When a bad guy runs, he runs. He doesn't return.

"You're there. You're seizing his stuff. He's in trouble. Why would he come back?"

MacLeod says the police deal with situations like this every day across Canada. "Occurrences like this are so common, it's off the chart.

"Do any of the bad guys come back?" he asks. "I don't think so. We have to get a warrant for their arrest and go out and look for them."

He continues, "Anyone can be a Monday morning second-guesser. But the facts did not indicate they should have done anything other than what they did. The guys in charge out there wouldn't be thinking he'd return. That would not even be a consideration for them."

An editorial in the *Edmonton Journal* seems to have hit the nail on the head.

"As eager as Albertans may be to understand and draw conclusions, we must wait—patiently and confidently—for them [the police] to complete their reconstruction and analysis of events.

"There is already too much uninformed second-guessing of decisions made by the four officers last Wednesday night and Thursday morning. RCMP spokesman Wayne Oakes is rightly frustrated by the 'armchair quarterbacking' of the investigation. 'How these people outside the process are able to offer expert opinion baffles me,' he told reporters Monday."

There was also a lot of discussion about why a violent person like Roszko, with such a criminal record, was not in jail. People were asking whether or not the justice system had failed in Roszko's case and had contributed to the four officers' deaths.

An Alberta government report released in the fall of 2005 summarized James Roszko's run-ins with the law and concluded that the ambush and murder of the Mounties was not preventable. The report noted that Roszko had been flagged as a possible dangerous offender in 1995, but police couldn't apply the distinction because he didn't meet the required criteria, even with his serious record that included forty-four charges and fourteen convictions.

Senior Crown prosecutor Gordon Wong, who wrote the report, told the media, "At no time did Roszko meet the criteria to be considered for a dangerous offender."

Wong said one more conviction for sexual assault would have brought Roszko to a level where he could have been considered for a dangerous offender distinction, which would have resulted in longer prison terms for further offences. "What you need to get a designation is a series of convictions," he said. "You need that to apply for dangerous offender designation. He simply did not have the subsequent convictions."

Kim Connell, a former commander of the Mayerthorpe Detachment who still lives in the town, said that the Alberta report was a whitewash. "The justice system let us down and that's why four members are dead. That's it!" He added that the provincial government issued the report "to cover their asses."

Gordon Wong denied that, saying, "I'm not interested in covering up anything."

Some people even began to complain about the expense of the investigation.

An RCMP press release supplied some answers to questions with regard to its cost. "This investigation involved the murder of four police officers and the death of one civilian. While we must be accountable for our financial expenditures we must also be accountable for the actions we take and the actions that are not approved. Given the size, nature and scope of this investigation, the cost is comparable to other large-scale operations. The purpose of conducting an investigation is to investigate. Only when this process is complete are they truly in a position to possibly know and understand all the circumstances."

On Wednesday, March 16, Superintendent Marty Cheliak, the officer in charge of the Western Alberta District, invited members of the slain Mounties' families to come out to a private meeting in the Quonset hut on Roszko's farm. With him, representing the RCMP, were Superintendent Brian McLeod and Rev. Bob Harper, "K" Division's full-time chaplain.

This type of information meeting is standard procedure in all homicide cases. Although this meeting was difficult for the RCMP representatives to conduct, they realized that many of the family members had questions about how their loved ones had been killed.

Prior to the actual meeting—outside the Quonset hut—the families met with all of the members of the Mayerthorpe Detachment search team. The families were introduced, then chatted with the members and thanked them for their efforts. After an appropriate amount of time, the Mayerthorpe contingent left and the families were invited to go inside the Quonset.

Using all the information at his disposal, Brian McLeod walked the group through the significant steps of the violent incident. Occasionally, either he or Marty Cheliak answered questions from the family members.

One of the things McLeod revealed was that forensic analysis indicated Roszko had been hiding inside the Quonset hut behind a large white plastic vat that was situated close to the human door in the southeast corner of the building. That's where he fired from initially. Then he apparently got off other shots while moving around inside the Quonset.

Cheliak remembers, "At one point, Don Schiemann said out loud, 'Evil is residing here. This is an evil place.'"

The most chilling moments in McLeod's presentation came when he pointed out the various places where the families' murdered loved ones had fallen.

Marty Cheliak says, "When Brian pointed out the spot where Peter Schiemann had lay murdered, Peter's entire family—Don, Beth, Michael, and Julia—went to that spot and stood there.

"That was a very powerful moment. They stood there absorbing their feelings at the spot where Peter had been killed."

After the Schiemanns did this, the various other family members followed suit—going to the spot where their loved ones had fallen.

Then they had a solemn candlelight service where everyone held a lighted candle in the darkness of the hut while Bob Harper offered a prayer for the fallen four.

After the meeting ended, the entire group went to the restaurant in Rochfort Bridge for coffee. The general feeling among the family members was

Chief Superintendent Marty Cheliak. (RCMP)

that the meeting, although painful at times, was needed. Many of their terrible questions had been answered. They appreciated all the inside information they had received.

The next day, March 17, Inspector Bob Williams locked the gate on Roszko's laneway and instructed Staff Sergeant Gary Radford to return all the keys to Warren and Stephanie Fifield. The property was now back under their control. The RCMP had completed their physical examination of the crime scene in two weeks.

Chief Superintendent MacIntyre stayed on at the command post continuously until March 16, when he went home for the long weekend. He came back on March 21 and officially left Mayerthorpe a week after that.

From then on, Bob Williams was officially in charge of the investigation.

A federal Human Resources and Skills Development Canada (HRSDC) investigation and an RCMP internal investigation into the police officers' actions of March 2 and 3, 2005, were completed at a later date. Both these reports stated that there was no way that the RCMP could have anticipated the slayings of the four RCMP officers.

The report compiled by the Human Resources (HRSDC) department concluded that the "immensely tragic event was the direct result of an unprecedented, premeditated act of murder."

The RCMP's internal report stated: "This was a premeditated act of murder. Roszko's behaviour was unprecedented and unanticipated.

"There was nothing available to the police at the time which would have suggested that Roszko had intent to plan and execute a deadly assault on officers."

Both reports agreed that this was a most unique case. Never before had a criminal fled the scene and then surreptitiously returned with the determined intent of killing police officers.

The lying and lack of co-operation by Shawn Hennessey and his family initially slowed the RCMP investigation, but in the end, the police got their break from the second man who had travelled with Roszko on the night of the ambush and murders.

A year after the murders, on March 17, 2006 — and during subsequent meetings — Dennis Cheeseman spoke to his boss at Sepallo Foods, Brad McNish, and confessed some vital information to him regarding the Roszko case. McNish, a former Calgary police sergeant, took this information directly to the RCMP.

McNish told Sgt. Terry Kohlhauser that he had held a meeting with his staff where they expressed concerns about some of the employees at Sepallo Foods working there while under the influence of drugs. After the meeting, Dennis Cheeseman approached McNish privately and revealed that there were times that he had come to work having smoked marijuana. As they talked, Cheeseman gradually became more and more distraught. Gradually he began to purge himself of some of the deep, dark secrets about his involvement in the Roszko incident.

Over the course of several meetings, Cheeseman told McNish that he had not been honest with the police. He said he knew more about the case than he was prepared to share with them. His main concern was that he hadn't told the police the truth and he was having difficulty dealing with the Mounties' murders.

Even at that, he lied to McNish.

Dennis tried to deflect the guilt away from his brother-in-law, Shawn Hennessey. Dennis said that Roszko had approached him a few days before the murders and told him he needed a rifle.

Cheeseman said he took him to John Hennessey's place and gave him the Winchester and some ammunition from the back of John's truck.

Cheeseman also revealed to McNish that Shawn Hennessey was involved in Roszko's marijuana grow-op. He said that on Wednesday, the day before the murders, Shawn knew the Mounties were searching Roszko's Quonset hut. Because of his connection with Roszko, Shawn was concerned that he would be implicated in charges related to the illegal grow-op.

Cheeseman told McNish that later that same day, Roszko came to Shawn's house and said he was going to kill some of the RCMP who were searching through his Quonset. Cheeseman admitted that he and Shawn followed Roszko to a farm where Roszko dropped off his truck. Then they drove him back to his farm. As they were driving, Cheeseman claimed that Roszko ranted about killing RCMP officers at his farm. He said, "They've made a mess of my life. They've got me and I'm going to get them." Roszko also told them he was going to burn down the Quonset hut because of the marijuana plants and the stolen goods that were in it.

While Cheeseman revealed all this information to Brad McNish, he refused to go to the police and tell it to them.

Nevertheless, his confession to McNish was the break the Mounties had been looking for. They now believed they had sufficient evidence to convict Dennis Cheeseman with aiding and abetting Roszko in the Mountie murders.

However, Cheeseman's confession would not suffice to convict Shawn Hennessey. In Shawn's case, Cheeseman's revelations would be considered hearsay and inadmissible. Therefore, after an extended conference among the RCMP investigators, a decision was made to deploy undercover operators to obtain more evidence from both Dennis Cheeseman and Shawn Hennessey.

An undercover operational plan or "sting" named Project Kourage was approved on March 21, 2006, and went into action a few days later.

In recent years, undercover operations have become a significant factor in the realm of police investigations. The RCMP has approximately 1,500 of its members qualified as trained undercover operators. At any given point in time, about 600 of them are engaged in undercover operations. About five percent of these operatives are female.

All those qualified as undercover operators with the RCMP across Canada are listed in a central registry in Ottawa. In each member's dossier, there are photos and up-to-date information regarding the operator's location, rank, responsibilities, education, interests, hobbies, areas of expertise, personality traits, languages spoken, etc.

When an undercover operation is required, the lead investigator in a case submits a request through the Division Undercover Coordinator for suitable undercover operators based on the specific needs of an investigation. The Coordinator then offers the assignment to chosen personnel in consultation with the various members' detachment commanders.

Undercover work is voluntary; therefore, members selected for a particular operation have the right to refuse. If they do accept the undercover assignment, they are still required to maintain their ongoing responsibilities at their present posting.

The first element of the Mayerthorpe sting was initiated when the RCMP sent an undercover operator[2] to Barrhead to befriend Shawn Hennessey. The new man in town posed as a welder and demonstrated to Shawn his interest in snowmobiling and quadding, two activities that Hennessey really enjoyed.

Shawn was leery of the operator, suspecting he might be an undercover cop. But despite his suspicions, Hennessey continued to associate with him and invited him to go snowmobiling and quadding.

Even when the new man's girlfriend came to join him, Shawn and his wife, Christine, remained cautious. Nevertheless, the Hennesseys did continue to associate with the new couple.

The second phase of the "sting," which ran parallel to and in conjunction with the first, focused on Dennis Cheeseman.

In October 2006, a female undercover operator managed to develop car trouble outside of Sepallo foods. As Dennis was

---

2   For obvious reasons, the names and aliases of undercover agents cannot be revealed.

leaving work, he stopped to help her. Actually, her car had been rigged with a kill switch that would disable the motor at just the right time.

Dennis tried his best to start the car, but he couldn't get it going. He gave the operator a ride to a nearby restaurant, where, during a brief conversation, the women revealed she had just broken up with her abusive boyfriend.

Cheeseman volunteered to keep an eye on her disabled vehicle until she could have it removed from the Sepallo parking lot.

Their meeting ended with their exchanging phone numbers.

In the weeks that followed, the female operator made numerous phone calls to Cheeseman in relation to her broken-down vehicle.

Early in the undercover operation, the Mounties wanted to set up listening devices in the Cheeseman and Hennessey residences. To get Dennis out of the house, the female operator invited him to her annual Christmas party. Dennis accepted her offer, and he, in turn, invited her to his Christmas party.

While they were at the operator's party — and the Hennesseys were away from the house, too — the bugs were installed in the home. The operator's Christmas party was an elaborate hoax. Everyone at the party was a Mountie — even Santa Claus, who made a late-night surprise visit to hand out a few gifts.

Cheeseman was a willing participant in these events that helped develop their relationship. Ultimately, he became smitten with the woman and came to think of her as his girlfriend. To cool the situation, the operation handlers introduced a reason for her to get away for a while. The story they devised was that her beloved grandfather was dying and the operator needed to leave to be with her family in Manitoba. But even while she was gone, she stayed in touch with Cheeseman.

The entire RCMP undercover operation was designed to ensure that a suitable distance was maintained between the female operator and Cheeseman. By design, they made sure that there was no opportunity for an intimate relationship between them. Including the Christmas party in December 2006, the female operator and Cheeseman saw each other only on five occasions. All of these meetings were in public places, and at three of these meetings, there were other undercover operators present. The remainder of their relationship was conducted on the phone.

It was at the staged Christmas party that the female operator introduced Cheeseman to "an old school friend." He was also an undercover operator.

After Cheeseman had been introduced to the female operator's old school friend, the RCMP effected a scenario whereby she was supposedly beaten and robbed by her abusive ex-boyfriend. A makeup artist distorted her appearance to make her look as if she had been badly beaten.

The operator's old school friend suggested to Dennis that he was going to deal with the ex-boyfriend. Cheeseman offered to go along. Although Dennis was told he did not have to get involved, he insisted that he go to help get back the money the boyfriend had stolen from the female operator.

On February 24, 2007, they tracked the ex-boyfriend to a hotel south of Calgary. While Dennis searched the room for money, the old school friend took the ex-boyfriend, who was also an undercover operative, into the bathroom and pretended to beat him up. Dennis could hear the banging and screaming as the boyfriend faked being hammered.

Having accomplished their mission, Dennis and the male operator left the hotel as real buddies. Not long after that, the operator offered Dennis employment, purported to be illegal, which Cheeseman readily accepted.

Although Cheeseman did not see the female operator again, they did communicate by text messages on a few occasions.

Shawn and Christine Hennessey watched Dennis and the new woman's relationship grow with mixed emotions. On one hand, they were happy for shy and reticent Dennis, who never seemed to have much luck with women. On the other hand, they were concerned that she might be an undercover cop who was plying Dennis with her attention for her own purposes.

Meanwhile, the male operator revealed to Cheeseman that he was a member of a criminal gang. Very soon after they met, he offered Dennis the choice of either participating or not in a simulated crime where the operator's gang was going to steal a mini-loader from a guy who owed them money.

Dennis made the choice to involve himself. During the heist, he used bolt cutters to sever a chain that secured the trailer and the mini-loader. He also hooked up the trailer as the undercover operator watched.

After the loader escapade, other assignments followed.

Dennis was invited to participate in a caper that involved the gang members' stealing a boat. He chose to be actively involved. Then he willingly took part in the theft of a truck full of cigarettes.

The biggest deal he was involved in was helping to unload crates of automatic weapons from a private plane that landed at the small airport in Edson, Alberta. Dennis assisted in transporting the weapons to an Edmonton warehouse and acted as security during the sale of the guns.

Dennis was paid for everything he did that involved a staged crime. They gave him $500 to unload the illegal gun shipment. They passed him $300 for participating while they stole equipment from people who owed the gang money. He got $700 for participating in the cigarette heist.

On every occasion that Dennis got together with the gang, they told him he didn't have to take part in any of the criminal activity. But they stressed that their gang operated under a strict code of honesty and trust. They expected every gang member to be completely honest with each other.

To this end, Cheeseman disclosed to five undercover operators on four separate occasions that he had been involved with the murder of four RCMP members at Mayerthorpe. The leader of the gang, "Mr. Big," was aware of Cheeseman's involvement in the Mayerthorpe murders and invited Dennis to attend a meeting with him to clarify the details of his participation in that crime. During their meeting, the leader of the gang congratulated Dennis for his good work. He said that gang members had told him that Dennis had a bright future with their organization.

Then Mr. Big told him the gang had connections with a major satellite company in the United States. He advised Dennis that this company constantly took detailed photos of the prairies. And if any pictures existed that would show Cheeseman driving James Roszko back to his farm on the night of the killings, the gang might be able to make the photos disappear.

It was then that Cheeseman disclosed the details of his involvement in the Mayerthorpe shootings.

On the drive home from this Kelowna meeting, Cheeseman reiterated his involvement with the Roszko incident to one of the high-ranking gang members. Dennis gave this undercover operator a lot of the details about what had happened that night when he and Shawn drove Roszko back to his farm.

Dennis told the man that when he saw the lights of the police cars at Roszko's property, he said he and Hennessey were sure Roszko was going to kill the police.

Dennis said, "Obviously we knew he was going back to kill RCMP officers. He said he was pretty much going to go and take care of business. He was pretty much going to burn the Quonset hut, burn down the trailer, and then just leave."

In May and June of 2007, Mr. Big pushed Cheeseman to recruit Shawn Hennessey to join the criminal gang. But Shawn resisted. He told Dennis that he had a young family and he didn't want to jeopardize his life with them by getting involved with criminal activity that could land him in jail.

Dennis Cheeseman continued to work with the criminal organization. He actually took a lead role overseeing undercover operators in a series of extortion-based scenarios.

Meanwhile, the undercover operators in Barrhead continued to socialize with Shawn and Christine on a regular basis. As they became friendlier, Shawn disclosed a version of his involvement in the Mayerthorpe shootings. The version he offered minimized his involvement to something less than criminal.

But on July 6, 2006, Mr. Big confronted Cheeseman and told him that his involvement in the Roszko case was bringing a lot of police heat down on the criminal organization. He proposed — almost insisted — that a meeting with Cheeseman and Hennessey be set up to discuss their mutual problem with the RCMP investigation.

Cheeseman was able to induce Shawn to join him at a meeting with the big boss at the Barrhead airport. And this was the reason why: In April and May of 2007, the gang had offered Shawn employment with the promise of a big payday. He turned this down. But this time, the incentive to get him to meet with the big boss was based on the fact that the RCMP investigation was closing in on Shawn. And Hennessey was aware, through Cheeseman, that Mr. Big could potentially make evidence disappear.

So Shawn Hennessey agreed to attend the meeting.

Because Shawn was concerned about being taped on a recording device, he didn't want to get into Mr. Big's car. Consequently, their entire meeting took place outside the vehicle.

As they walked along the runway, Shawn admitted to driving Roszko back to his farm.

Shawn told him that the Winchester rifle was to be used as a "scapegoat," by which he meant that Roszko would use the rifle if the Mounties caught him or had him under fire.

He also told Mr. Big that he had known Roszko for ten years. He said he had worked for four years with Roszko on his grow-op and auto chop shop. He claimed the money was good and he believed that he was the only person that Roszko trusted.

Shawn also advised him that in the two and a half years since the murders had occurred, he had never told anyone what had happened with him and Roszko. He said he hoped Mr. Big could be trusted.

The undercover operator, as Mr. Big, recorded every word that Shawn said.

Mr. Big told Hennessey that Cheeseman had admitted Shawn's involvement in the Roszko affair to him.

Shawn replied, "Which then brings another guy that knows that . . . which brings me a step closer to fucking years [in prison]."

Shawn told Mr. Big that all he knew was that Roszko was going to burn down the Quonset, which housed the marijuana plants and the chop shop. As for the Winchester rifle, he said, "He told me I had to give it to him. He didn't give me an option. He told me he had no intentions of using it. None."

Shawn also admonished himself for getting Dennis involved in the Roszko ride. He admitted that Dennis had nothing to do with the marijuana operation. He said to Mr. Big, "Why I ever went out and asked Dennis to come with me, I don't know. I do now know. Comfort!"

After the airport meeting, Shawn went back to Barrhead with Dennis and then he returned to work.

The next day, Hennessey had a second meeting with Mr. Big.

When Mr. Big asked Shawn if he believed Cheeseman's statement that it was Roszko's intention to kill police that night, Hennessey responded, "Yes."

Mr. Big said to Hennessey that it only made sense that with his guns and with his socks over his feet, it was clear that Roszko intended to "whack" the police.

Hennessey appeared to agree with that, saying, "Yeah."

That admission was what the police were looking for.

That same day — Saturday, July 7, 2006 — Dennis Cheeseman was arrested in the Edmonton suburb of Sherwood Park. He was charged with four counts of capital murder as a party to the offences committed by James Roszko. He was jailed in the Edmonton Remand Centre.

When Shawn Hennessey heard about Dennis's arrest, he knew he would be next.

On Sunday, July 8, he and his wife were visiting at her cousin's house in Barrhead. When Shawn went out to get something from his car, he was swarmed and taken down by the Edmonton ERT. Christine saw this and ran out to help him. She, too, was taken down by the emergency unit.

Shawn says, "There were rifles everywhere. They had my wife face down on the driveway, dragging her through the dirt."

Like Dennis, Shawn was charged with four counts of capital murder and incarcerated in the Edmonton Remand Centre.

After the arrests, RCMP Deputy Commissioner Bill Sweeney held a news conference at Edmonton Headquarters. He opened by saying, "Today we have been able to provide Canadians with the first significant update on the Mayerthorpe investigation."

Regarding the two accused, he said, "They were in the same community as James Roszko and were associates over an extended period of time."

He added, "It's not necessarily that they committed the crime directly, but they were somehow involved in facilitating the crime."

When Sweeney announced the charges against Hennessey and Cheeseman, Peter Schiemann's sister Julia whispered to him, "Thank you."

Anthony Gordon's mother was also in attendance and wiped a tear from her eye as the arrests were announced.

The families of the four dead officers had been contacted about the developments in the case a few days before the arrests went down.

Barry Hennessey, Shawn's father, told a reporter for the *Grande Prairie Herald–Tribune* that he just couldn't believe his boy could be involved in such a crime. "It's a huge loss to all of us. It's worse than a death. Everybody loved him. He didn't do nothing, as far as I'm concerned. I'm just a lost parent right now."

The RCMP investigation had taken twenty-eight months, using over 200 officers for various periods of time. The cost of the investigation was calculated to be in excess of two million dollars.

There was criticism of the RCMP investigation.

Some said it was far too costly. The police say that every investigation into multiple murder is expensive.

Others claimed that since Roszko, the killer, was dead, such a widespread investigation was unnecessary. The law says if there were persons who enabled Roszko to commit his heinous crime, they deserve to be punished.

Christine Hennessey said the police were just looking to blame someone and they settled for Shawn and Dennis.

The RCMP say they didn't want to blame just anyone. They wanted to determine whether or not someone had helped Roszko commit these multiple murders. And when they uncovered enough evidence to support a conviction in this regard, they closed in and made their arrests.

Some insist the Mounties tried longer and harder in this case than they would have if it had been civilians who were murdered. The RCMP disagree. They say that to solve this case, their investigators did nothing different from the normal operating procedure than they would have done on any major case investigation.

The author believes that the RCMP investigators would have worked equally hard to solve any major crime of this calibre. But surely the fact that their comrades were murdered would have given them an added incentive to do their very best work.

9 | Before the Courts

On July 9, 2007, Shawn Hennessey and Dennis Cheeseman were jointly charged with four counts of first-degree murder as parties to the offences committed by James Roszko.

As described in the Criminal Code of Canada, any of the offences listed below qualify as first-degree murder.

First-degree murder is planned and deliberate; contracted; committed against an identified peace officer; perpetrated while committing or attempting to commit one of the following offences: hijacking an aircraft, sexual assault, sexual assault with a weapon, aggravated sexual assault, kidnapping, and forcible confinement or hostage-taking; perpetrated while committing criminal harassment; committed during terrorist activity; committed while using explosives in association with a criminal organization; perpetrated while committing intimidation.

With regard to "Parties to Offence," the Criminal Code states: Everyone is a party to an offence who actually commits it, does—or omits to do—anything for the purpose of aiding any person to commit it, or abets any person in committing it.

Therefore, Hennessey and Cheeseman were charged with first-degree murder because four peace officers were murdered, and the two men allegedly abetted Roszko by driving him to the scene of the crime knowing he was going to kill the policemen. They also omitted to phone the police to warn them of the impending mortal danger.

On Thursday, July 12, Hennessey and Cheeseman were not present when the Crown appeared before Provincial Court Judge Ken Tjosvold to ask for an adjournment and to announce that the two accused would be prosecuted jointly (together).

None of the relatives of the murdered Mounties were in court. But the small courtroom was jammed full of family and friends of the accused who had come to show support for Hennessey and Cheeseman.

At times, the crowd became unruly, challenging the judge with comments and questions. One man even called out to the assembly, "I am an ambassador of Jesus Christ. We need to pray."

Those in attendance considered the murder charges to be extremely controversial, due to the fact that neither Hennessey nor Cheeseman was present at the crime scene when the killings occurred.

The judge adjourned the case until August 9, 2007.

There appears to be two distinct types of reaction to the arrests of Hennessey and Cheeseman.

Some people in Mayerthorpe were pleased, or at least relieved, that the case had been finally resolved with these arrests. Others just wanted to forget the horrible incident that had made their town notorious. They wanted to put the experience behind them and move forward.

Many residents of Barrhead and area were angry that these two nice young men were being used as scapegoats for the Mountie murders.

It wasn't long before Shawn's parents began to make their presence felt in support of their son and their daughter-in-law's brother. Barry and Sandy Hennessey helped Shawn select his lawyer. Initially, the Hennesseys retained an Edmonton criminal specialist named Edmond O'Neill. Then O'Neill brought in D'Arcy DePoe, a senior, more experienced criminal lawyer, a colleague in his law firm, to assist him with the case. Because of the massive size and intricacy of the file, DePoe soon became the lead defence counsel for Shawn Hennessey.

Cheeseman chose Peter Northcott as his defence counsel.

Raising the funds to pay the lawyers was a concern. The families of the two estimated their defence costs would run to approximately $100,000. Many of the residents of Barrhead knew this would be the case and did their best to help out. They organized yard sales and bake sales — some of them on a regular basis. Dennis's aunt, Marian Power, says she held either one type of sale or the other every weekend.

Barry and Sandy Hennessey opened an Internet site. Their home page began with a thank you.

Dear Friends,

First of all, let us thank everyone who has supported Shawn and Dennis, an enormous thank you to our community, for your kind words, your support, your generosity, and your prayers, which has made our lives a little easier during this indescribable time.

Further on in the Web site they wrote:

Since July 7th 2007 our lives have been drastically altered and will never be the same.

The families have had to begin selling their possessions that we worked so hard for in order to provide both Shawn and Dennis with the best legal representation as possible. Shawn's daughters ask us often why everything in their lives had to change . . . unfortunately we do not have an answer for them. We have asked ourselves that very same question *many times.*

And still further on:

Due to the enormous legal fees that the family is faced with, we need your help to protect the rights of these two young men.

You can donate directly via the PayPal link below, or mail your donation to

Barry Hennessey

(address withheld)

Even with the donations that came in from these different sources, it was Barry Hennessey who had to supply the majority of the money needed for his son's defence. He raised a significant portion of that by signing for a second mortgage on Shawn's home.

As the legal process dragged on, Dennis Cheeseman, who was shy and reserved by nature, became more and more depressed in prison. In July, he began refusing visitors. He became so distraught he was reported to be on a suicide watch for a period of time.

His aunt, Marian Power, told Eliza Barlow of the *Edmonton Sun*, "All we know is that Dennis really isn't seeing anyone. I really do believe he blames himself."

Ms. Barlow reported that when Christine Hennessey went to visit Dennis, her brother, at the remand centre, he broke down and went back into his cell.

On August 9, 2007, a judge in the Mayerthorpe courtroom announced that the two men's preliminary hearing would begin on May 12, 2008. He also advised that the hearing would be moved to a larger courtroom in Stony Plain, a town west of Edmonton.

During the time of their incarceration at the Edmonton Remand Centre, Shawn and Dennis shared the same cell. They were good company for each other, but still the long prison days passed slowly. Both of them spent a lot of their time reading. Most of the books in the prison library were quite old, but Shawn enjoyed any stories he could find about sports.

Their only reprieve from the boredom came on Sundays when the Hennesseys would come to visit. Everyone in the family took their turn — Barry, Sandy, Christine and her little girls, Shawn's sister Alecia and her husband, Neil Osland.

Each visit was to last no longer than thirty minutes, and a prisoner was allowed only two visitors at a time. When the Hennessey family arrived, they would split up. Half of them would see Shawn and the other half would visit with Dennis.

But that changed drastically in September when Shawn and Dennis were separated. Hennessey was sent to the Red Deer Remand Centre; Cheeseman remained in Edmonton. After that, the Hennesseys had to split up their group and make two separate trips.

The drive to Edmonton isn't too bad, but the trip to Red Deer takes two and a half hours. When the family went to see Shawn, they had to travel five hours for a thirty-minute visit. And all their visits were "closed," which meant the visitors and prisoner were separated by a glass window that prevented any physical contact between them.

The winter in prison was long and tedious. Both of them looked forward to the start of their preliminary hearing.

Then, on April 15, 2008, Shawn was released on $525,000 bail. His family and friends contributed a half-million-dollar surety. Shawn put up $25,000 in cash.

The judge stipulated that Shawn had to live at his home near Barrhead. He was required to report to his parole officer daily. He was not to use the telephone and he was not to have any contact whatsoever with Dennis Cheeseman.

Cheeseman did not apply for bail at that time. He was released almost a month later, just hours before his preliminary hearing was scheduled to begin.

His bail requirements specified that he put up $10,000 in cash and his family members were required to provide $245,000 as a surety. His bail conditions stipulated that he had to abide by a curfew, get a job, stay in Alberta, and have no contact with Shawn Hennessey.

The purpose of a preliminary hearing is to determine whether or not the Crown has sufficient evidence in a particular case to proceed to trial.

The proceedings pertaining to Shawn Hennessey and Dennis Cheeseman commenced on May 12 in Stony Plain before Provincial Court Judge Peter Ayotte. He ordered that all the evidence presented to the court in this matter be subject to a publication ban.

The hearing lasted a month and involved a lengthy list of witnesses.

Several Mayerthorpe RCMP members took the stand and told about the events that occurred before, during, and after the tragic incident. Rob Perry, the bailiff, spoke of his experiences with James Roszko on the day before the murders. Steve Vigor told about his confrontation with Roszko on that fateful day. He hushed the courtroom as he described how he and the killer stood face-to-face and shot at each other. Vigor became quite emotional as he recalled how he waited in vain to hear a response from his fallen colleagues.

Brad McNish gave testimony regarding Cheeseman's confession to him.

Part of the court transcript reveals McNish testified that Dennis told him, "I knew that Roszko was going to kill those RCMP officers."

Dennis told McNish, ". . . and he [Roszko] said they've got me and I'm going to get them."

McNish said he asked Dennis, ". . . and how did you know that? And he [Dennis] said, 'because Roszko told me.'"

Later in the transcript it is recorded that McNish testified: ". . . and I found out that he [Roszko] had told him [Dennis] that in ... when . . . when he was driving Roszko to the scene. And also at a time when he . . . prior to them leaving."

Still later McNish testified: ". . . when they were at his house . . . 'his' being Dennis's and Shawn's house . . . that Roszko indicated to them, while they were standing there, that he . . . that he was going to go and kill these RCMP officers."

Two pages later in the transcript, McNish told the court that Dennis told him: ". . . as we got closer to the farm we could see the RCMP cars . . . we were close enough that I could tell they were RCMP cars."

On that same page of the transcript, McNish testified: "And I recall asking if there were conversations going on at the time while they were driving and he [Dennis] indicated that Roszko . . . was definitely indicating that these guys have, again, made a mess of his life, that they're out there, and that, you know, this has to stop, this is . . . you know . . . I'm going to get these guys, I'm going to kill these RCMP."

Still further on, McNish testified he said to Dennis: ". . . do you actually recall Roszko saying, I'm going to kill those RCMP officers? And Dennis said, 'Yes, I do.'"

Later, on the same page, McNish testified: ". . . I asked Dennis if Shawn was there . . . when Roszko said that, and Dennis indicated that he was. Because, you know, as I said, he said that once when they were at the house and once again when they were in the car."

The substance of McNish's testimony appeared to be very incriminating.

John Hennessey, Shawn's grandfather, gave evidence that he had made up a story about how his Winchester rifle had been stolen from his truck when in fact he had given it to Shawn.

Neil Wiberg, general counsel of the Alberta attorney general, testified that he was convinced that the confession Dennis

Cheeseman made to Brad McNish was sufficient to have Cheeseman convicted on charges of first-degree murder. However, his remarks were not direct evidence admissible against Hennessey. Eventually, Hennessey made his own admissions to the undercover officers.

Many members of Project Kourage, including Mr. Big, testified about the various roles they played in the sting operations against the accused. Some of them played portions of their incriminating audio and videotapes for the court.

The result of the hearing was that both of the accused were committed for trial on four counts of first-degree murder.

Their trial was scheduled to begin on Monday, April 6, 2009, which meant the two men had eleven months before their case would come to court. Because the proceedings were expected to last approximately three months, the Hennesseys were worried about the financial demands of such a lengthy trial.

Barry Hennessey says, "The family finances were depleted. My wife and I had done everything we could do to raise money but we didn't have much left. It was going to be very difficult for us to finance the cost of a long trial."

Their concerns came to a head on January 1, 2009.

On that day, Barry Hennessey, his wife, Sandy, their daughter Alecia, Shawn, and Christine met with D'Arcy Depoe in his Edmonton office. Because Dennis was prohibited from speaking to Shawn, he was excluded from attending the conference.

Barry Hennessey says in that meeting, D'Arcy Depoe recommended that the two accused should consider pleading guilty to the lesser offence of manslaughter.

"He gave us an ultimatum. He said that if Shawn went to trial, he would be convicted of manslaughter. But he also said that Shawn would risk being convicted of first-degree murder with no chance of parole for twenty-five years."

DePoe, who had been defending people for twenty-seven years, including more than seventy homicide cases, categorically denies this.

"I don't issue ultimatums. Generally, I give advice on what I see as the issues, the pros and the cons of a trial versus the entry of a guilty plea, the potential defences, the likelihood of success at trial, and so on. I leave the decision as to how to plead to the client.

"I discussed the full range of sentence with the family several times. I advised them that if the judge saw things our way, and with the potential at least for early parole, he could be out in a year. I also said that this was unlikely, and that we ought to be satisfied with a sentence in the range of seven to eight years. I made it very clear that the sentence could be in the range suggested by the Crown . . . ten to fifteen years."

Shawn seemed to lean towards pleading guilty to manslaughter, but he wasn't sure.

Barry was adamantly opposed to the idea. "I thought it was crazy," he says. "Why should they plead guilty when they were not guilty of nothing."

In this regard, Mr. DePoe says, "The basis of party liability was explained to Barry Hennessey numerous times. And the facts of what the two accused had admitted to doing were explained to him several times. But it just didn't sink in."

In any case, Barry was so upset that he left the meeting in tears. "They all stayed there talking, and I went out in the parking lot and stood by my car crying. I knew it was wrong. You don't plead guilty to something you didn't do. The whole idea was tearing me apart."

The decision was left to Shawn, and it weighed heavily on his mind.

As the weeks passed, he remained undecided. It was a very difficult choice between the *possibility* of receiving four life sentences for first-degree murder or accepting a definite but lesser term for manslaughter.

Finally, Shawn decided to plead guilty to the manslaughter charges. The court date for the guilty pleas was arranged for Monday, January 19.

Long before that plea date was established, Linden MacIntyre and the CBC had come calling. Linden wanted to interview Shawn for *The Fifth Estate*, but the Hennesseys' lawyers were vehemently opposed to the accused having anything to do with the media.

It was only after the Hennesseys became profoundly uncomfortable with the compiled *Agreed Statement of Facts* that they became sufficiently concerned to defy the lawyer's instructions.

Even then, Shawn Hennessey needed to be convinced.

After a preliminary discussion with MacIntyre, Shawn and his wife, Christine, agreed to be interviewed for television. They spoke to MacIntyre on tape at Shawn's house on Sunday, January 18, the day before his plea date for manslaughter.

Barry claims, "Shawn remained undecided about pleading guilty right to the very end. Even during the course of that television interview with Linden MacIntyre when Shawn said he had decided to plead guilty to manslaughter, he wasn't sure he was going to go into court and do it."

Nevertheless, the next day, Shawn and Dennis appeared in the Court of Queen's Bench before Mr. Justice Eric F. Macklin and somberly pled "yes" to the accusations that they had committed four counts of manslaughter.

The courtroom was jammed with a standing-room crowd of over one hundred people who listened intently to the lengthy proceedings that followed their pleas.

As part of the public record, an *Agreed Statement of Facts* was read into the court transcript (Appendix A at the end of the narrative).

In this document, seventy-seven articles or facts are listed that were agreed to by both the Crown and the defence.

For example, the first article reads:

1. *On March 2, 2005 bailiff Rob Perry ("PERRY") set out to execute a warrant authorizing the seizure on behalf of Kentwood Ford of a 2005 Ford F350 Super Duty pickup truck, white in colour, Vehicle Identification Number 1FTWW31P55EA94067.*

For the purpose of this book, the most salient articles in the *Agreed Statement of Facts* are as follows:

49. *The RCMP commenced an extensive investigation to try to determine, among other things, how ROSZKO returned to his farm to ambush and murder the four peace officers and whether or not he had received any type of assistance. Additionally, the police wanted to determine how ROSZKO had armed himself with respect to the*

*.300 Winchester as it was discovered through the
National Firearms Registry that that particular rifle
was in fact, legally registered to John HENNESSEY who,
as previously noted, is the grandfather of the accused
HENNESSEY.*

50. *The police further conducted numerous interviews of
relatives of ROSZKO and executed search warrants with
respect to ROSZKO'S cell phone.*

51. *Red Deer ERT members had approached from the north
side of the Quonset. After their entry into the Quonset,
someone mentioned seeing a bed sheet on the north side
by the east corner of the Quonset. Later, in addition to
the bed sheet, a pillow case containing a pair of work
gloves along with a small water bottle and a can of "Bear
Scare" pepper spray was seized from the location.*

53. *The search of the Telus cell phone records relating to
ROSZKO'S cellular phone indicated that between 3:34
p.m. and 4:37 p.m. on March 2, 2005, ROSZKO placed
one phone call to Kal Tire in Barrhead and numerous
calls were made between ROSZKO and a "bag phone"
then utilized by the accused, HENNESSEY, by virtue of his
employment with Kal Tire. Additionally, numerous calls
were made to HENNESSEY'S residence. The last call made
by the bag phone was to HENNESSEY'S residence at 5:24
p.m. The bag phone was not used again until March 4,
2005.*

54. *ROSZKO asked HENNESSEY if he could hide his truck
at the HENNESSEY residence, however, HENNESSEY
steadfastly refused. At one point, HENNESSEY was
aware that ROSZKO was at his residence by reason of a
phone call received from his wife, Christine HENNESSEY.
HENNESSEY also spoke to ROSZKO at that time on the
telephone.*

55. *HENNESSEY stopped briefly at Jessie ZASIEDKO'S house
during the evening of March 2, 2005. HENNESSEY was
seeing his brother-in-law, the accused Dennis Keegan
CHEESEMAN ("CHEESEMAN"). HENNESSEY is married
to CHEESMAN'S sister, Christine. HENNESSEY was*

*apparently aware that CHEESEMAN was helping Jessie
ZASIEDKO move. HENNESSEY asked CHEESEMAN
to speak to him alone, and indicated that he needed
CHEESEMAN'S help because there were RCMP officers
at ROSZKO'S farm, and HENNESSEY was involved in
the grow operation located on ROSZKO'S property.
He further asked CHEESEMAN to get home as soon
as he could. CHEESEMAN knew ROSZKO as he, like
HENNESSEY, had done odd jobs from time to time for
ROSZKO on ROSZKO'S property. These jobs involved
menial labour such as the digging of holes for the
planting of trees. CHEESEMAN, unlike HENNESSEY,
had no involvement with respect to any of the illegal
operations on the ROSZKO property.*

60. *FIFIELD continued to watch the ROSZKO residence
    throughout the night. She could see vehicles driving in
    and out, and assumed that they were police vehicles
    based on what she had seen in the daylight. She also
    noted, at some point, that she saw lights on in ROSZKO'S
    trailer.*

61. *When CHEESEMAN returned home to the rural residence
    he shared with his sister Christine and his brother-in-law,
    HENNESSEY, in the later evening hours of March 2,
    2005, he found ROSZKO and HENNESSEY sitting at
    the kitchen table. It was evident to CHEESEMAN that
    Christine and her children were home. However, they
    were avoiding ROSZKO.*

62. *ROSZKO had arrived at the residence with the Luger
    handgun in the waistband of his pants, and was
    seeking the rifle that HENNESSEY had been given by his
    grandfather, John HENNESSEY, a few years prior.*

63. *HENNESSEY wiped the .300 Winchester Magnum
    down; he provided it to ROSZKO as well as a box of
    ammunition intended for use in that rifle.*

64. *When CHEESEMAN viewed that situation, he took it
    upon himself to go downstairs and retrieve a white
    pillowcase and some gloves. CHEESEMAN then put on the
    gloves and stuck the HENNESSEY rifle in the pillowcase.*

65. *It was clear to all present that ROSZKO was enraged at the police, and ROSZKO made comments to the effect that he intended to return to his property and burn down the Quonset that contained the illegal marijuana grow and chop shop operation.*

66. *Both HENNESSEY and CHEESEMAN knew that armed confrontation with the police was a real possibility and that the situation was clearly trouble.*

67. *ROSZKO decided that he would hide the sought after truck at CHAYKA'S residence, and the two accused agreed to follow him there in order to give him a ride back to his residence*

68. *HENNESSEY asked CHEESEMAN to accompany him for support and comfort. Both men were intimidated and fearful of ROSZKO. They followed ROSZKO to CHAYKA'S residence in HENNESSEY'S Dodge Neon. During that trip of approximately a half an hour, the two accused were relatively quiet. When they arrived at the CHAYKA residence, they pulled over and waited near the highway while Roszko drove the white truck and parked it down the CHAYKA driveway. During this time period, the two accused discussed leaving ROSZKO there, however, decided not to act upon that plan. ROSZKO ultimately reappeared on foot carrying the HENNESSEY rifle, with the handgun still tucked into the waistband of his pants. CHEESEMAN exited from the front passenger seat, vacating the seat for ROSZKO. ROSZKO slid the rifle with the pillowcase into the back seat next to CHEESEMAN.*

69. *During the trip from CHAYKA'S, CHEESEMAN and HENNESSEY did not converse with ROSZKO, but ROSZKO ranted and complained about the RCMP, and threatened to get even with them. He indicated that he was going to burn down the Quonset. CHEESEMAN described his rantings as "devil talk."*

70. *ROSZKO directed HENNESSEY to drive past the range road on which he lived, and to proceed to the next range road where his mother lived. He directed HENNESSEY to drive past his mother's residence and to stop across the*

field from where the police were located. The two accused could see the lights from police cars that early morning of March 3, 2005, and ROSZKO paused to pull socks over the outside of the boots he was then wearing. ROSZKO grabbed the HENNESSEY rifle from the back seat and proceeded off in the direction of the police, sometime in the early morning hours of March 3, 2005, and most likely between 1 a.m. and 3 a.m.

71. *HENNESSEY and CHEESEMAN departed and drove directly home. CHEESEMAN suggested that they should call the police and warn them about ROSZKO, however, HENNESSEY discouraged that idea, and felt that ROSZKO would come after them should he evade police. Neither accused made such a phone call.*

The last article in the *Agreed Statement of Facts* states:

Following an extensive RCMP investigation, the accused CHEESEMAN was arrested on July 7, 2007, and the accused HENNESSEY was arrested on July 8, 2007.

After the entire document was read into the court, Judge Macklin asked the Crown, the defence counsels, and each of the accused if they agreed with the accuracy and veracity of the facts submitted.

Everyone said they agreed.

Furthermore, Shawn and Dennis each submitted written instructions to the effect that they agreed with the *Agreed Statement of Facts*. Each man's submission was attached to his copy of the document.

According to the *Agreed Statement of Facts*, it seems clear that the two accused knew there were police on Roszko's property and they were aware that an armed confrontation, where Roszko intended to harm the police, was a real possibility.

An article written in the *Edmonton Journal* after the guilty pleas were entered said: "Hennessey and Cheeseman now admit they supplied Roszko with a rifle, heard him talk about revenge against the RCMP, drove him close to his farm, dropped him off, and decided against warning the RCMP about the grave danger Roszko presented."

Further in the article: "Hennessey and Cheeseman's families and friends had long stated they were innocent and didn't help Roszko. In the statement of facts that Hennessey and Cheeseman confirmed were accurate, a different story emerged."

On the basis of the *Agreed Statement of Facts*, it appears to be irrefutable that Hennessey and Cheeseman were complicit in Roszko's crime.

After the guilty pleas were submitted, Shawn Hennessey addressed the court.

Katherine O'Neill of the *Globe and Mail* reported that Shawn Hennessey made a tearful apology to the families of the slain Mounties. "I would like to apologize for my involvement in this tragic case," he said. "In no way did I mean for any harm to come to anyone. I'm truly sorry."

Ms. O'Neill wrote that, "Family members of the fallen officers who packed the courthouse to watch the proceedings appeared unmoved by his act of contrition."

Dennis Cheeseman declined the judge's offer to address the court.

Outside the courtroom, Don Schiemann said that for him Hennessey's apology was the most moving moment of the plea session. "Was he sorry that he got caught or sorry that he did it? I can't look into his heart. I take his sorrow at face value and I forgive him."

When a reporter asked him if he forgives Cheeseman, Schiemann answered, "I haven't heard anything from him yet."

The day after the accused entered their guilty pleas, family members of the deceased Mounties were invited to enter victim impact statements. It took hours for the thirteen impact statements to be incorporated into the record.

As each person addressed the court, the sorrow and anguish in their voices made their painful declarations extremely moving.

The following extracts of their statements are taken from Ryan Cormier's articles in the *Edmonton Journal*.

Anthony Gordon's widow, Kim, said, "Anthony was robbed of seeing the birth of his second son, Anthony Ashton J. Gordon.

He never got the chance to look upon his new son with pride and hold him close. Never heard his first cry, saw his first smile, or saw him take his first step. Anthony had the opportunity to be a good father and that was stolen from him. My two sons were robbed of knowing an amazing man."

Kelly Johnston spoke of her grief, saying, "When I lost my husband, I lost my purpose. When Leo's heart stopped beating, so did mine. It breaks my heart that Leo never got to see our wedding photos and we never got to go on our honeymoon."

Brock Myrol's fiancée Anjila Steeves told of her desolation. "I am so lonely for Brock it hurts. I feel lost, like a leaf that has fallen from a tree and been tossed in the wind. He was the one person I would have turned to to get through something like this. Brock was the air I breathed, and without him I am suffocating."

Rev. Don Schiemann presented the court with a series of snapshots of his son Peter beginning when he was just a young tyke. He spoke of him as the ten-year-old boy who would stick licorice up his nose to gross out his little sister.

With a quiver in his voice, he said, "March 3, 2005 was like having one's arm torn off. The pain is beyond words. Over time, the pain has subsided, the wound has healed, but there will always be the telltale scar tissue. The limb is always missed.

"I struggle to understand the incredible evil that would lead a man to end the lives of four others in such a brutal and heartless manner. For me, this is not an academic question. It hits home and it hits hard."

As Hennessey and Cheeseman sat dejectedly with their heads down, the mothers of Leo Johnston, Anthony Gordon, and both parents of Brock Myrol offered their poignant comments about the excruciating pain they endured with the loss of their beloved sons.

Colleen Myrol's comments were particularly touching. "My grief is every day, every night, every morning, every moment. It is every breath I take. I feel like my heart has been ripped out of my chest. My world is shattered. I am completely broken."

Crown prosecutor Dave Labrenz told the court, "James Roszko was only able to murder these four police officers as a direct result of the aid of Shawn Hennessey and Dennis Cheeseman. James Roszko never would have been able to commit these murders without their assistance."

He claimed the two guilty men acted selfishly, claiming they abetted Roszko in his crime because of their involvement with him in his the marijuana grow-op. He asked the judge to sentence the two accused to ten to fifteen years.

Labrenz argued they had the chance to prevent the murders with one phone call.

David Staples of Canwest News Service reported that both defence lawyers pleaded for mercy. Cheeseman's lawyer, Peter Northcott, argued for a four-year sentence, the minimum allowed for manslaughter.

Northcott said, "Taking into account time served, that should be cut to three years."

He claimed that Cheeseman's was a markedly different situation (from Hennessey's). "When Mr. Cheeseman got involved with Mr. Roszko, Mr. Hennessey had already handed over the rifle. All that Mr. Cheeseman knew was that Mr. Roszko was planning to burn down a Quonset hut. "He was never in control of the situation, nor was he part of any of Mr. Roszko's plans."

Staples's article stated that D'Arcy DePoe, Hennessey's lawyer, told the court that neither of the accused were the ones who shot the four police officers.

DePoe claimed that no one here (in the courtroom) gave Roszko a gun for the purpose of shooting someone. "These men didn't want this thing to happen.

"When Roszko came to Hennessey's house, just hours after the RCMP got onto his farm, he arrived uninvited and angry. Roszko's Luger pistol was in the waistband of his pants, but he had his gun in his hand at one point."

DePoe went on to say that Roszko was there for the purpose of demanding a rifle and ammunition, and that Shawn didn't feel he had any option, so he gave him the gun.

DePoe asked that his client receive a term of five years' incarceration. He argued, "Taking into account time served, that should be cut to three years."

Over one hundred letters were submitted in support of Hennessey's character. In them he was described as being trustworthy, reliable, and a hard-working father of two little girls.

DePoe told the judge, "Many people think very highly of him and they still do, despite where he is today."

Judge Macklin said he would hand down the sentences for the two convicted men in seven to ten days.

Corporal Wayne Oakes agreed with the manslaughter convictions, saying, "For law enforcement, for the people that worked with the fallen four, the people that knew them, the people who continue to stand beside them . . . they will see that justice was served today."

After these court sessions were concluded, the Canadian Press reported that Barry Hennessey was concerned that one of the tapes played at the preliminary hearing might unfairly influence Judge Macklin's determination of Shawn's and Dennis's sentences.

All the evidence from the preliminary hearing had been sealed. But when Hennessey and Cheeseman pleaded guilty, that evidence was unsealed and released to the general public.

The particular tape that Barry Hennessey was referring to is a recorded confession that Dennis Cheeseman had made to an RCMP operative during the Project Kourage sting.

This recording was neither played nor cited during sentencing arguments. But now that it was available for scrutiny, Barry feared Judge Macklin would use it to determine "the boys'" sentences. "You think the judge won't hear this?" Barry Hennessey complained. "It's not fair. It is not right that they released all of this."

Is this an example of Barry Hennessey's unschooled naiveté or an illustration of his subtle appreciation for the law?

On the surface, it appears to be the former, but in reality it could very well be the latter.

In this regard, Ken Johnson, an experienced trial lawyer from Port Elgin, Ontario, has expressed the opinion that Barry is probably correct. Insofar as Cheeseman's taped confession was not cited by the Crown in his arguments for sentencing, it is not the judge's prerogative to go looking for extraneous evidence relative to sentencing.

Ira Greenspoon, a Toronto lawyer, agrees with Johnson. He says the evidence in the preliminary hearing goes to guilt or innocence. Once a conviction is registered, evidence from the preliminary hearing is not relevant to determining the sentence.

In Judge Macklin's lengthy *Reasons for Judgment* (see Appendix B), he makes no reference to the taped confession in his determination of Hennessey's and Cheeseman's sentences.

As the day for sentencing drew near, there was a lot of commentary and speculation in the media about the penalty the boys deserved and the prison terms they would receive.

Barry Hennessey clearly was anxious about the boys' sentences too, and decided to have his say.

The day before the sentencing, in an interview with QR77's Dave Rutherford, Barry argued that as far as he was concerned the whole situation is unfair. "I don't think it's quite fair that nobody knows the real story. Tomorrow, the boys are being sentenced and all this [commentary] is coming out on the radio. I truly believe that this is a misfit of justice."

Barry claimed that the boys pled guilty to manslaughter because they feared spending the rest of their lives in prison for murder. "They pled guilty because they were told that if they didn't, they'd spend the rest of their living days in jail. They were fearmongered into it."

On Friday, January 30, Judge Macklin delivered his decision to a huge gallery that was packed in the courtroom with people standing in some of the aisles.

After making lengthy preliminary remarks and reading from his written document that detailed his reasons for judgment, he sentenced Shawn Hennessey to fifteen years in prison, and Dennis Cheeseman to twelve years. Macklin indicated their time would be reduced by approximately five years because of their time served and because the two had pled guilty instead of opting for trial.

He verbally chastised the two offenders, saying: "They let themselves down and their families.

"They let down four RCMP constables who put their lives at risk.

"They let down the communities where the officers lived, worked, and served. They let down the country the officers unselfishly agreed to serve and where the offenders are privileged to live under the rule of law.

"These four men were Canadian heroes and forever will be remembered as such."

Sketch of Dennis Cheeseman and Shawn Hennessey awaiting their sentences, January 30, 2009. (Illustration by Stephen Coffey for the *Barrhead Leader*)

In support of his decision, Judge Macklin distributed his twenty-four-page document entitled *Reasons for Judgment*, in which he

i)   Cited the facts of the case
ii) Analyzed his reasoning for the sentences
iii) Listed eleven similar cases and the sentences rendered
iv) Presented what he termed Aggravating and Mitigating Factors
v)   Commented on the Victim Impact Statements
vi) Demonstrated the calculation of the sentences
vii) Commented on the effect of the guilty plea
viii) Gave credit for time served
ix) Gave credit for time on bail
x)   Discussed their eligibility for parole
xi) Offered his conclusions

Some of his most crucial sentences in the document read as follows:

- Each of *the two accused pled guilty voluntarily.*
- *I was not bound by any agreement made between either of the accused and the Crown.*
- *It was clear to all present that Roszko was enraged at the police.*
- *Both Hennessey and Cheeseman knew that armed confrontation with the police was a real possibility.*
- *Cheeseman suggested that they should call the police and warn them about Roszko; however, Hennessey discouraged that idea.*
- *The sentences imposed on the two offenders must be proportionate to the gravity of the offence.*
- *Mr. Hennessey and Mr. Cheeseman were parties to Roszko's murders.*
- *Both Mr. Hennessey and Mr. Cheeseman say they were fearful of and intimidated by Roszko, who was known to be volatile. However, there is no evidence of any overt threats to either of them.*
- *Mr. Hennessey had to know that Roszko, in his enraged and heavily armed state, was a serious danger to the police officers who were already on his property.*
- *There was no good reason not to alert the police to danger.*
- *Mr. Cheeseman was little more than a bystander with knowledge of the danger to the police posed by Roszko.*
- *It is my view that Mr. Hennessey reaches the highest rung possible for a party to murder who did not participate in formulating a plan to murder, was not present, and was not the shooter.*
- *Mr. Hennessey appears to have been motivated exclusively by self-interest. The fact that he was fearful of Roszko reinforces the conclusion that he either knew or was willfully blind to the threat Roszko posed to others.*

The reaction to Judge Macklin's sentences was mixed, to say the least.

The media referred to the sentences as "harsh."

Crown prosecutor David Labrenz was quoted as saying, "The message sent today is that crimes of this type involving police officers have to be denounced, deterred, specifically and generally."

The families of the slain policemen appeared to be satisfied with the judge's decision.

Colleen Myrol spoke to Ryan Cormier of the *Edmonton Journal* and said, "Whatever the number of years in this sentence, the truth as we see it, for Dennis and Shawn, is that they have a life sentence.

"They caused all of us emotional pain and hardship, and for the rest of their lives, they will be branded by all of Canada as having been part of this horrific crime."

However, she did express some empathy for the families of the offenders. "We feel sadness; there are other families at stake, here. There are two children whose father has been sent to prison, and their uncle. You have to think of that also."

Don Schiemann said, "I've often been critical of our justice system. It often seems broken and ineffective. There are times when it works, and today it worked."

People from various communities reacted in diverse ways. Many from the Mayerthorpe region were glad that the prolonged and tragic saga was over. Some residents of the Barrhead area felt the two men were treated too severely. That division of opinion appeared to be sustained throughout Alberta and even across the country.

Corporal Wayne Oakes, who had followed the criminal proceedings carefully from beginning to end, said, "Judge Macklin was thorough. For each of the accused, he addressed the facts individually. Both of them and their lawyers agreed to the statement of facts that was read into the record and they signed it."

Christine Hennessey told the *Barrhead Leader* that while she didn't argue her husband's innocence and acknowledged his involvement with Roszko, she did think their severe sentences were unjustified. She had hoped that when her husband and brother pleaded guilty to manslaughter, both of them would receive lighter sentences.

The Hennesseys were outraged and devastated. Barry Hennessey had hoped the boys would be home by Christmas. Sandy Hennessey, Shawn's mother, told the same newspaper, "I'm devastated by the outcome of what happened in court today. Part of me feels like I'm numb. I'm totally numb. Another part of me feels like this is just a bad nightmare that continues to go on and on."

When she was asked what she had expected the sentence to be, Sandy replied, "Certainly not fifteen years. I had expected all along that it would probably be in the single digits . . . like five years, six years. I was really, really, shocked."

Barry Hennessey was outraged at the sentence and vowed to do everything in his power to get the boys out of prison.

Sandy agreed with her irrepressible husband.

"Now we start working on counting down to getting him out."

Those who opposed them were equally determined to ensure that justice would be done.

10 | Fair or Unfair

IT WASN'T LONG AFTER SENTENCING that the Hennesseys found two lawyers that agreed to appeal the severity of their punishments.

Hersh Wolch, a renowned trial lawyer from Calgary, offered to act for Shawn Hennessey. Peter Royal, an equally high-profile barrister from Edmonton, agreed to represent Dennis Cheeseman.

Wolch had established a stellar reputation across Canada. His successes in the criminal courts were numerous, but he was best known for helping to overturn two notorious wrongful convictions. One of those cases involved David Milgaard of Saskatchewan, who was released from prison after serving twenty-three years for a murder he didn't commit. Wolch had also served on the legal team that helped clear Steven Truscott of charges that he raped and murdered a young girl in Ontario in 1959.

Initially the legal team intended to appeal the length of the boys' sentences and to attempt to have their guilty pleas withdrawn so they could proceed to a new trial.

Hersh Wolch told the Canadian Press, "I really question the conviction and I question the outcome."

However, in the field of criminal law it is commonly held that the appeal of a guilty plea is a legal maneuver that is rarely used and seldom successful.

Wolch knew Hennessey's appeal would be difficult. After an exhaustive application of his legal skills, Hersh decided in January 2010 the appeal could not be done. "It's very hard to withdraw a plea," he said.

Nevertheless, the appeal of the boys' sentences will proceed. At the time of this writing, Hersh Wolch thinks these appeals will be heard in either February or March 2010.

Elsewhere, the public reaction to the Hennessey and Cheeseman sentences has been divided.

There was a great deal of support for them in Barrhead, where the general consensus among the residents held that the punishment meted out by the court was too severe and vindictive.

The manager of a Barrhead restaurant maintains the two men were innocent. "They didn't know what Roszko was going to do."

A receptionist at a Barrhead motel claims that Hennessey was a nice, quiet, dedicated family man . . . and a hard worker. "The conviction was bogus," she says. "They never should have gone down for it. They were guilty by association."

People in that community thought of Hennessey and Cheeseman as two guys with a bad friend who were at the wrong place at the wrong time. The boys were guilty only of making a series of bad choices that led them to Roszko's farm.

Mayerthorpe residents did not agree with that assessment. Generally they felt the court had done its job and meted out sentences appropriate to their crime.

Former mayor Albert Schalm says there were many people in Mayerthorpe who were hoping Hennessey and Cheeseman would get a stiff sentence.

A writer for the *Mayerthorpe Freelancer* conducted an informal survey in the town's business section and, although many of those surveyed did not want to be identified publicly, most of them said they agreed with the sentences.

One woman in one of the grocery stores said, "They deserved what they got. They'll have a long time in jail to consider the consequences of their actions."

Another person commented, "I think that the two men were sentenced fairly by the court, but I feel badly for their families. There are parents, wives, and children involved. They have to go on living with the knowledge that their kinfolk participated in one of the worst crimes in Canadian history."

A worker in a restaurant where the four dead Mounties had been regular customers said she feels sad. "We need to move on, but I still miss them. They were nice guys."

Mayerthorpe's Rev. Arnold Lotholz told the author that Hennessey and Cheeseman were definitely involved in some way. "They certainly bear some guilt."

Anthony Gordon's widow, Kim, says that with the appeal still pending, everything is still not over. "As far as their sentences . . .

justice has been somewhat served. It's hard to listen to them [the families] whining about their children are not going to see them for a long time. Because of their actions, my two children will never see Anthony. He [Shawn] should have thought of his children first . . . before getting himself involved."

Anjila Steeves, Brock Myrol's fiancé, told the writer: "No amount of time is ever enough. These were people's lives they were playing with. My lifetime with Brock is gone. I didn't want any of this to happen. It's too hard on families, but there have to be consequences for doing what they did, or what is going to deter people from doing the same thing in the future?"

Kelly Johnston says, "The sentences are appropriate. They didn't phone and they ruined countless other people's lives. They had the ability to save somebody's life and chose not to. They should be penalized . . . and face the consequences.

"I think they both should have received equal sentences. He [Cheeseman] suggested phoning, but suggesting and doing are two different things."

In a letter to the editor in the *Edmonton Journal* dated January 24, 2009, a man from Red Deer wrote:

> I praise the RCMP for their hard work and dedication in investigating the senseless massacre of four young Mounties on March 3, 2005 near Mayerthorpe.
>
> Shame on Shawn Hennessey and Dennis Cheeseman for their cowardly role in allowing James Roszko to commit his murderous rampage.
>
> These men deserve the maximum penalty for their crime, and hopefully will use that time to atone for their actions.
>
> Name withheld by the author.

On February 9, 2009, Joe McLaughlin, the managing editor of the *Red Deer Advocate,* wrote in part:

> After the Mounties were murdered, Hennessey and Cheeseman didn't act like they were innocent of any wrongdoing.

They lied about their whereabouts and activities. They denied assisting Roszko after police identified the rifle that Hennessey had given to Roszko as belonging to his grandfather.

It took 28 months and a $2-million police investigation before Hennessey and Cheeseman would admit the truth.

Now facing lengthy jail terms, they have a different version of the truth. Shocked by the severity of the sentences, they claim they were wrongfully convicted and plan to appeal.

Hennessey's family blames his lawyer for misleading them into guilty pleas; they expected him to be home with them in time for Christmas

That would have been an affront to justice and to the families of the slain Mounties.

Even in Barrhead, not everyone was sympathetic to Hennessey and Cheeseman.

An editorial in the *Barrhead Leader* dated January 27, 2009 said that Hennessey's and Cheeseman's guilty plea was an admission by them that they had aided and abetted James Roszko, and any further speculation in that regard should be "laid to rest." The reality is that these two men will go to jail based "purely on their own admission of guilt."

A letter to the editor in that same issue reads as follows:

Dear Editor,

I wonder if the Hennessey/Cheeseman families and all their supporters are still proud of them? It's really too bad they did not have the guts to maintain their innocence and go to trial where they would have received a life sentence like they deserve.

Name withheld by the author.

One week later, in that same newspaper, a relative of Shawn Hennessey wrote a response to that letter:

Dear Editor,

Mr. (name withheld) you need not wonder any longer—the Hennessey/Cheeseman families are still very proud of our boys. I cannot speak for all their supporters, but if all the people who have stopped me in the streets and all the phone calls I have received from across the province are any indication, there are still many out there.

I wish you had introduced yourself to us at the courthouse as I assume you must have attended court daily and heard both sides in order to make such a judgmental statement. It is people like you with your lynch mob mentality, combined with legal advice that stopped these boys from coming forward sooner.

I can only hope and pray that you never find yourself in the position of having an armed man show up at your door, waving a gun in your face, making demands and threatening your family because I fear your family would lose.

Name withheld.

The editorial in this issue said:

"Shawn Hennessey and Dennis Cheeseman are not going to prison for anything they've done. They are behind bars for what they didn't do."

It goes on to say that the two men didn't "pull any triggers . . . didn't know the size of the police contingent on Roszko's property . . . and couldn't have possibly known five men would die the following morning. But they didn't make the phone call."

The article concludes with the statement that "both Hennessey and Cheeseman can be relatively certain had they made even the smallest effort to signal the threat posed by Roszko they wouldn't have been sentenced to a combined 27 years in prison last Friday."

In an interview with Shawn's mother, Sandy, in that issue of the *Barrhead Leader*, she is asked the question: "When you look back, is there something that you would have done or not done?"

Sandy Hennessey: "Well, I wish we had spoken out a lot sooner. But we were told by counsel not to speak. Don't speak to the press.

So we're going by what Shawn's attorneys had told us. And yeah, I really regret that."

Question: "People want to know if Shawn was innocent, why did he plead guilty?"

Sandy Hennessey: "He pled guilty because he wanted the quickest way to get out from underneath all this. And he thought that by pleading guilty at this point, this was [saving time] going to court, waiting till spring, going through all that process you know, and he just thought it would speed up the process. Certainly not expecting fifteen years by any stretch of the imagination."

Both Sandy and Barry Hennessey were very involved with their son's case and supportive of him throughout the course of his legal problems. Barry was more publicly prominent and certainly much more vocal than his wife.

It appears that both of them were responsible or at least integrally involved with the formulation and circulation of an Internet newsletter under the banner *The Friends and Family of Shawn Hennessey and Dennis Cheeseman*.

After the sentencing, it included an update that read:

Today's events [the sentencing] changed our lives forever. Shawn and Dennis agreed to plead guilty to manslaughter because they were told that it would be the quickest route home to their families. Their choice was tough. They were also told that going against a very powerful machine with unlimited resources on first degree murder could possibly result in 4 X first degree murder charges which could result in 4 X 25 year sentences. Which may possibly mean that they could be behind bars for the rest of their natural lives. It appeared that the only option they had was to plead guilty to manslaughter and take that chance of receiving a lesser sentence so that they could come home to their families within the next couple of years. The choice they made was not easy for them to admit guilt to something they disagreed with.

Then as the 12 year and 15 year sentences were handed out we were all in total shock. Strange though as it was noted [sic] that day by the crown [sic] that they had insufficient evidence for a first degree murder conviction at trial.

All we ask is that the justice system look at this and give the boys the chance at a fair trial with all the evidence out in the open.

A "Free Shawn and Dennis" petition was also circulated. It stated:

In regards to Shawn Hennessey and Dennis Cheeseman

We are asking that the Minister of Justice please release Shawn Hennessey and Dennis Cheeseman immediately from prison. These two men are presently serving 15 and 12 years for crimes they had no idea were going to happen. March 3, 2005 four police officers lost their lives in Mayerthorpe. The 2 men that are in prison had zero idea what James Roszko was about to do. He did the killings 10 hours after the boys dropped him off at his mother's house. Shawn has never to this day said he heard this madman say he was going to hurt anyone. It took a several million dollar (Mr. Big Sting) to get a false confession from Dennis Cheeseman. These boys only walked in a courtroom to plea [sic] guilty to a manslaughter charge (even though they knew they were inocent [sic]) they would face life sentences for capital murder. They were told the crown would possibly give them the minimum sentence which could have them home within a year if they agreed to the agreed statement of facts and plea [sic] guilty of manslaughter. Later it was said by the crown that they had insufficient evidence against them on capital murder charges to get a conviction. Their council [sic] should of gone to trial, and all we all ask is these 2 boys get a fair day in court. Please release them and set a trial date. They now have lawyers they have faith in and that believe in them. Don't let this matter get any further out of control than it already is. Please release them immediately.

The petition asks the reader to submit a name and an e-mail address, and then to answer yes or no to two questions:

Do you think they should get a chance at a trial?

Should they be released until a trial date can be set?

In a column on the same page beside the petition, there was a list of comments that included the following items:

- "Barry Hennessey told the CBC News that the two men shouldn't have entered guilty pleas."
- "I know the position he [Shawn] was in was very tough. I respect his decision . . . that decision was very difficult for him and I have to think I might have made the same decision," Hennessey said.
- "Nobody agreed with him whatsoever. I don't know a person who agreed with what happened to him, doing what he did. No friends, no family, nobody agreed to it."
- "Obviously, we had run out of money and we didn't know what way to turn . . . we spent every cent we had to try to help him through and he seen the pressure, and when the money was gone, it seemed like we didn't have much more chance," Hennessey said.
- "The choices were [to] roll the dice [and] do 25 years times four, or take a chance on telling people what everybody wants hear: that you're guilty of something you didn't do and take a chance on . . . maybe coming home in two to three years to raise your family."
- "Shawn has never spoke to anybody about this but yet he's sentenced to 15 years." Hennessey said, "Nobody wanted to listen to Shawn's story. Shawn tried to tell exactly what happened in that house and how it all took place and nobody wants to listen to him."
- "His [Shawn's] heart is broke, as well as the rest of our hearts are broke for everything that happened in Mayerthorpe," Barry Hennessey, father of Shawn Hennessey, said.

Many of the above comments speak to Barry Hennessey's dogged determined to free his son from prison. In this regard he is steadfast, relentless, intractable, and ultimately irrepressible for the love and devotion he has demonstrated for Shawn. During the course of Shawn's legal problems he has been fearless in his defence.

But he can also be highly emotional, overly aggressive, and reckless in his pronouncements and accusations. In that regard, it seems he will say almost anything to inflame emotions or arouse a reaction. Many of his remarks have been over-the-top exaggerations, false generalizations, or out-and-out distortions.

His most egregious assertion is that there is a vast legal conspiracy against Shawn—a cover-up that encompasses the RCMP, the courts, the Crown, the defence lawyers, and Correctional Services Canada. He claims that Correctional Services Canada was vindictive in initially assigning Shawn to a penitentiary placement in far-off Prince Albert, Saskatchewan.

He says the judge at the sentencing was vicious, unreasonable, and lost his composure. He maintains his lawyers and the Crown were "together"—whatever that means.

Steve Vigor, the Mountie who shot James Roszko, says, "Barry Hennessey's talk of a conspiracy is laughable. It's an example of a society that does not accept consequences for their actions. The family feels justified for blaming others."

Barry Hennessey does admit it was an error for his family to make up a story about the grandfather's gun being stolen. "I agree 100 percent we shouldn't have lied about the Winchester rifle being stolen."

And he does ask several reasonable questions.

"Why would you give a guy who's going to kill a policeman a gun registered in your grandfather's name?"

"Why did Roszko get two hicks to drive him if he was going to kill cops?"

"Why would he tell Shawn and Dennis what he was going to do?"

Barry claims, "It makes no sense."

His biggest complaint is that no one has heard Shawn's side of the story—other than the police, of course.

So the author asked him to tell Shawn's side of the story.

This is what he said:

1.   The boys never knew Roszko was going to kill any cops.
2.   Roszko was withdrawn and silent in the car and Dennis never heard him say anything. Barry says, "Dennis couldn't hear Roszko say 'nothing' anyway because the car was old and rickety and they were driving mostly on bumpy, gravel roads."
3.   All along the way, Shawn was hoping they'd run into a police roadblock, or a police helicopter would hail them down from overhead.
4.   They dropped Roszko off one hundred yards from his mother's driveway.
5.   When Roszko got out of Shawn's car, he pulled socks over his boots.
6.   Roszko took the Winchester rifle, which was in a pillowcase, out from the back seat so he could shoot the fuel tanks and burn down the Quonset hut.
7.   Shawn didn't see any police cars at Roszko's farm.
He saw only the light from his Quonset in his yard.

The problem with Shawn's story (as told by Barry) is that the *Agreed Statement of Facts* that Shawn signed and confirmed before the court contradicts points number 1, 2, and 7, above.

And the story about burning down the Quonset hut makes no sense.

Jim Guiry, a Professional Engineer, says that a fired bullet puncturing a gas tank or diesel tank will not cause it to ignite. The sparks from a bullet hitting a metal gas tank will only ignite the gas fumes. Both of those conditions might have been possible.

But Guiry says, "When the gas or diesel tank exploded, it would project a wild spray of burning globs into the air in all directions."

Roszko's gas/diesel tanks were at least thirty yards away from the Quonset hut, which was constructed of steel. Guiry states that the chances of these globs of burning fluid igniting a steel Quonset hut range from minimal to impossible. He insists that the suggestion that this would happen is extremely unlikely.

It doesn't matter whether Roszko said he could do it or that Shawn claimed he said that. Both of them were knowledgeable in mechanical and technical matters. Surely Shawn knew that burning down the Quonset hut with rifle fire was virtually impossible.

Beyond Shawn's story, there are other glaring questions.

Why didn't they call the police that morning?

Barry says, "Because they didn't think anything was going to happen other than Roszko was going to shoot at the fuel tanks and blow them up."

Yet Cheeseman suggested to Shawn they should call the police. But Shawn declined his suggestion.

Why did Dennis Cheeseman admit to all the items on the Agreed Statement of Facts?

Barry explains: "Because he was confused. He's all mixed up. He was for starters and the sting really screwed him up. He thought he had caused Mounties to die. Dennis should have been sent to a psychologist. He was petrified. He thought the sting gang was the Mafia and he was afraid they were going to kill him."

But Dennis voluntarily said the very same things to his boss, Brad McNish. What's more, Dennis's statements to McNish appear to vindicate the integrity of the Mr. Big Sting.

Why did Shawn tell the judge he agreed to all the Agreed Statement of Facts, *and why did he sign it and the instructions attached to them, thereby legally agreeing to them?*

Barry says, "He signed under pressure. The lawyers convinced him to sign. He didn't care. He said that he'd sign anything. He said, 'I'll sign that I'm a child molester if I can get out this year.' He would have signed anything to get himself out of jail in a reasonable period of time."

Why didn't Shawn co-operate with the RCMP *during their investigation?*

D'Arcy Depoe at a speaking engagement, Jasper, Alberta, February 2009.

Barry: "Because our lawyers, Ed O'Neill and D'Arcy DePoe, told us not to say anything to the police. We were told to give them the lawyers' business cards and refer the police to them. In fifteen conversations with the police, Shawn told them over and over to see my lawyer. The cops didn't like it."

Several of Barry's claims seem to impugn D'Arcy DePoe and they need to be addressed.

D'Arcy DePoe, fifty-six, is a highly respected and successful criminal lawyer. After graduating in law from Dalhousie University, he came to Alberta and has been practising criminal law there since 1981.

Although he has been attacked in the media by Barry Hennessey, DePoe has not responded to any of Hennessey's vilification. Prior to this book's being published, DePoe maintained his silence — especially in the media. But he feels he's been repeatedly slandered by Barry Hennessey and is now prepared to speak to the author.

His reply to Barry's last point about Shawn's remaining silent with the police is as follows:

"It is my standard advice to a client I am defending not to talk to the police. First of all, it gives the police an opportunity to acquire information with which they can convict you. Secondly, you don't know what they know and they can induce you to admit to evidence they might not have or confirm suspicions about which they are unsure.

"If you have a story to tell, tell it to a judge or a jury. And only do that after you have reviewed all the Crown's evidence, received legal advice, and been properly prepared to testify and to be cross-examined."

In fact, all of Shawn's interviews with the police took place before Mr. O'Neill was retained. Mr. DePoe spoke to Shawn for the first time in October of 2005. So Shawn, on his own, chose to speak to the police. And in so doing, he had every opportunity to tell them his side of the story, but unfortunately he chose to lie to them.

On March 9, 2005, the RCMP came to Shawn and asked about his involvement with James Roszko on the day and night of March 2, 2005. Shawn denied he'd had anything to do with Roszko on that day or night.

Two days later, on March 11, after the Mounties discovered the list of Roszko's cell phone calls, the same officer went back to see Shawn. This time he asked him about Roszko's cell phone calls to Kal Tire and to his "bag" phone.

This time, Shawn said "he guessed" he did talk to Roszko. He said that was the case because the bailiffs wanted to repossess Roszko's vehicle and he was asking to store it at Shawn's house. Shawn told the investigator that he refused to let Roszko do that.

The RCMP investigation continued for almost a month and then another Mountie came back to see Shawn for a third interview on April 5, 2005.

On this occasion, the investigator had a lengthy conversation with Shawn about his relationship with Roszko. He asked whether or not Shawn had had any contacts with Roszko the afternoon before the day of the murders, or on the evening before the murders, or early the next morning.

Shawn denied seeing Roszko that day or night. He denied that Roszko had come to his place. He denied that he drove Roszko to his farm. Shawn not only lied about those instances but he made the fatal error of creating his own false alibi.

Shawn told the RCMP officer that he came home from work, had supper, played with the kids, and put them to bed. Then he and Christine watched TV and went to bed because he had a work-related conference the next morning in Edmonton.

The investigator asked Shawn if he would swear to that on a bible and Shawn answered, "Absolutely." Yet in the deposition of that interview, there are approximately two dozen proven lies.

Shortly after Shawn's third interview, the same investigator who had spoken to Shawn on April 5 interviewed Christine Hennessey.

She wove the same identical alibi as her husband had previously spun. After hearing Christine's story, it was obvious to the police that the identical alibi had been concocted between them.

A false alibi or any false statement by an accused is very problematic when the Crown puts it before a jury. It can totally destroy the credibility of the accused, and a jury will often take it to infer guilt.

One is then left to wonder how any lawyer would defend Hennessey and Cheeseman in court. After all of Shawn's lies and his false alibi, and Cheeseman's numerous admissions of guilt to both McNish and to Mr. Big, what jury would believe them? What would the defence be?

Nevertheless, Barry Hennessey told the media that when their money ran out, their lawyer lost interest in the case. "The lawyers were our biggest problem," he said. "When we ran out of money, the lawyers convinced him to sign."

D'Arcy DePoe denies this allegation. He considers it to be not only defamatory but ridiculous.

"My interest didn't change a whit when their money ran out. Their money ran out before the preliminary hearing, yet we carried on without a nickel from them in my trust account. Months later, Shawn applied for legal aid coverage and got it. I applied to get extra coverage and was granted 500 extra hours on top of what the Tariff allows.

"This may be the biggest case I've ever worked on. I have eighty large binders of discovery, plus dozens of CDs, tapes, and wiretaps that I had to examine. We needed those 500 extra hours to adequately defend the accused at trial.

"So I certainly deny Barry Hennessey's accusations. I defended Shawn Hennessey in good faith and to the best of my ability without regard for the remuneration I would receive at the end of the day."

DePoe says that Barry Hennessey is a very difficult person to deal with. "There is no reasoning with the man. Barry hears what he wants to hear. And no matter what he was told about the law or the evidence it simply didn't sink in.

"I could not reason with him or explain anything to him."

On one occasion, Barry came to speak to DePoe about Dennis Cheeseman's being depressed and contemplating suicide. His comments and questions to DePoe in this regard were not based on any concern about Dennis. They were, however, so outrageously offensive that DePoe immediately terminated their conversation. "I was so shocked, I put him out of my office."

DePoe says, "By mid-2008, I was no longer prepared to speak to him because it was a waste of my time trying to talk to him.

"The Hennesseys' complaints are based on the severity of sentence Shawn received. It was higher than I expected. I thought something in the range of eight years would be fair. But I told them in a worst-case scenario the judge might decide to give Shawn the top of the range that the Crown had asked for.

"I did recommend a sentence appeal."

Barry Hennessey told the media that the sentences were ridiculous. "I just don't understand the sentences they received. They got more time than Karla Homolka.[3] It's just a no-brainer."

The "Mr. Big" sting is another issue that Barry Hennessey assails. He contends that in 40 to 60 percent of the cases where this sting has been used, the end results are wrongful convictions. The range of the percentage of cases that Barry quotes is so broad it defies credibility.

In any case, RCMP Cpl. Wayne Oakes disagrees with Mr. Hennessey. He says that as of 2008, the Mr. Big sting has been used across the country over 350 times. In seventy-five percent of those operations, success has been achieved by either clearing or charging a suspect. In the cases prosecuted, ninety-five percent have resulted in convictions.

The Canadian Press notes that the RCMP has been using Mr. Big sting operations since the 1980s. The evidence from Mr. Big stings is admissible in Canadian courts, but it is not admissible in the United States or Great Britain.

Lawyer David Brodsky, who is part of the Toronto-based Association in Defence of the Wrongly Convicted, states that stings are not used in those two countries because of the potential for false statements. He says, "They don't use it because they know it is so effective they will get a statement in every case. But they won't necessarily be getting the truth."

---

3   Karla Homolka received a twelve-year sentence in exchange for her
     testimony against Paul Bernardo for the murders of Kristen French and
     Leslie Mahaffy in Ontario in the early 1990s.

In the *Red Deer Advocate*, Lee Giles wrote an article entitled, "Let's Outlaw Mr. Big Stings." In it he claims, "There is no need for our law enforcement officials to engage in questionable conduct to uphold the rule of law."

In part of his piece, Giles writes, "The suspect is often told—by pretend gang members—he will only be allowed to participate in future lucrative crimes if he confesses to past misdeeds, such as murder. Not surprisingly, with a potential king's ransom in the offing, many suspects are quick to confess—whether or not they are guilty."

He quotes John Cotter of the Canadian Press as saying in part, ". . . there is some concern that Mr. Big tactics could lead to false confessions that could send an innocent man to jail."

Steve Cormack, writing in the RCMP *Vet's Net*, replies to Lee Giles's article:

"As I sit down to write this letter, I am literally trembling in anger. The 'Mr. Big' undercover technique has led to literally hundreds of successful conclusions to homicide investigations that would have otherwise gone unsolved.

"They are . . . a legitimate investigative tool that has withstood legal challenges up to the Supreme Court of Canada. . . . The proper application of this technique is not, as Giles states 'questionable conduct.' It is an innovative and proper investigative method."

Criminologist Rob Gordon of Simon Fraser University states that Mr. Big operations are an effective law enforcement strategy to glean intelligence and information about crimes. He says the challenge is to ensure that statements from such operations are accurate and admissible in criminal cases.

Gordon maintains, "As an investigative tool it is very effective. If you go the next step and try to use it as evidence it gets wobbly. People get caught up in the activity that they are alleged to be involved in."

He claims that to impress Mr. Big, they will say things that are not true.

Another writer who opposes stings claims they can be a form of brainwashing. He says they can play to a subject's ego. Men brag and make up stories of how dangerous they are. Consequently, some of the evidence garnered from a sting can be as believable as a drunk in a bar bragging about his fantastical sexual exploits.

Others in support of stings claim that the burden of proof is now so high that the police have had to become more and more creative when it comes to collecting evidence or getting confessions. They do admit, however, that it is important to have checks and balances to ensure the evidence, and admissions are confirmed as true. They conclude that there is no problem with stings as long as due diligence is maintained in assessing their veracity.

In a letter to the *Red Deer Advocate*, Brian Lowe comments about the sting that caught the two men who were complicit in the Mayerthorpe murders. Under the headline "Bleeding hearts oppose Mr. Big stings," he wrote: "The RCMP got their men through a sting—men that would otherwise still be roaming free and unknown to the public."

Lowe ends his letter by stating: "My hat's off to the RCMP. They got their men—too bad not before four of their own were murdered."

The public debate about the use of the Mr. Big sting against Shawn Hennessey remains controversial and unresolved.

Another somewhat contentious component in the Shawn Hennessey saga emanates from a one-hour segment of the CBC's *Fifth Estate* that was broadcast on February 4, 2009.

In that program, the host, Linden MacIntyre, interviewed Shawn Hennessey and his wife, Christine, the day prior to Shawn's going to court to enter his guilty plea to manslaughter.

It has been said of the CBC that they have never met a cop they liked. Whether or not that is a fair imputation, the program seemed to be moderately unbalanced in favour of the accused.

In that interview, Shawn and Christine Hennessey claimed that Roszko had a pistol in his waistband and posed a real threat to them and their family if Shawn refused to help him hide his truck from the police.

During the taping, the Hennesseys appeared to be a nice young couple that was being treated unfairly by the justice system.

Shawn stated that he was going to plead guilty to manslaughter because it was the easiest course for him to take.

"I believe this is the way to go," he said. "Put this behind me and move on with life and be at home with my family. They mean the world to me. I just can't risk a life sentence. I don't know. I have no faith in the justice system."

The major problem with the interview is that parts of the story that Shawn Hennessey related to Linden MacIntyre absolutely contradict his already signed admissions in the *Agreed Statement of Facts*. And this was the document that was slated to be entered into the court records the next day after his interview on the *Fifth Estate*.

Several Canadians from various walks of life were invited to watch a tape of that show and submit their reactions to the author. Almost all of them felt that although Shawn Hennessey bore some responsibility for his actions in this tragedy, it seemed that he had received unfair treatment by the police and the courts.

From Shawn's performance on the *Fifth Estate*, they judged him to be a good and decent husband and the father of two little girls, who was railroaded into a long prison term by an unfair justice system.

Tom Tweedie, a retired physician living in Ancaster, Ontario, had this to say:

"My reaction to the program was that I felt some empathy for Hennessey being forced to go with Roszko, but he still had a responsibility to phone the police.

"It's a sad situation . . . not knowing what Roszko would do but knowing he was going to do something bad. Still, they went ahead and drove him out to his farm.

"I think Hennessey is remorseful and sorry that it ever happened. I had empathy for a young husband and wife in a horrible mess. But the bottom line is they were responsible. When someone is threatened with a gun you can understand their problem. But he should have gone ahead and called the cops."

Tom's wife, Barbara, a retired teacher, says, "Yes, I had empathy for him, too. He had no idea he was aiding and abetting a murderer . . . a guy who is off his rocker. It was one of those things where he had a moment to make a choice. And then it turned out, 'Oh my God. What have I done?'

"I also had the uneasy feeling that their excuses were a bit phony. And they never admitted that calling the police was an option."

Tom Tweedie also questioned Hennessey's character. "Because he did muck around selling dope, it made me wonder whether he was a person on the other side of the law. He didn't seem to have the mindset that told him this is really bad. He had kind of a macho . . . almost criminal . . . attitude.

"He saw the lights, and there was Roszko crossing the field with a powerful gun in his hands. I mean, why didn't he phone the police? Why the hell didn't he call the police?

"Maybe he was worried about being implicated in the marijuana . . . in the trafficking."

A retired teacher from southwestern Ontario who wishes to remain anonymous watched the *Fifth Estate* program and was disturbed by what he saw.

"I saw a couple anguishing. A young husband and father of two young children. The impression I got was that he [Hennessey] turned over the gun to Roszko out of fear. He and his wife were both afraid if Roszko ever came back, their family would be wiped out. They were living in the same community with the guy.

"In hindsight Hennessey said he should have tackled the man and subdued him.

"He was a family man with children. They seemed like good people. I think the authorities are looking for a scapegoat. They have to punish somebody.

"Manslaughter normally gets ten years. He got fifteen and his partner got twelve.

"They [the police] figure we can't do anything about Roszko; he's dead . . . so punish an accomplice. There's a difference between being an accomplice and aiding and abetting someone out of fear. An accomplice carries the connotation of co-operation and bonding. No. They did it out of fear.

"The police told them plead guilty and we'll take it easy on you."

When it was pointed out to this viewer that it's the Crown that makes and/or accepts plea-bargains, he replied, "Crown and police are in the same bag. The Hennesseys were the picture of innocence. Why would he just give a gun to a psycho?"

Bill Fowler, a retired McMaster University professor, thought that Hennessey seemed like a confused kid. "He had conflicting sides to him. He kept saying could have, should have, if it happened again . . . it's too late for that now."

Fowler emphasized one very discerning observation: "From what I saw on the program, he had everything covered. Why did he plead guilty? I'm wondering why anyone advised him to plead guilty? He didn't do anything."

Glenn Dowell, a business executive residing in Dundas, Ontario, said that the interviewer seemed to lead the conversation towards Hennessey's innocence. "But I still was left to wonder why Hennessey didn't call the police. And afterwards, he lied to the police. He should have come forward."

Carl MacLeod, a retired RCMP Staff Sergeant and one-time commander of the Joint Forces Unit in Hamilton, Ontario, said: "Linden MacIntyre was very soft on Hennessey. Hennessey did a lot of lying and equivocating during the interview. His attitude betrays the guilty mind. After Roszko threatened Hennessey and his family, a regular John Doe would have gone to police immediately.

"In my opinion, Hennessey did the *Fifth Estate* interview for free publicity, public sympathy, and an early release on his sentence."

Peter Dunn, a retired municipal director, made the observation: "At the end of the program, I thought that the two men were set up by the RCMP. However, I felt that I was brought to that conclusion by program design. The interviewer led some of the statements made by the man and his wife and summed up their comments with more concrete statements than they had made.

"Further, I thought the technique of introducing an idea that would be later enlarged on was done in such a way so as to bring about a conclusion sought by the *Fifth Estate*."

In Dunn's opinion, "Very little came from the police."

Andy Garlatti, a retired accountant with Chrysler Canada commented: "Fifteen years is a bit much.

"Why didn't they make a better effort to present the prosecution's case?

"I'd have to hear the Mounties' side of the story. But if Hennessey is lying on camera, he's guilty."

Bobbi-Lee Keermaa, a certified dental assistant from Hamilton, Ontario, watched the show and volunteered her opinion to the author: "I thought he was innocent. He seemed so nice. The poor guy, he didn't do anything. And his wife was in such pain. I felt bad for them."

At the time that all these people watched the program, none of them—including retired Staff Sergeant Carl MacLeod—were aware of what was contained in the *Agreed Statement of Facts*. Consequently, they didn't know that Hennessey was making statements on the *Fifth Estate* that flatly contradicted what he had signed and what he was prepared to admit the next day in court.

Readers of this book are left to ask themselves why Hennessey would do that. Their answer should help them draw their own conclusions about Shawn Hennessey's guilt or innocence.

Moreover, Linden MacIntyre had fourteen days between the time of the program's taping and the date it went to air to edit the tape and add either voice-over comments or on-camera appearances to point out the inconsistencies in Shawn Hennessey's televised statements versus the *Agreed Statement of Facts*.

His decision not to do this left the viewing audience with an unbalanced presentation of Shawn Hennessey's story.

Linden MacIntyre's response to this observation is that he deduced from pre-interview conversations that they (the Hennesseys) were profoundly uncomfortable with the "facts" (*Agreed Statement of Facts*) as defined by his lawyers—because these facts didn't accurately represent the coercive nature of Roszko's behaviour when he showed up at the Hennesseys' on the night of March 2. They (the Hennesseys) also felt that the facts misrepresented a lot of what Roszko had said to them—especially about his intention to harm policemen.

MacIntyre emphasizes, "My piece was not intended to be the final record but just another element."

The meaning gleaned from this comment is that this interview was intended to be another part of the puzzle of whether or not Shawn Hennessey was dealt with fairly or unfairly.

And that is a reasonable approach.

The issue remains: Was the judicial process fair or unfair?

That is the burning question.

11 | In Memoriam

DURING THE WEEK OF THE FOUR funerals and the National Memorial Service in Edmonton in March 2005, Margaret Thibault spent time on the chartered funeral buses and at home thinking about what could be done to honour the four slain police officers.

As the Coordinator of Victims' Services for the areas of Mayerthorpe and Whitecourt, she had maintained an office in the Mayerthorpe Detachment. Although her job was to assist and support victims and witnesses of crime, Margaret was in daily contact with the RCMP in one detachment or the other. Over the years she had come to know all the members in both places and was a close friend to many of them — including some of those who died . . . and their families. And during the investigation after the murders, she proved to be a tower of strength for all the members working out of Mayerthorpe.

Corporal Wayne Oakes says, "She was tremendously helpful. She's an absolutely wonderful woman."

Margaret was well aware that the pain and grief in the two communities was almost unbearable. Residents of both towns deeply mourned the loss of the four good young men who had been their neighbours and their friends.

Many Mayerthorpe residents were also concerned that the name of their community would forever be tied to one of the worst mass murders ever to occur in Canada.

Margaret says, "I knew we had to take that heavy grief and turn it into something positive."

She began sharing her thoughts with several members of the community.

One of them was Jurgen Preugschas, a local farmer who was very active in the Mayerthorpe Kinsmen and other community projects. More than just a farmer, Jurgen was an entrepreneur who owned and ran an enormous pork operation on his 3,000-acre spread southwest of town. Annually, he and his son Niko marketed some 20,000 hogs on three different farm lots. They leased one-third of their acreage for custom grazing and cropped the remaining land in barley, wheat, and canola.

Jurgen was a former chairman of Alberta Pork and in 2008 went on to become president of the Canadian Pork Council. In this position, he retains an office in Ottawa and travels around the world representing Canadian interests in his specialized field.

"I knew most of the members in the Mayerthorpe Detachment . . . and I was friends with a couple of the boys who were killed. It was an awful thing that happened.

"Margaret and I are good friends. We got together shortly after the tragedy occurred and talked about doing something to honour these four members."

Margaret recalls, "At first we had no real vision . . . we hadn't sorted out our thoughts. But I knew we had to take that heavy grief in the community and make something positive out of a very negative situation.

"Our little town had been thrust on centre stage for all the wrong reasons of a horrible tragedy. But that's not who we are, and I didn't want us to be remembered for that."

Another person that Margaret contacted was Colette McKillop, a very active member of the Mayerthorpe community who owned and operated Grigg Insurance, a family business that had been handed down to her through three generations since 1947.

Colette and Charlotte Arthur were the two residents who made up the red and white ribbons that were distributed around town immediately after the tragedy had taken place.

Margaret Thibault says, "People from all over were sending money in cards and letters . . . to the town office, to the detachment office, to 'K' Division Headquarters in Edmonton. Many of them were addressed only to 'The Town of Mayerthorpe.' Most of the envelopes contained either five or ten dollars. But lots of people sent more than that. A few contained cheques for one thousand dollars or more.

"The cards and letters came from all across Canada . . . from every province, the north, the Northwest Territories, the United States, England, Ireland, Scotland. I distinctly recall one letter coming from Sweden. They came from people in all walks of life . . . including children.

"The money in those envelopes specifically addressed to the families of the four was given to 'K' Division for the family fund. Other non-specific or general donations were banked in a special account under the Victims' Services umbrella."

Colette recalls, "People were driving into town off the highway wanting to donate to a fund. It was as if they were expecting us to do something special."

After some preliminary discussions with Jurgen and Colette, Margaret decided to call a meeting. She issued invitations to those two, and to Jim Martin and Joe Sangster of the RCMP, delegates from local businesses, plus government representatives from Mayerthorpe and area, Lac Ste. Anne County, the province of Alberta, and the government of Canada.

In total, she asked fourteen people to attend.

The first meeting was held on April 1, 2005, in the back meeting room of Shorty's Restaurant just off "Main Street" in Mayerthorpe.

"We did a lot of brainstorming . . . the objective was to determine how could we best remember those who died," Colette recalls.

Margaret says, "We discussed what we could do . . . what we should do to remember the boys properly. We wanted to find something that would address their honour and their bravery . . . something beyond the horror of the tragedy we had witnessed. We wanted to erase the horror, the dark side of the episode, and the sad memory of the event.

"In the give-and-take of that meeting, I saw the best qualities of people come out. There was such goodness in those around the table. Their motivation was very clear. You could see they were thinking: 'Four wonderful young men are dead. We can't let that be the end of it.'

"They all wanted to take steps to keep their memory . . . their goodness alive in a positive way . . . and always with dignity."

Colette agrees. "Sometimes when you get people together, their egos can get in the way and they become difficult. But there was none of that in our meeting. They were all totally unselfish and co-operative. It was absolutely a dream working with all of them. And it was wonderful to be a part of it."

Margaret makes it clear: "We also wanted to protect the good name of our community. We said from the start we would not be defined nor defeated by the shootings."

When the meeting ended, everyone went away to think about the best way to achieve this goal. The next meeting was scheduled for May 6.

The first order of business at this gathering was to elect an executive. The positions were filled as follows:

President – Margaret Thibault
Vice-President – Constable Joe Sangster
Secretary – Colette McKillop
Treasurer – Charlotte Arthur and Hendrickson Black
     Accounting

The assembly adopted an official name for their group: The Fallen Four Memorial Society.

Then a discussion ensued in which members of the Society put forth their suggestions for ways to remember the fallen four.

Some liked the idea of a perennial garden, others wanted to plant four trees in a designated area, someone suggested they commission individual busts of the fallen four to be displayed in a building close to the detachment office.

It was soon decided that whatever the society did, they wanted the commemoration to stand alone. They didn't want it housed in an arena or in a new swimming pool, or at the town hall, or even in the RCMP detachment building. The focus was to be on the fallen four alone

And the committee wanted the commemoration to be in an open area that was accessible to everyone. They didn't want it tucked away in a location that was difficult to find or a site to which it would be awkward to gain entry.

Prior to the fourth meeting, Margaret's son Tony, who is an artist, conceived the idea of a park. He drew a design that showed a circular area with four statues of Mounties standing around the

Margaret Thibault, Sgt. Jim Martin, and Colette McKillop in the
Fallen Four Memorial office at Mayerthorpe, May 2009.
(The Fallen Four Memorial Society)

circumference of the circle in various poses. The four different poses represented the individuality each fallen officer had in life.

Margaret liked his concept. With more discussion, they came up with the idea of having one more statue in the middle of the circle to honour all the police officers across the country who have died in the line of duty.

She brought Tony's drawing to the next meeting.

The group liked the idea of having bronze statues raised in a public park to honour the fallen four.

"We loved the idea right away," says Colette. "We knew right away it was perfect. It was a place everybody could use and appreciate . . . not only members of our community but people from outside, too. It would be a positive place for people to come and visit.

"We had received so many gifts and cards and letters. They showed us that it wasn't just our little town that was suffering. All those items we received were symbolic of how Canadians felt about the RCMP and were sent to demonstrate they were sharing in our grief. With these statues, people could come and see what their thoughtfulness had created.

"They all could share in the park."

Jurgen Preugschas, whose business travels had taken him around the world, was very much in support of raising the statues. "In various countries, I had seen statues of people erected to commemorate unfortunate circumstances.

"I felt in our small town the RCMP were important and I wanted to show our respect by honouring them for what they gave our country and our community.

"One hundred years from now, people can come and see what these four men did . . . and remember their sacrifice.

"As the years go by, their deaths will not have been in vain."

So the basic idea was immediately accepted. After that, the concept needed to be refined and detailed, and an appropriate property needed to be acquired for the park. The committee looked at several locations, but none of them were deemed to be entirely satisfactory.

Finally, Jurgen, who had let it be known that the society was looking for a property, was approached by his friend Gil Greenwood, who owned a couple of empty commercial lots around town. One of them, a six-acre parcel, was adjacent to the RCMP detachment office. Greenwood agreed to sell the land to the society for a modest price, and the purchase was made in July 2005.

It is worthy of note that as the park and the visitors' centre began to take shape, Gil Greenwood contributed much of the sale price of the property back to the building fund.

The acreage had to be converted from commercial zoning to parkland, and the committee had to go through a lot of paperwork to have the designation changed.

In October 2005, Megan Sangster and Haley Martin, who were both eleven years old and Grade 5 students at Mayerthorpe's Elmer Elson Elementary School, conceived the idea of Kids 4 Cops. Their organization wrote letters and went on radio and national television in Edmonton challenging all students from every school in Canada to donate a loonie towards the Fallen Four Memorial.

In this endeavour, they were helped immensely by Megan's mom, Heather Sangster, and Pat Lakeman, the detachment's long-time office manager. These two women worked with the girls, helping them to form and register their society. They also set up and scheduled their fundraiser activities and their radio and TV appearances.

Megan and Haley were daughters of Mayerthorpe RCMP officers and had been close with the three local detachment members who were killed at Roszko's farm.

Haley says, "There was a lot of work involved . . . especially at first . . . writing speeches and setting up exhibits for shows and fairs. But we had a lot of fun, too. Opening the cards we received from all over the country was really fun."

Working with Katherine Lakeman, Katie Mattson, and Megan's older sister Laura Sangster from Mayerthorpe High School, Kids 4 Cops raised approximately $200,000 towards the building of the Memorial Park. Their contribution to the success of the fundraising was so significant that their group was integrated into the society as a subcommittee.

It was this type of community effort and the assistance of hundreds of other avid volunteers that enabled the society to raise the funds required to create the Memorial Park.

After the land was purchased, the word began to spread that the society was going to build a park. PCL Maxam, a mammoth worldwide construction firm with offices in Edmonton, got in touch with Joe Sangster. Joe took the name of the firm to the society, and it was contracted for the job. PCL is the company that, while working on a building project near University Hospital in Edmonton, hoisted four large black ribbons high in the air on one of their cranes during the time of the RCMP National Memorial Service.

PCL assigned Matthew Greenwood as the supervising manager for the park and he worked closely with the group as the project developed.

Meanwhile, Margaret, Jurgen, Jim Martin, and Joe Sangster were travelling around the province, looking to hire a sculptor.

"Our committee wanted a Canadian to do it," Colette says, "and, if possible, an Albertan."

The sculptors they settled on were a husband and wife team named Don and Shirley Begg, who run Studio West Ltd. in Cochrane, Alberta, just west of Calgary. Their studio and foundry building encompasses 16,000 square feet on one acre of land.

Inside the huge edifice there are three overhead bridge cranes that are used to move and position the extremely heavy statues that they create there.

The Beggs have many famous statues to their credit. One of their most imposing works is the 2,600-pound (1,180-kilogram) statue of Colonel James Macleod that graces the lawn outside of RCMP Headquarters in Ottawa. Macleod, who is portrayed mounted on his horse, was an early commissioner of the Northwest Mounted Police and the founder of Fort Calgary. The names of all the members of the RCMP who have died in the line of duty since the inception of the Force in 1873 are inscribed on the base of Macleod's statue.

Another famous personage the Beggs have cast in bronze is Lord Strathcona (Donald Smith), who drove the last spike for the CPR at Craigellachie, British Columbia, in 1885. They also created the bronze of General Andrew Hamilton Gault, who founded the Princess Patricia Canadian Light Infantry in 1914. His statue stands to the west of the magnificent National War Memorial located in Ottawa's Confederation Square.

Initially, the Mayerthorpe committee commissioned Don and Shirley to produce fifty copies of *On Guard*, a sixteen-inch bronze Mountie in full uniform that the society could sell to help raise funds for the Memorial Park.

Margaret Thibault's group was already sold on the Beggs' artistry even before they produced the miniatures, but the authenticity and meticulous attention to detail they detected on those bronze miniatures confirmed the validity of their selection.

Early on, the sculptors recommended that the Mayerthorpe statues be created at life-size plus 10 percent. Apparently this would give the figures more impact. Shirley Begg says, "It gives the statue more presence."

At the beginning of the process, the artists looked through countless family photograph albums of each fallen member, as well as official photos provided by the RCMP.

During their discussions with various family members, Shirley recalls, "There were many tears over many cups of tea."

Jim Martin and Staff Sergeant Scott Beck from the Cochrane Detachment worked closely with the Beggs, providing uniform items such as belts, boots, breeches, and a Stetson. Don and

Shirley also travelled to Calgary to confer with the artisans there who make the Mounties' boots and hats.

"Details are very important to us . . . the marksmanship badges, the RCMP buttons and collar badges. We want that to be precisely accurate."

Their next decision was to determine the various poses that each of the fallen four would assume. Don and Shirley discussed this together at length and finally came up with a recommendation that was approved by RCMP Headquarters in Ottawa.

Their idea was to portray the fallen members in the four positions of readiness looking outward from the four quadrant points of the compass. The stance assumed by each member would be determined by his seniority. Each man's rank, name, and regimental number would be engraved on the bronze base of his statue.

Brock Myrol would stand facing south towards his hometown of Red Deer. As a recent graduate of Depot Division, Brock would be portrayed in the "stand easy" position, adjusting his kit and preparing for duty on his troop commander's orders. His feet would be twelve inches apart.

Anthony Gordon would face west toward the Whitecourt Detachment, where he served. Anthony would stand in the "at ease" position, ready to be called to attention. His body is stiffened with his hands behind his back. The right hand is in the palm of his left hand, right thumb over left thumb. His fingers are extended and pointing towards the ground. His head and eyes are to the front, elbows in, and his shoulders back. His feet are twelve inches apart.

Leo Johnston would face north toward his hometown of Lac La Biche, Alberta. As the second-longest serving member of the four, Leo would stand "at attention," ready for orders. His heels are together and in line, feet turned out in a "V" at a thirty-degree angle. His arms hang straight down from his shoulders, elbows close to the side, wrists straight. His fists are clenched at his sides with his thumbs placed at the seam of his trousers, pointing to the ground. His shoulders are back and square to the front. His head is up with his eyes looking straight forward.

Peter Schiemann would face east toward his hometown of Stony Plain, Alberta, and his birthplace of Petrolia, Ontario. As the most senior in experience of the four, Peter would stand in the "salute" position, a formal stance of respect and courtesy. From the attention position he has brought his right hand up for a salute. His arm is bent at the elbow. With his open right palm to the front, his fingers are extended and close together, with his thumb close to his forefinger. His fingers, wrist, and elbow are in line. His saluting hand is positioned so the brim of his Stetson is between his pointer and middle finger, and that part of the brim of the Stetson aligns with the outside corner of his right eye.

With all the research and planning at their disposal, the Beggs then discussed with each other the images they were about to create. When they came to a mutual agreement of that vision, the sculpting began.

Shirley explains, "We have a rather unique approach to our work. We sculpt together. I start from one side, Don starts from the other, and we work towards each other. We like to think we use four hands to make our vision come to life."

Don says their method works well for them. "We've been doing this together since 1970."

The process sounds long and complicated.

First, it takes them approximately six months to sculpt a clay model.

Then it takes another two weeks to make a rubber mould from which they form a hollow wax pattern with a ceramic core.

Their final four to five weeks is spent casting the bronze from the clay model using what Don calls "the lost wax method."

The total time involved in creating all four statues took well over two years.

The Beggs were also responsible for designing and casting the eleven doves that flew free from the top of the twenty-four-foot (7.32-metre) obelisk that would stand in the middle of the circular area from which the four Mounties faced outwards.

While the sculpting process was in progress, the society's work in Mayerthorpe continued to move forward. In March 2006, the Alberta Lottery Fund gave the Memorial Society a grant of $300,000 for their park project. On February 8, 2007, the society turned the sod to officially initiate the building of the Mayerthorpe

Fallen Four Memorial Park. In March, the Society was successful in applying for a major grant from the Canada, Alberta Municipal and Rural Infrastructure Funding program.

By October of 2007, the Visitors' Centre was completed. This one-storey building is 3,000 square feet in size. One third of its space is allocated to an information centre where there is a digital guest book and a fifty-two-inch television that displays a power point scroll. Memorabilia such as books, tee shirts, pins, and mugs are on sale here. Another one-third of the building is used as a museum for the fallen four. Among the items displayed here are hundreds of cards and gifts from around the world that were sent in sympathy to the Mayerthorpe Detachment. These include teddy bears and dolls, woodcarvings, special moulded glass items, beautiful handmade quilts, and unique paintings.

One of the paintings that adorns a wall in the museum was done by a local artist, Deanna Jackson. It depicts four RCMP officers in red serge and Stetsons integrated with another Mountie on horseback, an RCMP bugler, and the Canadian flag.

Margaret Thibault says, "It's so moving. The first time I saw it, I burst into tears."

The remaining third of the building is set aside as a boardroom that is used by the society but also available as a community meeting place and a staging area for local weddings and other celebrations.

By June 10, 2008, the statue plinths were completed and the central obelisk installed. On July 3, the fallen four statues, each weighing 800 pounds, were manoeuvred onto their plinths.

The grand unveiling occurred on Friday, July 4, 2008.

This was a grand affair attended by 3,000 enthusiastic citizens. The luminaries on hand included the mayors of Mayerthorpe and Whitecourt; members of provincial and federal Parliament; RCMP Deputy Commissioner Bill Sweeney; Ed Stelmach, the Premier of Alberta; and the Honourable Stephen Harper, Prime Minister of Canada.

Those most touched by the ceremony were the family members of the fallen four and the men and women who had served with the four Mounties and remembered them fondly.

Since that day, over 15,000 visitors have come to see the park and the statues and to pay tribute to the fallen four. Over 9,000 people have signed the guest registry in the park. Drivers travelling along Highway 43 can see the monuments and the obelisk from their cars. It's an easy exercise for them to pull off the road and spend a few minutes among the statues.

But it's more than just the casual drop-ins that are fuelling the interest in Mayerthorpe's Memorial Park. Travel Alberta did a survey indicating that to date seventy percent of the guests at the park went there as a target destination. Only thirty percent were drive-by visitors.

Colette McKillop says, "Travel Alberta told us that the results of this survey are incredible. And I can see why. I mean, we're not Niagara Falls or Jasper. It's amazing. We started with just a plain prairie field. And we're just tiny little Mayerthorpe.

"The most beautiful thing is that these visitors will no longer remember Mayerthorpe because of that Quonset hut. They leave here with the wonderful statues of the fallen four foremost in their minds.

"We're so pleased that the interest has been strong and we hope that it continues to grow."

Surely Colette need not be concerned about that. There's every possibility that as time goes by, this site will become an attraction for Canadian families to visit . . . a historic place where parents and grandparents can bring their little ones and tell them about the sacrifice these four men made in the service of their country.

Another worthwhile Mayerthorpe memorial that continues to flourish is the annual charity hockey game between the Mounties and the Wranglers. The idea for the first game originated in a conversation among Jim Martin, Clayton Seguin, and Al Starman. All three of these members played for a local senior team named the Wranglers. The three Mounties wanted to form an RCMP team to play against the Wranglers so they could raise some money to make improvements to the arena.

"We thought we might be able to raise about $500," says Martin.

They approached Lyle Johner about playing a fun game, he agreed, and the contest was scheduled for March 7, 2005. Martin

Opening ceremonies at the fallen Four Memorial Park in Mayerthorpe, July 4, 2008. (The Fallen Four Memorial Society)

formed a team that included himself, Seguin, Starman, Joe Sang-ster, Julie Letal, and Cindie Dennis (now Christians).

Martin says, "Cindie was a really good sport. She wasn't much of a skater and she certainly wasn't a hockey player, but she gave it everything she had. From that first year right down to our most recent game, Cindie always gets the biggest applause from the fans."

Peter Schiemann agreed to play. He had no hockey equipment and had to borrow everything but he was willing to give it a try. Leo Johnston was prepared to help out in any way he could.

Then, of course, the tragedy struck.

Jim remembers, "When that happened, the hockey game was the last thing on my mind. No one even thought the game was going to go. But somehow it did."

With all the Mounties coming into town for the funerals, Martin was able to get a number of them to borrow equipment and play for the RCMP team. Chris Pittman, who had lived with Peter Schiemann, came back and suited up for the RCMP team.

When word got out that the game was going to be played, the interest in the venture spread like wildfire. Every media outlet in Edmonton covered the game live. CTV was there with their cameras. Radio station 630 CHED brought in Rod Phillips and Morley Scott, the announcers of the Edmonton Oilers, to broadcast the game play-by-play.

Jim says, "Playing that game was one of the best decisions we ever made. It pulled the community together. The place was jammed to the rafters. There wasn't even any place for people to stand. That really tugged at my heart because it showed us that so many people cared.

"All the families of the fallen members were in attendance. There was a beautiful candlelight remembrance service before the game. It was wonderful."

The game itself was a great release of tension and pent-up emotions.

"There was a lot of kidding around . . . I even think the RCMP team won. But that didn't matter. There's no doubt the Wrangler guys were lenient with us. They allowed us to score some pretty soft goals. It was just a lot of fun."

In August 2005, the famed RCMP Musical Ride came to Mayerthorpe to help ease the community's pain and thank them for their support. Many families from the town and beyond came out and joyously watched the thirty-two riders on their splendid black steeds execute their intricate manoeuvres.

But it was the RCMP hockey game against the Wranglers that became an ongoing annual event. In 2006, the game drew another sold-out crowd. This time RCMP members from all across Canada came to play. The Mounties had a roster of twenty-five players. The Oilers broadcast crew did another play-by-play.

Martin recalls, "We had a moment of silence before the game and a service where four children were escorted on the ice by local celebrities to light four candles on stands at centre ice."

In 2007, the Fallen Four Memorial Society took over the sponsorship of the game. They initiated a sports memorabilia auction in conjunction with the game to raise money for the Memorial Park.

The next year, the crowd was as big as ever. Craig MacTavish, the Oilers' head coach, handled the bench duties for the Mountie team. The Fallen Four Memorial Society had another sports memorabilia auction and all the proceeds went towards the park building fund.

When the Mayerthorpe arena burnt down in 2008, the game committee decided to hold the game in Edmonton at Rexall Place, the home of the Oilers. Northlands Coliseum donated the use of the facility and covered the cost of the ticket service. Craig MacTavish was back at the helm of the RCMP team, along with his assistants, Charlie Huddy and Pete Peters.

This game evolved into a gala event.

Donations for the auction of sports items arrived in droves. Don Cherry had one of his on-air garish jackets framed and signed and donated it to the cause. The Oilers contributed a full package that included four tickets for a game in the head coach's private seats, autographed team jerseys, and a private tour of the Oilers' dressing room. Sydney Crosby signed one of his jerseys and sent it to the auction. All of the Canadian NHL teams donated hockey sticks signed by their players. A travel agency donated a four-day holiday at the Fairmont Hotel in Cairo, Egypt.

Over two thousand fans attended the game, and the Memorial Society collected $25,000 for their building fund.

Jim Martin says, "In the future, we hope to have our arena rebuilt in Mayerthorpe and move the game back there. And we'll keep playing the game as long as the people come out and support it."

Those series of games are a marvellous example of how something wholesome and beneficial arose from a tragic event that shook the very soul of a small Canadian community.

And the memory of that terrible March day in 2005 extended beyond Mayerthorpe.

The night before the RCMP game at Rexall Place, in a nationally broadcast game between the Toronto Maple Leafs and the Ottawa Senators, the CBC devoted one of its Coach's Corner segments to the Fallen Four and the game to be played in their honour in Edmonton.

In that part of the telecast, details of the 2005 tragedy were recalled while photos of the four slain Mounties were shown on camera. And later, Don Cherry, in his traditional gaudy jacket and snazzy, high-collared shirt, reminded the listening audience, "We gotta get out there and support the Mounties."

Even detractors of the irreverent broadcaster rate his segment of that program as one of Don Cherry's better moments on television.

These memorial activities have been helpful to the Mayerthorpe community.

Residents of the municipality know that the sad and infamous chapter in their town's history will not be forgotten. But the Memorial Park, and, to a lesser extent, the annual hockey game have helped the people of Mayerthorpe put the tragic affair behind them and move on with their lives.

Ex-mayor Albert Schalm says, "The community has healed now . . . we're back to normal. The Memorial Park helps but the entire community has done a lot of things right. They've dealt with their pain in a considerate, sensible way and we've maintained a good relationship with the detachment."

The RCMP team at Rexall Place, March 1, 2009. Front row L to R: Adam Cook (CTV celebrity coach), Jim Martin, Adam Schedlosky, Alex DaSilva, Don McDermid, Clayton Seguin, Troy Heystek with his daughter Emma, Mark Hennig, Joe Sangster, Lindsay Carter, Bill Robinson. Back row L to R: Eddie Bourque, Devon Bateman, Steve Bereza, Cindie Christians, Trevor Josok, John Kirkman, Blaine Rahier, Gabe Graham, James Murray, Travis Harkness, Doug Lee.

Rev. Wendell Wiebe agrees, "Many towns might have collapsed because of the tragedy. But our people banded together with love and respect for each other and we found the strength to carry on."

12 | Epilogue

JAMES ROSZKO LEFT a huge wave of destruction in the wake of his murderous rampage. Not only did he seriously ravage the lives of the families of the four Mounties he killed, he left deep scars on many others.

Anjila Steeves, Brock Myrol's fiancée, has been badly affected by Brock's death. She can't seem to get over her loss and has even legally changed her last name to Steeves–Myrol. She now lives in Red Deer, Brock's hometown, and, as an artist who has always loved painting, has managed to get a job as an assistant teacher of art at Red Deer College.

"The past four years have been difficult. After Brock died, I stayed in Mayerthorpe until August. I was so depressed I seldom left the house. I still don't want to socialize.

"Before Brock was killed, I was very active. I got out and worked every day. I went to the gym; we went camping and hiking and fishing. Brock was my best friend.

"I hardly know anyone here in Red Deer. I don't see much of my old friends because most of them are married with children and families."

Anjila has been asked out on dates, but, she states, "I always say no. I have no desire to go out with anyone. It wouldn't be fair for me to go out with someone else. I'm in love with Brock. He was so perfect for me . . . wonderful in every way."

Her primary focus continues to be on Brock. She often speaks of him as if he were still alive. There is a mystical side to this attractive woman. "I feel we met in another life before this and loved each other even then."

For the past four years, on Valentine's Day, Anjila has gone to the cemetery and put flowers on Brock's grave.

In October 2008, she took what she calls a "memorial trip" to the Antares Training Centre in South Africa where Brock had qualified to be a field guide for Kruger National Park. While Anjila was there, she met Ian Owtram, the instructor who had trained Brock and who still remembered him very vividly.

"Brock loved it there. Being there as a guide was his passion.

"He always wanted to take me there. We planned to come here on our honeymoon.

"I wanted to see the Centre and the grounds . . . and the places where Brock had taken his course and where he ate and slept."

Although Anjila seems to be preoccupied by her tragic past, she does sustain a glimmer of hope for the future. "I went to the police memorial services in Ottawa and found that I liked it there. I discovered an area in Quebec province where there are a lot of artistic people . . . musicians and artists, and I've made some good friends there."

She purchased some property near Val Des Monts, about twenty-five minutes north of Ottawa, and plans someday to live in the quaint town of Wakefield, Quebec. "It's beautiful there. Brock would have loved it there."

It's very apparent that Anjila is struggling to get over her loss, but she says, "I find it very hard to do."

Kim Gordon has been left to raise her two sons on her own. Her older boy, Spencer, is seven and in school. He doesn't remember his dad. Her second son, Anthony, who was born after his father died, is four.

Kim says, "It's very difficult when I think about the fact that my sons will never know their father.

"And I'm tired of talking to the media. It's been four years now since my husband was killed and with every anniversary of his death the phone starts ringing for interviews or my comments.

"People don't realize how time goes by. Everyone wants to go back over it. I want to look ahead . . . and raise my children. I'm trying to get on with my life. I want a happy life and I'm determined that my sons will have a happy life, too."

There is a tired sadness in her voice when she says to the author, "You're my last interview. After this, I don't want to say any more."

Kelly Johnston stayed in Mayerthorpe until June 2007, when she moved to Airdrie, Alberta.

"I wanted a fresh start. I hoped for something positive and I've always loved the view of the mountains."

Her friend Andria Reid says that Kelly needed to get out of Mayerthorpe. "She needed to be away from the centre of attention. Every person in town knew she was Leo's widow . . . she couldn't get away from their comments and their concern."

And Kelly thought about Leo constantly. "I still do . . . and I always will.

"And I still think about how Roszko snuck into the Quonset hut."

She says she went out to the crime scene many times. "I just wanted to be where Leo died.

"For months and years after the incident I drove the Range Road by Roszko's property, trying to figure how Roszko got by Leo and Tony. I always went alone. That was just for me. I would stand at the farm gate for hours trying to satisfy my curiosity as to how he did it.

"And now I think I know."

But Kelly says her theory about that is something she is not willing to share with anyone. "That's private . . . something I just want to keep to myself."

When Leo died, his father, Ron Johnston, asked Kelly to have him buried in Leo's hometown of Lac La Biche, Alberta, and Kelly agreed. But later, when Kelly went to Depot to meet Queen Elizabeth II, she visited the RCMP cemetery there and knew that this was the place where her husband should be buried.

Kelly made application to have Leo's body exhumed and was granted permission. But Leo's parents, Ron and Grace Johnston, opposed the disinterment. They wanted their son's body to remain near his Metis ancestors in Lac La Biche. As a consequence, a legal battle ensued at several court levels, where Kelly's request to move her husband's remains was always upheld. The dispute ultimately went to the Supreme Court of Canada, but they refused to hear the case.

An attempt was made to disinter Leo's body in the fall of 2007 but the Johnstons and several of their supporters blocked access to the grave.

With all the legal hurdles crossed in Kelly's favour, arrangements were made to have Leo's body exhumed on the bitterly cold day of December 15, 2008. As a sign of respect for Leo Johnston's service with the Force, and to ensure that those in attendance kept the peace, the RCMP stationed vehicles at the gates of the cemetery. Kelly stood at the gravesite with six Mounties by her side while the disinterment process ensued.

The Johnstons, with their son Lee and his wife, watched the procedure from a hotel across the street from the cemetery. When Leo's casket was lifted onto the vault truck, Kelly sat in a funeral car while the Johnston family came over to pay their final respects.

Although the Johnstons were deeply traumatized by the exhumation of their son's remains, they maintained their decorum, and the transfer of the casket proceeded as smoothly as possible.

Leo's remains were taken to a funeral home in Edmonton.

Kelly says, "The next morning, I spent an hour of very special time with my husband in a private room."

Leo's body was then cremated. His ashes were deposited in one side of a heart-shaped urn.

Kelly told the author, "We used to cuddle and spoon every night, even during afternoon naps. Someday my ashes will be in the other chamber of the urn, and we'll be able to spoon together every night for eternity."

Their vessel will be ensconced in the columbarium at the RCMP cemetery in Regina at some undisclosed time in the future.

"It will be a very private ceremony. That's when I will walk my Leo across the parade square one last time and see him put to rest with his fellow officers."

Don Schiemann, his wife, Beth, and their children, Michael and Julia, were crushed by Peter Schiemann's death. As a close-knit and deeply religious family, their only consolation is that they will be with him again in heaven.

After Peter's death, Don was very active, attending many of the legal proceedings that took place. On occasion he was quite vocal about various aspects of the Mayerthorpe tragedy, particularly those pertaining to the fact that a man of James Roszko's criminal history was allowed to remain out on the streets.

RCMP Chapel, Regina Training Academy (Depot)

In his desire to reform the Canadian justice system, Don initiated a campaign entitled Vision for Justice in Canada. To date, he has written over sixteen newsletters that address the weaknesses and flaws that he feels plague our laws and judicial policies, particularly in the domain of sentencing and parole.

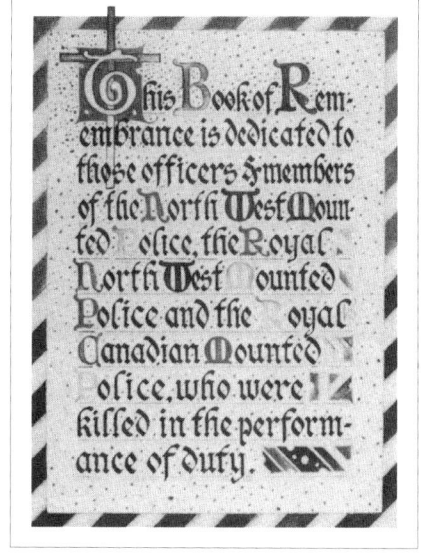

Page one of the Book of Remembrance located inside the Chapel at Depot.

Although the families of the murdered Mounties have suffered immensely, they did participate in two events that were intended to lift their spirits.

On May 19, 2005, members of the families were invited to the Training Academy (Depot) in Regina to meet Queen Elizabeth II and Prince Philip. The meeting took place in the old and revered chapel on the base. This small, white building with its bright red spire that is located on the edge of the parade square holds a special niche in the hearts of all Depot graduates. It is the only structure on the base that remains from the original Northwest Mounted Police supply depot. Back then, it was one of four barracks that housed the Mounties who served in the Riel Rebellion.

It was from the second floor of one of these buildings that once stood near the chapel that Louis Riel was hanged in November 1885.

Inside the chapel, the walls are lined with numerous plaques that honour many Mounties from the past who lost their lives while in the performance of their duties. These tablets—such as the marker for the four members of the Royal Northwest Mounted Police who are remembered as the famed "Lost Patrol"—offer an observer a virtual lesson in Canadian history.

A Book of Remembrance is on display near the entrance to the chapel. Each page in this ornate tome is dedicated to a member of the RCMP Honour Roll. Every week, a page is turned to feature one of these fallen officers.

It was near the chapel entrance that the queen and her consort were introduced to the family members of the fallen four.

Kelly Johnston says, "The queen was lovely . . . beautiful blue eyes, skin like porcelain. In the brief time I spoke to her, I found her to be a wonderful, compassionate lady."

In October, the families travelled to Ottawa to meet with Prime Minister Paul Martin and two of his government associates. During this meeting, Don Schiemann presented them with demands for mandatory minimum sentences and the elimination of reduced parole and statutory release provisions for criminals of serious crimes.

Back in Alberta, all the members of both the Mayerthorpe and Whitecourt detachments have been reassigned to new postings.

Sergeant Brian Pinder was transferred to a staffing assignment at Edmonton Headquarters.

Jim Martin was promoted to sergeant and transferred to the Spruce Grove Detachment in Alberta, where he supervises twenty-three members and seven support staff. He still lives on his acreage south of Mayerthorpe with his wife, Melanie, and his daughter, Haley. And he continues to be involved with the Fallen Four Memorial Society and the annual hockey game they sponsor against the Wranglers. It's hard to imagine a Mountie who is more dynamic than Jim at his job and enthusiastic about his involvement with his community.

Clayton Seguin was transferred to Claresholm, Alberta, in June 2006. He says, "I was kind of disappointed they didn't move us quicker. It was difficult staying in Mayerthorpe. Everywhere you turned, there were reminders of the incident. It brought back a lot of painful memories.

"What's worse, some of the local petty criminals would say antagonizing things to your face. I gave one of these guys a speeding ticket, and he said, 'He should have got more of you.' Another told me, 'It should have been you.' Some of the bad kids in the area would say terrible things to the members' kids."

Clayton says he knows that there are Mounties from other jurisdictions in Alberta who have received the same kind of insults and verbal abuse.

Corporal Jeff Whipple agrees with Clayton. He insists, "They should have moved us right away. I would go into work one day, then I had to go home the next day. I'd see the psychologist, then go back to work. That first week after the killings, I can't remember a thing about it. I don't have a clue about what was going on. I was off work, then back, then off. Everything is a complete blur. This went on for fifteen months after the incident."

Whipple is still an active member of the Force, but he's off duty with full pay and benefits.

Both Whipple and Al Starman of the Mayerthorpe Detachment are suing the RCMP for the trauma they experienced as a result of the massacre. They claim they are permanently disabled and suffer from nightmares, flashbacks, and post-traumatic stress disorder (PTSD).

Starman's suit claims he witnessed the aftermath of the shootings and suffered significant nervous shock. He was medically discharged from the RCMP in 2007. His claim states that instead of recognizing his health problems and transferring him out of Mayerthorpe, the RCMP continued to involve him in the investigation, where he had to deal with the relatives of the dead officers.

Speaking on behalf of the RCMP, Cpl. Wayne Oakes says that under the Force's member assistance program, all the Mounties were offered stress counselling following the Mayerthorpe shootings. He adds that services were provided to every member that was impacted.

Clayton Seguin found it very difficult to talk to me about the incident. When I spoke to him on the phone, I could hear the anguish in his voice.

Cindie Dennis was married to Kevin Christians on June 7, 2008, at her grandparents' ranch near Lundbreck, Alberta. She is now serving at Leduc and is still bothered by her memories of the tragedy. But she was willing to try and talk about them, especially about her fond memories of her close friend Peter Schiemann.

But there are many members from both the Mayerthorpe and Whitecourt detachments who cannot bring themselves to discuss their recollections of that terrible time in their lives.

Joe Sangster, Leo Johnston's close friend, who was transferred to Killam, Alberta, was so traumatized by the incident that he still finds it too painful to talk about.

Julie Letal, who is now at the Peace River Detachment, feels much the same as Joe Sangster.

Supt. Marty Cheliak was promoted to Chief Superintendent in July 2006 and transferred to Iqaluit, where he is in command of "V" Division (Nunavut), a huge area that stretches across the top of Canada and encompasses twenty percent of the country's land mass. More recently, he has been transferred to RCMP Headquarters in Ottawa.

Margaret Thibault stayed on at Victims' Services until 2007. Then she left and volunteered to work for the Fallen Four Memorial Society, where, for a year, she helped supervise the development and creation of Mayerthorpe's Memorial Park.

In April 2008, she became the secretary for George Vander-Burg, the sitting MLA for Whitecourt–Ste. Anne.

Staff Sergeant Tom Pickard and virtually all the members of the Whitecourt Detachment will not talk about the tragic incident. Those from Whitecourt whom I contacted were polite but simply said something to the effect that, "I respect what you're trying to do, but I prefer not to talk about this." Or, "That was a very painful time in my life and I want to put it behind me."

Whenever I encountered this type of response, I made it a point to respect the individual's feelings and accept his or her silence. Many of them are suffering from PTSD and several are still receiving professional help.

As a writer of several books about police murders, I have often come upon witnesses of these sad events—especially principals in the stories—who are either unwilling or unable to speak about their memories of the incidents. On many occasions—for this book and others that I have written or wanted to write—I have spoken to widows, family members, and friends of the deceased who simply cannot bring themselves to relive the agony of their experiences.

There have been times when some of these individuals *have* agreed to speak to me but cancelled out when the time came for their interviews. When this has happened, I have either discontinued my attempt to write the book or moved on to other principals who were able to speak about their experiences.

However, it is my contention that these tragedies are very much part of the fabric of our history and, as such, are stories that need to be told. As horrible a catastrophe as the Mayerthorpe incident was, it is a tale that needed to be thoroughly researched and recorded. And it's a book that belongs on the shelves of every library in the country—including those in our schools.

Furthermore, even in the woeful saga of Mayerthorpe, there are some positive residual features. The creation of the Mayerthorpe Memorial Park is a wonderful, uplifting residuum of the tragedy.

Mayerthorpe's present mayor, Doug McDermid, says, "The day we dedicated the park for the Fallen Four . . . the day when Prime Minister Harper spoke to us of our courage and determination was a turning point. From that day on, we stopped looking back and started to look forward."

The park is truly place of honour where people from around the world can come to reflect on the sacrifice of the four slain Mounties.

Constable Steve Vigor's bravery under fire is also worthy of the high honour he received. On February 29, 2008, he was summoned to Rideau Hall in Ottawa to meet Governor General Michaelle Jean who presented him with the Medal of Bravery, a tribute that is Canada's third highest recognition for courage.

The substance of Vigor's citation reads: "While another officer took cover in his car to call for assistance, Constable Vigor returned fire, hitting the suspect and forcing his retreat back into the Quonset. He maintained on watch until the arrival of backup. Tragically, four other RCMP officers had been ambushed and killed by the suspect, who later took his own life."

As the Governor General awarded Vigor his medal, she quietly said to him, "Congratulations. You deserve this. It was a wonderful act of bravery."

Steve says, "That was a very emotional moment for me . . . one that I will never forget. I'm just sorry that Garret Hoogestraat didn't receive one, too. He deserves it. He protected me with our vehicle and while he was doing that, he could have easily been shot and killed by Roszko."

From the Hennessey side of the ledger, it must be noted that Barry Hennessey's constant love and concern for his son is an example of a father's undying devotion to his child. He says he will not rest until his son is granted a trial. And it is through his resolute striving that he has found two high-profile lawyers who are willing to appeal Shawn's and Dennis Cheeseman's guilty pleas.

The bar for a successful appeal of a guilty plea is high. One of the few ways it can be overturned is to prove that these two men did not completely understand the essence and import of their guilty plea. And even if the guilty pleas are successfully appealed, Shawn and Dennis will face a trial where the evidence seems to be heavily weighted against them.

But Barry Hennessey is prepared and willing to attack one obstacle at a time. First he wants to have the lawyers deal with the pleas. If that is successful, he then will pursue their going to trial. No matter the odds against these two difficult endeavours, Barry says he and his wife, Sandy, will not give up.

Against all odds, it was Barry who managed to get his son and Dennis transferred from their original penitentiary placements. After the two men were sentenced, Correctional Services Canada (CSC) sent Shawn to the Saskatchewan Federal Penitentiary west of Prince Albert and Dennis to Stony Mountain in Manitoba.

Barry claimed their placement was a case of pure vindictiveness and persecution. He complained that it would be extremely difficult for those who loved Shawn to visit him. The long drive to Prince Albert and back would be extremely difficult, especially for Shawn's wife and children. And for those who wanted to see Dennis, the drive to Stony Mountain north of Winnipeg would be almost impossible.

Both Shawn Hennessey and Dennis Cheeseman wrote letters to CSC appealing their "pen" placements.

Portions of Shawn's letter read as follows:

My name is Shawn Hennessey. I am writing this letter because I am in strong disagreement with being pen placed out of province. To be sent out of province will make it extremely difficult for contact with my family. I am 29 years old, married with 2 small children. My wife will have to travel quite some distance for a visit witch [*sic*] will mean pulling the children from school to bring them along so they can see their father.

. I have spent 10 months in custody between the Edmonton and Red Deer Remand centers. I have been in no trouble whatsoever.

. I am in the process of appealing my sentence and not being in Alberta will complicate things. I will have limited access to my legal counsil [*sic*].

. The decision made to send us out of province may un-necessarily [*sic*] expose me to negative associations that may also hinder my rehabilitation. This appears to be unusual and by far un-necessary punishment that will violate CSC policy and your routine procedure for pen placement by housing us so far away from all of our support.

Mr. Cheeseman and myself have been cell mates while in custody in the Edmonton Remand Center. We have been a great source of support for one another and to split us up and send us to different penitentiaries will illuminate [*sic*] any further support we will be able to give each other.

I hope you reconsider your decision to send us out of province and consider Grand Casch [*sic*] or Bowden Institute for they are much closer.

Thank you.

Parts of Dennis Cheesman's letter are presented below.

My name is Dennis Cheeseman . . . I've been in the Edmonton Remand Center for about 11 months now with no problems whatsoever. I am waiting to be shipped out now and hoping to be rehabilitated properly and fairly.

. My family, friends, legal council [*sic*] all support, even my appeal will be in Alberta. I have no criminal record besides this, as I'm not a repeating offender.

. Being out on bail, there was no problems. I stayed employed, followed all the conditions and rules. My probation officer had nothing bad to say about me. I'm wanting to work, take courses, finish my school, etc. So I thought that by sending me to Grand Cache or Bowden was a good start. But I've been told that might not be the case, that I could be going to out of province to Stoney [*sic*] Mountain. This means a number of things. I'm appealing and it will be difficult traveling back and fourth [*sic*]. I will have no visits at all. 0 [zero] - no family there, no legal council [*sic*] no community support at all. I know I will not handle Stoney Mountain very well, mentally, emotional, physically.

. You are uneccessarily [*sic*] exposing me to a lot of bad associations in a place that has a bad reputation for violence and gangs.

. If you send us out of province, then it's not right and it violates CSC policy and routine procedures for placement.

. Please reconsider this decision for you need to take proper steps when dealing with our lives to get rehabilitated. Thank you for taking the time to read this.

Their parole officer, Jay West, who had assessed Shawn and Dennis, agreed with their requests and supported them. West wrote a letter to CSC that spoke against their placements. He argued that because the two were first-time offenders who appeared to be naïve, they would be susceptible to the wiles of more hardened criminals in these prisons. West indicated that he had recommended the two men be kept together in a lower security prison in Alberta.

Barry Hennessey got involved, too. He called CSC in Ottawa and told the secretary who answered the phone that he wanted to speak to someone at the "top of the ladder . . . somebody who makes the decisions."

She referred Barry to Paul Urmson, who was in charge of CSC's Western region.

Barry sent Urmson an e-mail complaining that CSC was violating their own placement policies to persecute Shawn and Dennis. Barry argued, "These boys need support from their communities and family's [*sic*] more than ever now. Please send them back to Alberta for the remainder of their assessments before they lose their mental states."

Elsewhere in the e-mail he stated: "If everything is done according to CSC's policies, this should be no issue."

Two days after Barry's phone call, Urmson phoned Barry and told him he had received his letter. According to Barry, Urmson said, "I've made the decision to reverse their placement decision back to Alberta where they belong."

When Barry heard that, he began to cry. He thanked Urmson and told him, "I don't know what to say—I'm so happy."

Barry told the author, "I'll never forget that day as long as I live."

After that, Shawn phoned his father from the Prince Albert penitentiary and said, "Dad, what did you do? You pulled it off! I'm going to Grand Cache."

Four days later, Shawn was transferred to the penitentiary at Grand Cache, west of Edmonton near the B.C. border. Dennis was sent to Drumheller, south and east of Red Deer. So it appears that the boys' letters and Barry's persistence and determination had paid off.

On June 19, 2009, David Staples wrote a story in the *Edmonton Journal* revealing that Dennis Cheeseman may have been sexually molested by James Roszko at a time prior to the Mountie murders. Such an accusation was contained in a letter that Barry Hennessey wrote to Prime Minister Stephen Harper.

Barry Hennessey had told me about this sexual exploitation during one of my earlier interviews with him but, in deference to

Dennis Cheeseman's feelings, he did not want me to include the information in this book.

Apparently, he has now changed his mind about going public with it. Barry seems to think this revelation will have a significant impact with regard to Dennis's and Shawn's possible future trial.

Neither the Prime Minister's Office nor Alberta Justice Minister Alison Redford would comment on Barry's latest revelation, because the two men's criminal appeals are now being considered by the court.

Kelly Johnston doesn't think this new information should change anything at all. David Staples quotes her as saying that her heart goes out to Cheeseman if he was in fact sexually assaulted by Roszko, but she feels that Cheeseman and Hennessey are still criminally responsible for assisting in the mass murder.

"They are victims of their own poor judgment . . . I understand they were afraid, even terrified, but all it takes is you go and you tell the police your story.

"I don't have sympathy for anybody, or for anybody's reasoning and fear, that prevented them from saving my husband when it was so simple to do . . . Roszko might have pulled the trigger, but they enabled him . . . the blood is on their hands."

Whether or not Barry Hennessey's new information will prove to be significant or even relevent remains to be determined.

The only element of government business that remains in the Mayerthorpe story is a mandatory provincial fatality inquest. That can only take place after all the appeals (and the possible subsequent trial) are completed.

As a conclusion to this book, I must add that the tragedy at Mayerthorpe has focused on a problem that continues to linger across Canada: There are violent, lawless, antisocial people like James Roszko who present a menace in many communities across the country. But these angry misfits seldom do enough to be imprisoned and even when they are jailed, they don't stay there very long. Within weeks or months, they return to their communities more abusive and perverted than they were before they were sent away.

After researching and writing about James Roszko, it seems to me that our country needs a special designation for people like him who do not qualify for "dangerous offender" status. I believe we need another classification for repeat criminals like him—a status that might be termed "serious offender."

Under this designation, our police would be granted an open-ended warrant that would allow them, for a stipulated but extended period of time, to search a serious offender's property without warning. And any violations of the law detected by these warrants would lead a serious offender to lengthy terms of incarceration.

Just think what this might have meant in Roszko's case. The police might have found his assault rifle that killed the four police officers. The authorities certainly would have discovered his marijuana grow-op and his chop shop.

As a serious offender, these operations would have kept him off the streets for a long time. And when he did get out, he'd continue to be classified as a serious offender and thereby subject to further searches and a step closer to being designated a "dangerous offender."

Then again, such a draconian measure as I have suggested would have to pass the challenge of Canada's Charter of Rights and Freedoms. It would also have to withstand an onslaught of legal challenges from our civil libertarians, most of whom do not have to live among the likes of repeat criminals like James Roszko.

Be that as it may, we have now come to the end of this narrative of the "Mayerthorpe" story. There may be still more to come, but as it now stands, it is surely one of the most violent, lengthy, and complex tales of crime and punishment in the annals of Canadian history.

APPENDIX A
Agreed Statement of Facts

Docket No. 070845441Q1

IN THE COURT OF QUEEN'S BENCH OF ALBERTA
JUDICIAL DISTRICT OF EDMONTON

Between:

HER MAJESTY THE QUEEN

- and -

SHAWN WILLIAM HENNESSEY and
DENNIS KEEGAN CHEESEMAN

Accused

AGREED STATEMENT OF FACTS

1. On March 2, 2005 bailiff, Rob PERRY ("PERRY"), set out to execute a warrant authorizing the seizure on behalf of Kentwood Ford of a 2005 Ford F350 Super duty pickup truck, white in colour, Vehicle Identification Number 1FTWW31P55EA94067.

2. Based on information he received regarding the person identified in the warrant, James Michael ROSZKO ("ROSZKO"), PERRY decided to bring a partner, Mark HNATIW ("HNATIW"), along.

3. On March 2, 2005 at approximately 3:00 p.m., PERRY and HNATIW arrived at N.E. 18 – 58 – 7 W5th meridian, County of Lac St. Anne, near MAYERTHORPE, Alberta. This property is one of three quarter-sections owned by Warren and Stephanie FIFIELD. ROSZKO, Stephanie FIFIELD's son, occupied a mobile home on this property.

4. The bailiffs observed a man standing outside of the man-door of a Quonset hut located on the property. Based on the photographs of ROSZKO seen later, the bailiffs believe this individual was ROSZKO. As they did not immediately see the vehicle in question, they proceeded to drive past the entrance to the property to get a more complete view of the property.

5. The bailiffs performed a U-turn and returned to the driveway of the property. They observed a locked steel gate across the entrance to the property, a second gate and chain-link fence further up the driveway, as well as a metal Quonset and

a mobile home on the property. They saw a new white Ford truck parked near the trailer that they suspected was the vehicle they were there to seize.

6. As they returned, they observed ROSZKO enter the Quonset through the pedestrian door and close it. The bailiffs honked their horn to get ROSZKO's attention. Shortly thereafter two large dogs, one believed to be a Rottweiler, appeared from the opposite end of the Quonset and ran toward them barking and growling.

7. The bailiffs decided to call the Mayerthorpe Detachment of the Royal Canadian Mounted Police ("RCMP") for assistance. They spoke with Corporal Jim MARTIN ("Cpl. MARTIN), who advised them not to enter the property until the RCMP arrived.

8. Prior to the arrival of the police, the white pick up truck parked near the trailer was started and initially was driven towards the bailiffs at the gate, however, it veered off and travelled south across country. Both bailiffs observed the vehicle to stop at one point. ROSZKO disembarked from the truck and appeared to be opening a gate, drove forward, disembarked on further time to close the gate and appeared to be digging in the snow. He then drove across the field and out of sight.

9. The bailiffs suspected that the departed truck was the one that they were there to seize.

10. PERRY directed HNATIW to contact the Mayerthorpe RCMP to advise that the suspect vehicle was being driven off of the property.

11. The police investigation would subsequently determine that the truck ROSZKO departed in was the subject of the civil enforcement order.

12. At approximately 3:40 p.m., Cpl, MARTIN and Constable Peter SCHIEMANN ("Cst. SCHIEMANN") arrived at the ROSZKO property. After speaking with the bailiffs, they departed to search the surrounding roads for ROSZKO and the white pickup truck. Constable Julie LETAL ("Cst. LETAL") arrived and assisted the bailiffs in getting through the first locked gate.

13. Cpl. MARTIN and Cst. SCHIEMANN returned at approximately 3:45 p.m. Pepper spray was used on the dogs inside the second gate, and the dogs were backed into a granary/shed behind the Quonset. A doghouse was positioned in front of the door to the shed, and Cst. LETAL backed her police vehicle against the doghouse to pin the dogs inside.

14. PERRY proceeded with the others to the front of the Quonset with the intention of checking the interior for the vehicle they were attempting to seize. A padlock was hanging in the clasp of the door to the Quonset, but was not locked.

15. The bailiffs and the Mayerthorpe RCMP officers entered the Quonset, with at least one officer drawing their weapon. An odour of marihuana was detected. A number of vehicles or vehicle parts were observed, consistent with a "chop shop" or a place where stolen vehicles are altered.

16. The groups proceeded through the Quonset toward the back plywood and black plastic enclosed area. Peering through a flap in the plastic, a marihuana grow-op operation was observed.

17. At approximately 4:05 p.m. Cpl MARTIN left with Cst. SCHIEMANN to obtain a Search Warrant for the ROSZKO property, leaving Cst. LETAL and Constable Trevor JOSOK ("Cst. JOSOK"), a member of the Whitecourt RCMP, to secure the scene. Cst. JOSOK had arrived while the members were inside the Quonset.

18. At approximately 5:00 p.m. contact was made with the Auto Theft Section of the Edmonton RCMP. It was determined that due to the length of time it would take to get a Search Warrant and given the lighting conditions, Constable Steve VIGOR ("Cst. VIGOR") and Constable Garrett HOOGESTRAAT ("Cst. HOOGESTRAAT") would not attend until morning.

19. Cst. SCHIEMANN returned to the ROSZKO property with Constable Brock MYROL ("Cst. MYROL"). Cst. JOSOK departed.

20. At approximately 6:30 p.m., bailiffs PERRY and HNATIW left ROSZKO's property and returned to Edmonton, Alberta. At some time prior to departing, PERRY placed a Notice of Seizure between the outside and inside doors of the mobile home located on the ROSZKO property.

21. At 7:55 p.m., Cpl. MARTIN was granted a Search Warrant for ROSZKO's property. The search team comprising of Cpl. MARTIN, Cst. LETAL, Cst. STARMAN, Cst. SANGSTER, Cst. SCHIEMANN and Cst. MYROL was assembled.

22. The search team arrived at the ROSZKO property and at approximately 8:40 p.m. commenced the search. It was discovered that the grow operation was larger than originally thought.

23. At approximately 9:30 p.m., Cpl. MARTIN made contact with Corporal Lorne ADAMITZ ("Cpl. ADAMITZ") of the Edmonton RCMP Green Team. The Green Team is a specialized unit responsible for the investigation and processing of relatively large scale commercial drug operations. Cpl ADAMITZ agreed to put together a team and attend immediately.

24. Between 9:30 p.m. and 10:00 p.m., Uptown Towing was contacted to remove stolen property from the Quonset and between 10:00 p.m. and 10:30 p.m., they removed the following: a Wermac generator, a 1997 motorcycle, two 1998 Honda motorcycles, a 2003 red GMC truck, a 2002 Grey Ford F350 truck, a 1990 John Deere garden tractor and automotive parts.

25. At 00:30 on March 3, 2005, the Green Team arrived with Cpl. ADAMITZ, Cst. Al GOULASH, Cst. Ray SAVAGE and a member of the Edmonton City Police Green Team Unit. By 2:30 a.m. they had dismantled the grow operation and seized 280 plants of marihuana along with other grow operation paraphernalia, including harvesting books and other documents relating to the grow operation.

26. On March 3, 2005 at 3:00 a.m., the search was complete, except for the removal of the John Deere garden tractor, some automotive parts, chopped up truck frames and a truck shell in the back of the property. Constable Lionide

JOHNSTON ("Cst. JOHNSTON") of the Mayerthorpe RCMP and Constable Anthony GORDON ("Cst. GORDON") of the Whitecourt RCMP were called in to maintain security of the ROSZKO property until the arrival of members of the Edmonton RCMP Auto Theft Unit later that morning.

27. At 9:30 a.m., Cst. SCHIEMANN (not dressed in RCMP uniform as he was to attend Edmonton on other police business) drove from Mayerthorpe to ROSZKO's property to drop off Cst. MYROL who was going to assist in the search effort that morning.

28. At approximately 9:56 a.m. Constable Garrett HOOGESTRAAT (Cst. HOOGESTRAAT) and Constable Steven VIGOR (Cst. VIGOR), both of the Edmonton RCMP Auto Theft Unit arrived at ROSZKO's property.

29. Upon their arrival, they noted Cst. GORDON, Cst. JOHNSTON, Cst. MYROL and Cst. SCHIEMANN behind the Quonset in the area of the small shed feeding drugged meat to ROSZKO's dogs in an effort to sedate them. They parked toward the southwest corner of the Quonset near the shed. Cst. VIGOR remained in the vehicle for about a minute writing notes while Cst. HOOGESTRAAT exited the vehicle.

30. Cst. HOOGESTRAAT spoke briefly with Cst. GORDON. Cst. GORDON along with Cst. JOHNSTON, Cst. MYROL, and Cst. SCHIEMANN then walked toward the front of the Quonset. Cst. VIGOR exited the vehicle and joined Cst. HOOGESTRAAT at the rear of his vehicle where they were about to change into coveralls and commence their investigation.

31. Cst. VIGOR and Cst. HOOGESTRAAT heard two loud bangs, but were unsure what had caused the noise. Immediately thereafter, they heard a further quick succession of bangs. In addition, they heard screams. Cst. HOOGESTRAAT and Cst. VIGOR now recognized the sounds as gunfire. They both drew their weapons and ran toward the east end of the Quonset.

32. Cst. VIGOR directed Cst. HOOGESTRAAT to call for backup. Cst. HOOGESTRAAT returned to their vehicle to call 9-1-1. That call was received at 10:01 a.m., Cst. VIGOR then ran around one of the parked police vehicles and approached the open doors of the Quonset.

33. ROSZKO walked out of the Quonset from the large door carrying what Cst. VIGOR believed to be a hunting rifle, and what appeared to be a semi-automatic assault rifle. ROSZKO appeared to be surprised, raised the assault rifle and discharged two rounds at Cst. VIGOR, narrowly missing him by six to eight inches. The passenger's window and side view mirror of the police cruiser were struck in the process.

34. Cst. VIGOR returned fire with his service sidearm, directing two shots at ROSZKO. ROSZKO was noted by Cst. VIGOR to stumble back into the Quonset. It was later determined ROSZKO was hit twice by Cst. VIGOR, once in the hand and once in the thigh. Both of these wounds were non-fatal. ROSZKO returned, out of sight, to the interior of the Quonset.

35. Cst. HOOGESTRAAT backed their police vehicle near an adjacent sand pile giving Cst. VIGOR cover to retreat. The vehicle was parked in a position to maintain visual observation of the Quonset awaiting the arrival of the RCMP Emergency Response Team (ERT). At the south end of the main door, the leg of one of the peace officers was partially visible. Requests were made over the police radio for communication from the officers inside the Quonset, however, the only sound heard was from the officer's portable radios.

36. Once Cst. VIGOR joined Cst. HOOGESTRAAT in their vehicle, he contacted the ERT team and Cst. HOOGESTRAAT called in a request for an Explosive Disposal Unit Remote Mobile Investigator (EDU-RMI).

37. At approximately 12:05 p.m. the ERT team arrived on scene. At approximately 12:20 p.m., the EDU team arrived on scene.

38. The EDU unit robot was deployed at approximately 1:40 p.m. to video the inside of the Quonset in an attempt to ensure that no continued threat existed. The robot's video depicted Cst. GORDON near the entrance to the Quonset. ROSZKO was located a little further inside and toward the northeast side. Cst. JOHNSTON and Cst. SCHIEMANN were located near the centre of the Quonset. Cst. MYROL could not be seen by the robot. No indications of life were observed.

39. ROSZKO was observed lying on his back. A 9 mm semi-automatic Luger handgun, make Beretta, model 92 FS, was tucked into the waist band of his pants. Laying to the right side of ROSZKO was a .300 Winchester Magnum, bolt action, repeating rifle, model 70 XTR Sporter Magnum ("the RIFLE"). It was later determined that the RIFLE was owned by John HENNESSEY, the grandfather of the accused, Shawn William HENNESSEY ("HENNESSEY"). A semi-automatic .308 Heckler and Koch, model HK 91, assault rifle was between his legs.

40. The ERT team was then deployed and entered the Quonset. The weapons were removed from the proximity of ROSZKO, and he was rolled over and handcuffed. Cst. MYROL was eventually located near a rear door which was padlocked from the outside. Two of the officers were dragged outside in the hope of possible resuscitation. It was then determined that all four peace officers and ROSZKO were deceased.

41. A forensic examination of the crime scene later determined 19 shell casings were positively associated to the Heckler and Koch, along with 13 fired bullets that could have been fired from that semi-automatic rifle. Neither the .300 calibre rifle nor the 9mm Luger pistol was fired by ROSZKO.

42. A firearms expert determined that Cst. JOHNSTON had discharged a round from his 9 mm Luger Smith & Wesson at ROSZKO, however that bullet struck the butt plate of the handgun tucked in ROSZKO's waist band. Cst. JOHNSTON's service handgun failed to properly eject the shell casing, thereby preventing Cst. JOHNSTON from firing again.

43. Autopsies were performed by a Provincial Medical Examiner, Dr. Bernard BANNACH, on March 3, 2005.

44. In relation to Cst. SCHIEMANN, Dr. BANNACH found that there were multiple gunshot wounds. There was a perforating gunshot wound of the right side of the chest and another perforating gunshot wound of the left thigh. In addition, there was a superficial penetrating gunshot wound of the left wrist. In Dr. BANNACH's expert opinion the cause of death was as a result of multiple gunshot wounds.

45. In relation to Cst. GORDON, Dr. BANNACH determined that there were two perforating gunshot wounds of the torso, one of the chest and one of the abdomen. Similarly, Dr. BANNACH was of the opinion that Cst. GORDON died as a result of multiple gunshot wounds.

46. In relation to Cst. JOHNSTON, Dr. BANNACH noted four gunshot wounds with involvement of the chest, neck, face, upper extremities, pelvis, abdomen and lower extremities. Similarly, the cause of death was noted to be as a result of multiple gunshot wounds.

47. Finally, in relation to Cst. MYROL, Dr. BANNACH noted a perforating gunshot wound of the head, with massive damage to the skull and scalp, and evisceration of the brain. Dr. BANNACK also noted a second superficial grazing type gunshot injury to the lateral left hip region. It was Dr. BANNACH's opinion that Cst. MYROL died as a result of a gunshot wound to the head.

48. Dr. BANNACK also performed the autopsy on ROSZKO and determined that ROSZKO died of a self-inflicted gunshot wound to the left side of his chest, with the entrance wound being consistent with the Heckler and Koch. There were also gunshot wounds to his hand and his thigh, neither of which would have been fatal. Those latter two wounds were consistent with the two shots fired by Cst. VIGOR at ROSZKO.

49. The RCMP commenced an extensive investigation to try to determine, amongst other things, how ROSZKO returned to his farm to ambush and murder the four peace officers and whether or not he had received any type of assistance. Additionally, the police wanted to determine how ROSZKO had armed himself with respect to the .300 Winchester as it was discovered through the National Firearms Registry that that particular rifle was in fact, legally registered to John HENNESSEY who, as previously noted, is the grandfather of the accused HENNESSEY.

50. The police further conducted numerous interviews of relatives of ROSZKO and executed search warrants with respect to ROSZKO's cell phone.

51. Red Deer ERT members had approached from the north side of the Quonset. After their entry into the Quonset, someone mentioned seeing a bed sheet on the north side by the east corner of the Quonset. Later, in addition to the bed sheet, a pillow case containing a pair of work gloves along with a small water bottle and a can of "Bear Scare" pepper spray was seized from the location. These items were seized by Cst. Garry LOTOSKI ("Cst. LOTOSKI"), and continuity of the items was maintained by the RCMP. They were personally delivered by Cst. LOTOSKI to the RCMP Forensic Laboratory in Edmonton on March 31, 2005. Subsequently, it was forensically determined that an area of the left glove between the index

finger and middle finger contained DNA which was a DNA match to the accused, HENNESSEY.

52. Sometime between 2:00 p.m. and 3:30 p.m. on March 2, 2005, ROSZKO called his aunt, Ann CHAYKA, ("CHAYKA") looking for his mother, Stephanie FIFIELD ("FIFIELD"). ROSZKO called again about an hour later, sounding somewhat anxious and indicating that there was a situation occurring in his yard. Subsequent discussions occurred between FIFIELD and CHAYKA wherein FIFIELD sought permission on behalf of her son to park the white truck at CHAYKA's residence. CHAYKA didn't give her permission, however, when she awoke in the morning, she noted that ROSZKO's truck that the police were seeking had in fact been parked in her yard over night. ROSZKO was no where to be seen, however, CHAYKA did know via further contact from her sister, FIFIELD, that there were helicopters, police cars and ambulances in ROSZKO's yard. The distance from the CHAYKA property to ROSZKO's property was later determined to be 38.5 km.

53. The search of the Telus cell phone records relating to ROSZKO's cellular phone indicated that between 3:34 p.m. and 4:37 p.m. on March 2, 2005, ROSZKO placed one phone call to Kal Tire in Barrhead and numerous calls were made between ROSZKO and a "bag phone" then utilized by the accused, HENNESSSEY, by virtue of his employment with Kal Tire. Additionally, numerous calls were made to HENNESSEY's residence. The last call made by the bag phone was to HENNESSEY's residence was at 5:24 p.m. The bag phone was not used again until March 4, 2005.

54. ROSZKO asked HENNESSEY if he could hide his truck at the HENNESSEY residence, however, HENNESSEY steadfastly refused. At one point, HENNESSEY was aware that ROSZKO was at his residence by reason of a phone call received from his wife, Christine HENNESSEY. HENNESSEY also spoke to ROSZKO at that time on the telephone.

55. HENNESSEY stopped briefly at Jessie ZASIEDKO's house during the evening of March 2, 2005. HENNESSSEY was seeking his brother-in-law, the accused, Dennis Keegan CHEESEMAN, ("CHEESEMAN"), HENNESSEY is married to CHEESEMAN's sister, Christine. HENNESSEY was apparently aware that CHEESEMAN was helping Jessie ZASIEDKO move. HENNESSEY asked CHEESEMAN to speak to him alone, and indicated that he needed CHEESEMAN'S help because there were RCMP officers at ROSZKO's farm, and HENNESSEY was involved in the grow operation located on ROSZKO's property. He further asked CHEESEMAN to get home as soon as he could. CHEESEMAN knew ROSZKO as he, like HENNESSEY, had done odd jobs from time to time for ROSZKO on ROSZKO's property. These jobs involved menial labor such as the digging of holes for the planting of trees. CHEESEMAN, unlike HENNESSEY, had no involvement with respect to any of the illegal operations on the ROSZKO property.

56. As previously mentioned, CHAYKA received a telephone call from FIFIELD at approximately 8:00 p.m., wherein CHAYKA advised FIFIELD that ROSZKO had called looking for her. FIFIELD advised CHAYKA that there were a number of police vehicles in ROSZKO's yard.

57. ROSZKO's cell phone records indicate that he initiated calls to FIFIELD's residence at 8:13 p.m., 8:28 p.m., 9:59 p.m., 10:21 p.m., and 11:55 p.m. on the 2nd of March 2005.

58. At approximately 10:30 p.m. on March 2, 2005, that CHAYKA received a phone call from FIFIELD wherein she received ROSZKO's request to park his white pickup truck at CHAYKA's residence. CHAYKA indicated that ROSZKO did not have her permission.

59. After watching the driveway for a period of time, CHAYKA telephoned FIFIELD to report that ROSZKO had not arrived with his truck at her residence, and that CHAYKA was going to retire for the evening.

60. FIFIELD continued to watch the ROSZKO residence throughout the night. She could see vehicles driving in and out, and assumed that they were police vehicles based upon what she had seen in the daylight. She also noted, at some point, that she saw lights on in ROSZKO's trailer.

61. When CHEESEMAN returned home to the rural residence he shared with his sister Christine and his brother-in-law, HENNESSEY, in the later evening hours of March 2, 2005, he found ROSZKO and HENNESSEY sitting at the kitchen table. It was evident to CHEESEMAN that Christine and her children were home, however, were avoiding ROSZKO.

62. ROSZKO had arrived at the residence with the Luger handgun in the waist band of his pants, and was seeking the rifle that HENNESSEY had been given by his grandfather, John HENNESSEY, a few years prior.

63. HENNESSEY wiped the .300 Winchester Magnum rifle down; he provided it to ROSZKO as well as a box of ammunition intended for use in that rifle.

64. When CHEESEMAN viewed that situation, he took it upon himself to go downstairs and retrieve a white pillow case and some gloves. CHEESEMAN then put on the gloves and stuck the HENNESSEY rifle in the pillow case.

65. It was clear to all present that ROSZKO was enraged at the police, and ROSZKO made comments to the effect that he intended to return to his property and burn down the Quonset that contained the illegal marihuana grow and chop shop operation.

66. Both HENNESSEY and CHEESEMAN knew that armed confrontation with the police was a real possibility and that the situation was clearly trouble.

67. ROSZKO decided that he would hide the sought after truck at CHAYKA's residence, and the two accused agreed to follow him there in order to give him a ride back to his residence.

68. HENNESSEY asked CHEESEMAN to accompany him for support and comfort. Both men were intimidated and fearful of ROSZKO. They followed ROSZKO to CHAYKA's residence in HENNESSEY's Dodge Neon. During that trip of approximately a half an hour, the two accused were relatively quiet. When they arrived at the CHAYKA residence, they pulled over and waited near the highway

while ROSZKO drove the white truck and parked it down the CHAYKA driveway. During this time period, the two accused discussed leaving ROSZKO there, however, decided not to act upon that plan. ROSZKO ultimately reappeared on foot carrying the HENNESEY rifle, with the handgun still tucked into the waist band of his pants. CHEESEMAN exited from the front passenger seat, vacating that seat for ROSZKO. ROSZKO slid the rifle with the pillow case into the back seat next to CHEESEMAN.

69. During the trip from CHAYKA's, CHEESEMAN and HENNESSEY did not converse with ROSZKO, but ROSZKO ranted and complained about the RCMP, and threatened to get even with them. He indicated that he was going to burn down the Quonset. CHEESEMAN described his rantings as "devil talk".

70. ROSZKO directed HENNESSEY to drive past the range road on which he lived, and to proceed to the next range road where his mother lived. He directed HENNESSEY to drive past his mother's residence and to stop across the field from where the police were located. The two accused could see the lights from the police cars that early morning of March 3, 2005, and ROSZKO paused to pull socks over the outside of the boots he was then wearing. ROSZKO grabbed the HENNESSEY rifle from the back seat and proceeded off in the direction of the police, sometime in the early morning hours of March 3, 2005, and most likely between 1 a.m. and 3 a.m.

71. HENNESSEY and CHEESEMAN departed and drove directly home. CHEESEMAN suggested that they should call the police and warn them about ROSZKO, however, HENNESSEY discouraged that idea, and felt that ROSZKO would come after them should he evade police. Neither accused made such a phone call to police.

73. Later the same morning, HENNESSEY departed his residence for a Kal Tire meeting at the Mayfield Inn in Edmonton that commenced at 7:00 a.m. or 8:00 a.m. HENNESSEY remained at that meeting for the majority of that day and did not learn what had transpired at the ROSZKO farm until he heard it on the radio on his way home to his Barrhead area residence. HENNESSEY indicated that he would have arrived home between 4:00 to 5:30 p.m.

74. Similarly, CHEESEMAN went to work at Sepallo Foods at 7:00 a.m. that same morning and left work at 1:30 p.m. claiming a family emergency. In fact, CHEESEMAN left work when he had heard about the murder of the four peace officers on the ROSZKO farm.

75. HENNESSEY was aware that the rifle he had provided to ROSZKO was in fact registered to his grandfather, John HENNESSEY. The senior HENNESSEY had provided the rifle to Shawn HENNESSEY when he believed the Government planned upon eliminating the gun registry requirements. John HENNESSEY believed that he gave the rifle to HENNESSEY in early 2003 or late 2002.

76. HENNESSEY and his mother, Sandy HENNESSEY, discussed the fact that the rifle was registered to John HENNESSEY and that the RCMP would undoubtedly follow-up on that aspect of the investigation by questioning John HENNESSEY. As

a result, contact was made with the senior HENNESSEY, and the accused told John HENNESSEY that ROSZKO had the .300 Winchester Magnum. John HENNESSEY indicated that he was quite sure that it was his own suggestion that they all "story" to the police the notion that the rifle had been stolen from the back of John HENNESSEY's welding truck.

77. Following an extensive RCMP investigation, the accused CHEESEMAN was arrested on July 7, 2007, and the accused, HENNESSEY, was arrested on July 8, 2007.

Pursuant to the provisions of Section 655 of the Criminal Code of Canada, the above paragraphs contain facts, which are alleged by the Crown and admitted by the Accused, Shawn William HENNESSEY, and the Accused, Dennis Keegan CHEESEMAN, for the purpose of dispensing with formal proof thereof at trial.

_____

SHAWN WILLIAM HENNESSEY

_____

D'ARCY DEPOE
Counsel for the Accused, Hennessey

_____

EDMOND O'NEIL
Counsel for the Accused, Hennessey

_____

DENNIS KEEGAN CHEESEMAN

_____

PETER NORTHCOTT
Counsel for the Accused, Cheeseman

_____

DAVID A. LABRENZ
Agent of the Attorney General

APPENDIX B
Reason for Judgment

Court of Queen's Bench of Alberta

Citation: R. v. Hennessey, 2009 ABQB 60

Date:
Docket: 07084544lQl
Registry: Edmonton

Between:

Her Majesty the Queen

- and -

Shawn William Hennessey and Dennis Keegan Cheeseman

Accused

Reasons for Judgment
of the
Honourable Mr. Justice Eric F. Macklin

I.   Introduction

[1]   On March 3, 2005, near Mayerthorpe, Alberta, Royal Canadian Mounted Police Constables Anthony Fitzgerald Gordon, Peter Christopher Schiemann, Lionide Nicholas Johnston and Brock Warren Myrol were ambushed and murdered by James Michael Roszko who then killed himself. It was the worst loss of life suffered by the RCMP in a single incident in over 100 years.

[2]   On January 19, 2009, Shawn William Hennessey and Dennis Keegan Cheeseman pled guilty to four counts each of manslaughter in relation to the deaths of the four RCMP Constables. In accordance with s. 606 of the *Criminal Code*, I satisfied myself that each of the two accused pled guilty voluntarily, understood that his plea was an admission of the essential elements of the

offence, understood the nature and consequences of the plea and that it now fell upon the Court to impose a punishment on them, and understood that I was not bound by any agreement made between either of the accused and the Crown. The guilty pleas were then accepted by the Court and convictions for manslaughter as parties to a murder were entered against each accused. It remains for the Court to determine appropriate sentences.

II.   Facts

[3]   The following facts are contained in the Agreed Statement of Facts entered by the parties as an exhibit. It is only these facts, and the inferences that can reasonably be drawn from them, that are properly before this Court for consideration in sentencing.

[4]   On March 2, 2005 a bailiff, Rob Perry, set out to execute a warrant authorizing the seizure of a white 2005 Ford pickup truck. He brought along a partner, Mark Hnatiw. At around 3:00 p.m., Perry and Hnatiw arrived at property near Mayerthorpe, Alberta, on which Roszko occupied a mobile home. The bailiffs observed a man, probably Roszko, standing outside of the man-door of a Quonset hut located on the well-secured property, and a new white Ford truck that they suspected was the vehicle to be seized. When two large dogs ran toward them barking and growling, they decided to call the Mayerthorpe Detachment of the RCMP for assistance. Cpl. Jim Martin advised them not to enter the property until the RCMP arrived. Before the police arrived, Roszko drove the white pick up truck across the field and out of sight.

[5]   Cpl. Martin and Cst. Schiemann arrived at the Roszko property at around 3:40 p.m. The dogs were contained and Perry and the RCMP officer entered the Quonset. They observed a number of vehicle parts, consistent with a "chop shop" or a place where stolen vehicles are altered, and a marijuana grow operation.

[6]   At around 4:05 p.m., Cpl. Martin and Cst. Schiemann left to obtain a Search Warrant for the property, leaving Cst. Letal and Cst. Josok to secure the scene. Cst. Schiemann later returned to the Roszko property with Cst. Myrol. Cst. Josok departed. At around 6:30 p.m., bailiffs Perry and Hnatiw left and returned to Edmonton. At 7:55 p.m., Cpl. Martin was granted a Search Warrant for Roszko's property. A search team comprised of Cpl. Martin, Cst. Letal, Cst. Starman, Cst. Sangster, Cst. Schiemann and Cst. Myrol was assembled.

[7]   The search team arrived at the Roszko property and commenced the search at around 8:40 p.m. At 9:30 p.m., Cpl. Martin made contact with Cpl. Adamitz of the Edmonton RCMP Green Team, a specialized unit responsible for the investigation and processing of relatively large scale commercial drug operations. Cpl. Adamitz agreed to put together a team and attend immediately. A towing company attended and removed a number of stolen vehicles and other items. At 00:30 on March 3, 2005, the Green Team arrived and by 2:30 a.m. they had dismantled the grow operation and seized 280 marijuana plants along with other grow operation paraphernalia. At 3:00 a.m., the search was complete, except for the removal of some remaining items. Cst. Johnston and Cst. Gordon were called in to maintain security of the Roszko property until the

Page: 3

arrival of members of the Edmonton RCMP Auto Theft Unit later that morning. At 9:30 a.m., Cst. Schiemann drove from Mayerthorpe to Roszko's property to drop off Cst. Myrol who was going to assist in the search effort that morning. At around 9:56 a.m. Cst. Hoogestraat and Cst. Vigor of the Edmonton RCMP Auto Theft Unit arrived at Roszko's property.

[8]   After some initial contact with the RCMP officers on site, Cst. Vigor and Cst. Hoogestraat heard gunfire and called for back up. Roszko walked out of the Quonset carrying what appeared to be a hunting rifle, and a semiautomatic assault rifle and discharged two rounds at Cst. Vigor. Cst. Vigor returned fire, hitting Roszko in the hand and in the thigh. Roszko returned, out of sight, to the interior of the Quonset. Cst. Hoogestraat and Cst. Vigor awaited the arrival of the RCMP Emergency Response Team, which arrived on scene at around 12:05 p.m. A robot was transported to the scene at 12:20 p.m. and was deployed at approximately 1:40 p.m. No signs of life were detected. The ERT team entered the Quonset and it was determined that all four peace officers and Roszko were deceased. The officers died as a result of gunshot wounds. Roszko died as a result of a self-inflicted gunshot wound.

[9]   The RCMP commenced an extensive investigation to try to determine, among other things, how Roszko returned to his farm to ambush and murder the four peace officers and whether or not he had received any assistance. Additionally, the police wanted to determine how Roszko had armed himself with a .300 Winchester which was legally registered to John Hennessey, the grandfather of Shawn Hennessey.

[10]   A bed sheet and a pillow case containing a pair of work gloves along with a small water bottle and a can of "Bear Scare" pepper spray were noted in the Quonset. Subsequently, it was forensically determined that an area of the left glove between the index finger and middle finger contained DNA which was a DNA match to Shawn Hennessey.

[11]   The police conducted numerous interviews of relatives of Roszko and executed search warrants with respect to Roszko's cell phone. Sometime between 2:00 p.m. and 3:30 p.m. on March 2, 2005, Roszko called his aunt, Ann Chayka, looking for his mother, Stephanie Fifield. Roszko called again about an hour later, sounding somewhat anxious and indicating that there was a situation occurring in his yard. Subsequent discussions occurred between Fifield and Chayka wherein Fifield sought permission on behalf of her son to park the white truck at Chayka's residence. Chayka didn't give her permission, however, when she awoke in the morning, she noted that the truck the police were seeking had in fact been parked in her yard overnight. Roszko was nowhere to be seen, however Chayka learned from her sister, Fifield, that there were helicopters, police cars and ambulances in Roszko's yard. The distance from the Chayka property to Roszko's property was later determined to be 38.5 km.

[12]   The search of the Telus cell phone records relating to Roszko's cellular phone indicated that between 3:34 p.m. and 4:37 p.m. on March 2, 2005, Roszko placed one phone call to Kal Tire in Barrhead and numerous calls were made between Roszko and a "bag phone" then utilized by Shawn Hennessey, by virtue of his employment with Kal Tire. Additionally, numerous calls

Page: 4

were made to Hennessey's residence. The last call made by the bag phone was to Hennessey's residence at 5:24 p.m. The bag phone was not used again until March 4, 2005.

[13]   Roszko asked Hennessey if he could hide his truck at the Hennessey residence, however Hennessey steadfastly refused. At one point, Hennessey was aware that Roszko was at his residence by reason of a phone call received from his wife, Christine Hennessey. Hennessey also spoke to Roszko at that time on the telephone.

[14]   Hennessey stopped briefly at Jessie Zasiedko's house during the evening of March 2, 2005. Hennessey was seeking his brother-in-law, Dennis Cheeseman. Hennessey was apparently aware that Cheeseman was helping Jessie Zasiedko move. Hennessey asked Cheeseman to speak to him alone, and indicated that he needed Cheeseman's help because there were RCMP officers at Roszko's farm, and Hennessey was involved in the marijuana grow operation located on Roszko's property. He further asked Cheeseman to get home as soon as he could. Cheeseman knew Roszko as he, like Hennessey, had done odd jobs from time to time for Roszko on Roszko's property. These jobs involved menial labor such as the digging of holes for the planting of trees. Cheeseman, unlike Hennessey, had no involvement with respect to any of the illegal operations on the Roszko property.

[15]   When Cheeseman returned home to the rural residence he shared with his sister Christine and his brother-in-law, Hennessey, in the later evening hours of March 2, 2005, he found Roszko and Hennessey sitting at the kitchen table. It was evident to Cheeseman that Christine and her children were home, however, were avoiding Roszko.

[16]   Roszko had arrived at the residence with a Luger handgun in the waistband of his pants, and was seeking the rifle that Hennessey had been given by his grandfather, John Hennessey, a few years prior. Hennessey wiped the .300 Winchester Magnum rifle down; he provided it to Roszko as well as a box of ammunition intended for use in that rifle.

[17]   When Cheeseman viewed that situation, he took it upon himself to go downstairs and retrieve a white pillow case and some gloves. Cheeseman then put on the gloves and stuck the Hennessey rifle in the pillow case.

[18]   It was clear to all present that Roszko was enraged at the police, and Roszko made comments to the effect that he intended to return to his property and burn down the Quonset that contained the illegal marijuana grow op and chop shop operation. Both Hennessey and Cheeseman knew that armed confrontation with the police was a real possibility and that the situation was clearly trouble.

[19]   Roszko decided that he would hide the sought after truck at Chayka's residence, and the two offenders agreed to follow him there in order to give him a ride back to his residence.

Page: 5

[20]   Hennessey asked Cheeseman to accompany him for support and comfort. Both men were intimidated and fearful of Roszko. They followed Roszko to Chayka's residence in Hennessey's Dodge Neon. During that trip of approximately a half an hour, the two offenders were relatively quiet. When they arrived at the Chayka residence, they pulled over and waited near the highway while Roszko drove the white truck and parked it down the Chayka driveway. During this time period, the two offenders discussed leaving Roszko there, however, decided not to act upon that plan. Roszko ultimately reappeared on foot carrying the Hennessey rifle, with the handgun still tucked into the waistband of his pants. Cheeseman exited from the front passenger seat, vacating that seat for Roszko. Roszko slid the rifle with the pillow case into the back seat next to Cheeseman.

[21]   During the trip from Chayka's, Cheeseman and Hennessey did not converse with Roszko, but Roszko ranted and complained about the RCMP, and threatened to get even with them. He indicated that he was going to burn down the Quonset. Cheeseman described his rantings as "devil talk".

[22]   Roszko directed Hennessey to drive past the range road on which he lived, and to proceed to the next range road where his mother lived. He directed Hennessey to drive past his mother's residence and to stop across the field from where the police were located. The two offenders could see the lights from the police cars that early morning of March 3, 2005, and Roszko paused to pull socks over the outside of the boots he was then wearing. Roszko grabbed the Hennessey rifle from the back seat and proceeded off in the direction of the police, sometime in the early morning hours of March 3, 2005, and most likely between 1 a.m. and 3 a.m.

[23]   Hennessey and Cheeseman departed and drove directly home. Cheeseman suggested that they should call the police and warn them about Roszko, however Hennessey discouraged that idea, and felt that Roszko would come after them should he evade police. Neither offender made such a phone call to the police.

[24]   Later the same morning, Hennessey departed his residence for a Kal Tire meeting at the Mayfield Inn in Edmonton that commenced at 7:00 a.m. or 8:00 a.m. Hennessey remained at that meeting for the majority of that day and did not learn what had transpired at the Roszko farm until he heard it on the radio on his way home to his Barrhead area residence. Hennessey indicated that he would have arrived home between 4:00 p.m. and 5:30 p.m.

[25]   Similarly, Cheeseman went to work at Sepallo Foods at 7:00 a.m. that same morning and left work at 1:30 p.m. claiming a family emergency, when he heard about the murder of the four peace officers on the Roszko farm.

[26]   Hennessey was aware that the rifle he had provided to Roszko was in fact registered to his grandfather, John Hennessey. The senior Hennessey had provided the rifle to Shawn Hennessey when he believed the Government planned upon eliminating the gun registry

Page: 6

requirements. John Hennessey believed that he gave the rifle to Hennessey in early 2003 or late 2002.

[27]   Hennessey and his mother, Sandy Hennessey, discussed the fact that the rifle was registered to John Hennessey and that the RCMP would undoubtedly follow up on that aspect of the investigation by questioning John Hennessey. As a result, contact was made with the senior Hennessey, and Shawn Hennessey told John Hennessey that Roszko had the .300 Winchester Magnum. John Hennessey indicated that he was quite sure that it was his own suggestion that they all "story" to the police the notion that the rifle had been stolen from the back of John Hennessey's welding truck.

[28]   Following an extensive RCMP investigation, Cheeseman was arrested on July 7, 2007, and Hennessey was arrested on July 8, 2007.

III.   Analysis

A.   General Comments

[29]   The Crown seeks a sentence of between 10 years and 15 years imprisonment for each offender with credit given for time served. Mr. Hennessey and Mr. Cheeseman seek a sentence in the range of 5 years and 4 years imprisonment respectively, with credit given for time served and the fact that each pled guilty.

[30]   It is not uncommon to see a great disparity in cases of sentencing for manslaughter as there is a wide range of conduct that may fall within the definition of manslaughter and consequently significant variance in terms of the moral culpability of the offender.

[31]   The purpose and principles of sentencing are set out in ss. 718, 718.1 and 718.2 of the *Criminal Code of Canada*. The fundamental purpose of sentencing is to have respect for the law and the maintenance of a just, peaceful and safe society. When imposing sanctions, the Court should strive to achieve the objectives of denouncing unlawful conduct, deterring the offender and other persons from committing offences; separating offenders from society where necessary, assisting in rehabilitating offenders; providing reparations for harm done to victims or to the community and promoting a sense of responsibility in offenders and acknowledgement of the harm done to victims and to the community.

[32]   With respect to the offence of manslaughter, the *Criminal Code* provides in s. 236:

> 236. Every person who commits manslaughter is guilty of an indictable offence and liable

Page: 7

(a) where a firearm is used in the commission of the offence, to imprisonment for life and to a minimum punishment of imprisonment for a term of four years; and

(b) in any other case, to imprisonment for life.

[33]   The Alberta Court of Appeal highlighted the wide range of cases encompassed by the offence of unlawful act manslaughter in *R. v. Laberge* (1995), 165 A.R. 375. The Court stated at para. 6:

> 6   All unlawful act manslaughter cases have two common requirements: conduct which has caused the death of another; and fault short of intention to kill. However, despite these common elements, the offence of unlawful act manslaughter covers a wide range of cases extending from those which may be classified as near accident at the one extreme and near murder at the other... Different degrees of moral culpability attach to each along a continuum within that spectrum. It is precisely because a sentence for manslaughter can range from a suspended sentence up to life imprisonment that the court must determine for sentencing purposes what rung on the moral culpability ladder the offender reached when he committed the prohibited act. The purpose of this exercise is to ensure that the sentence imposed fits the degree of moral fault of the offender for the harm done.

[34]   The Court in *Laberge* emphasized the need to distinguish between fault determined by the offender's *mens rea* and fault in terms of his overall moral blameworthiness for the crime. The sentencing court is not limited to considering the offender's blameworthiness in terms of his mental state. It must consider other factors such as the "nature and quality of the unlawful act itself, the method by which it was committed and the manner in which it was committed in terms of the degree of planning and deliberation . . ." (at paras. 7 and 8).

[35]   The Court in *Laberge* (at para. 9) divided unlawful acts into three broad groups: those which are likely to put the victim at risk of, or cause, bodily injury; those which are likely to put the victim at risk of, or cause, serious bodily injury; and those which are likely to put the victim at risk of, or cause, life threatening injuries. The overall moral blameworthiness of the offender is greater where the offender knew or was wilfully blind to the fact that his conduct would put the victim at risk of serious harm.

[36]   In addition to considering the moral blameworthiness of Mr. Hennessey and Mr. Cheeseman in the deaths of the four RCMP Constables, the Court must also consider any mitigating and aggravating factors applicable to the circumstances of the killings and to the individual offenders themselves. It is also necessary to bear in mind the fundamental principle of proportionality mandated by s. 718.1 of the *Criminal Code*. The sentences imposed on the two offenders must be proportionate to the gravity of the offences and their respective degrees of

responsibility. The sentences must be within the range imposed for similar offences. While tragic consequences must be considered in the context of the nature of the offence, those consequences cannot unduly distort determination of the appropriate penalty (see *R. v. Mellstrom* (1975), 22 C.C.C. (2nd) 472 (Alta. S.C.A.D.)).

B.   Authorities

[37]   As stated above, s. 236 prescribes a four year minimum term of imprisonment for manslaughter where a firearm is used in the commission of the offence. Therefore, the potential sentences in this case range from four years to life in prison. It is the Court's task to determine where along that wide spectrum the proper sentences fall for these two individuals, as sentencing is ultimately a highly individualized process. In reaching a decision, the Court is guided by decisions in other cases where the offenders had similar moral culpability.

[38]   The parties each submitted cases relating to sentencing for manslaughter where the offender did not directly kill the victim, but where the activities of the offender amounted to entering into a common unlawful purpose or aiding or abetting the actual killer. I will not review all of the cases referred to, but in my view the following manslaughter cases provide some guidance:

> (1) *R. v. Bell*, 2003 CarswellMan 594, leave denied 2006 CarswellMan 42, 2006 MBCA 19: An RCMP officer was shot following a violent crime spree, while Bell and two others, heavily armed, were resisting arrest and fleeing in a stolen truck. Bell was not the driver, nor did she fire the gun, but was convicted of manslaughter and sentenced to 10 years imprisonment. There was no guilty plea, and she expressed animosity toward the police. There was no duress. With credit for time served, her sentence was reduced to 7 years.

> (2) *R. v. McLeod*, 2006 ABQB 217, aff'd 2008 ABCA 31: McLeod was hired by Chung to conduct an assault on a suspected police informant, which turned into a shooting by a third person that neither intended. McLeod was present at the time of the killing and was convicted of manslaughter. McLeod and Chung were young and were subject to firearms prohibitions at the time. Slatter J. sentenced McLeod to 9 years and Chung to 11 years imprisonment. With credit for time served, McLeod's net sentence was 3 years and 8 months and Chung's net sentence was 8 years and 4 months.

> (3) *R. v. McWhirter*, 2005 NBPC 6: McWhirter and a friend decided to rob a taxi driver as his friend needed money to pay off a drug debt. McWhirter did not want to participate in the robbery but agreed to be a lookout. He gave his friend a gun he had stolen from his parents' home. His friend pulled the gun on a driver, and killed the victim. McWhirter helped dispose of the body. He had no previous

Page: 9

record, strong family and community support, was remorseful, and had not used the firearm. He was sentenced to 7 years, after credit was given for time served.

(4) *R. v. Cooney* (1995), 80 O.A.C. 89: Cooney had participated in luring the victim for the purpose of robbery, and benefitted from property stolen. However, it was not clear that he was the perpetrator of the killing or was present when it was committed. Cooney was young with a minimal record. The Court of Appeal reduced the sentence from 12 years to an effective sentence of 10 years and 9 months, after credit for pre-trial custody.

(5) *R. v. Phillips*, 2008 ONCA 688: Phillips was jealous of his girlfriend's relationship with Wilman. Phillips loaded a gun owned by Wilman. His girlfriend took the gun and shot Wilman while he sat in his truck. Phillips and his girlfriend disposed of the body, stole Wilman's car and hid for a few weeks, and later returned to live in Wilman's home. Phillips denied any role in planning the shooting. The dangerous and reckless conduct of Phillips in loading the gun, his knowledge of his girlfriend's unstable temperament, Wilman's vulnerable position and kind treatment of Phillips and his girlfriend, the disrespectful manner in which Wilman's body was treated, the couple's flight from the jurisdiction, and Phillip's feigned surprise at the discovery of Wilman's death and his role in it were all aggravating factors. The Court of Appeal reduced the sentence to 9 years less credit of almost 4 years for time served, citing Phillips' lack of a significant criminal record and his lack of participation in the actual killing.

(6) *R. v. Dhak*, 2003 BCSC 595: Dhak was the driver of a vehicle involved in a drive-by shooting after a dispute at a nightclub, repositioning the vehicle to give the shooter a better advantage, but possibly only intending that the gun be used to threaten the individuals who were banging on the vehicle or to scare them away by firing the weapon. He had a record and was on probation at the time. He was sentenced to 7½ years less credit for time served for a net sentence of 1 year and 4 months.

(7) *R. v. Espadilla*, 2005 BCSC 358: Two groups became involved in an altercation at a nightclub. Espadilla knew one member of his own group (the killer) to be violent and to carry a firearm at times. Espadilla had recognized the vehicle driven by the victim as belonging to a person who lived in the adjoining apartment complex, and he guided the killer to the parking lot where he knew the victim parked his car. Espadilla was not present at the time of the killing but cleaned up the scene and stole items from the victim's apartment. He was young and had a minor unrelated criminal record. The court reluctantly accepted a joint submission amounting to what was effectively a 6 year sentence less credit for time served for a net sentence of 2½ years.

Page: 10

(8) *R. v. Uppal*, 2004 BCSC 414: Uppal was a bright promising young man who involved himself in the drug trade. The victim was his friend who trusted him. Uppal was told to make sure that his friend was in his apartment at the time appointed for the murder and that there were no other people there who might interfere or subsequently be witnesses. Uppal went along with this scheme because he was afraid of the principal and believed that if he did not comply he would himself be in danger. He attempted in the very last moments to prevent his friend's death. He was sentenced to 7 years, less credit for time served for a net sentence of 5 years.

(9) *R. v. Walcot*, 2001 BCCA 342: Walcot and Gamblin had been out shooting with a prohibited firearm. Walcot knew that Gamblin intended to "settle a score" and Walcot drove the car to the scene of the crime in order to enable Gamblin to carry out that purpose. Walcot gave the keys to Gamblin to unlock the trunk in order that Gamblin could obtain the rifle to carry out his purpose. Walcot was present when his friend walked into the home of the victims and shot them in the head. When the shots were fired Walcot was standing in the door of the house. Walcot turned himself in to the RCMP and assisted in the investigation. He pled guilty to two counts of manslaughter. He was minimally involved in the offence, had no prior record, and received the minimum sentence of 4 years.

(10) *R. v. Almarales*, 2008 ONCA 692: Prieto accused his girlfriend of having an affair with one of the deceased, and asked Almarales to drive him to his old apartment to retrieve some items. Prieto threatened Almarales with a gun prior to entering the apartment and took his car keys. Almarales was present when his friend Prieto shot three men in the apartment. Prieto later killed himself. Prieto was a very difficult, dangerous and unpredictable man. Almarales was a drug user and trafficker, and an alcoholic, rarely held lawful employment, and had a long record including crimes of violence, drug offences and failures to appear or to attend court. On appeal, a net sentence of 12 years for manslaughter was imposed (Almarales having served 21 months pre-trial custody), recognizing Almarales' secondary participation in the killings.

(11) *R. v. Mackhan*, [2005] O.J. No. 5959 (Sup.Ct.Just.): Mackhan was 18 years old when he participated in a near murder for which he was convicted of manslaughter. Watt J. noted that general deterrence, although significant in cases of fatal violence, does not trump every other sentencing principle and justify the imposition of artificially lengthy penitentiary terms for each and every youthful first offender. Watt J. stated that 15 to 18 years is a range of sentence available but infrequently imposed in manslaughter cases, especially on a plea of guilty of a youthful first offender, with no history of violent disposition and reasonable prospects for rehabilitation, who was a principal but not the prime mover in the

Page: 11

offence. An effective sentence of between 10 and 11 years was imposed less credit of 4 years and 2 months for pre-trial custody.

C.   Aggravating and Mitigating Factors

1.   Moral Blameworthiness of Mr. Hennessey and Mr. Cheeseman

[39]   It is now my duty to analyse and determine the overall moral blameworthiness of Mr. Hennessey and Mr. Cheeseman for the deaths of the four RCMP Constables so as to determine which rung of the moral culpability ladder each stands on. In doing so, it is necessary to examine the circumstances surrounding the involvement of the two offenders in the events of March 3, 2005.

[40]   Mr. Hennessey and Mr. Cheeseman were parties to Roszko's murders. They did not fire a gun. Nor were they present when Roszko killed the officers. There is no evidence before the Court that they participated in the initial formulation of Roszko's plan to return and burn down the Quonset or in any plan of his, whenever formulated, to kill RCMP officers.

[41]   Both Mr. Hennessey and Mr. Cheeseman say they were fearful of and intimidated by Roszko, who was known to be volatile. However, there is no evidence of any overt threats to either of them. Further, I note that Mr. Hennessey succeeded in refusing to allow Roszko to leave his truck on Mr. Hennessey's property, from which I infer that he had some negotiating power. Regarding Mr. Cheeseman, it is unclear what demands, if any, were ever placed on him by Roszko. He did not own or possess a rifle demanded by Roszko, nor was he the owner of the car Roszko presumably demanded be used to transport him to his property. In other words, Mr. Cheeseman seems to have become a party to the events of March 3, 2005 largely out of his desire to help his brother-in-law assist in the destruction of the Quonset by Roszko, and possibly out of concern for the welfare of Mr. Hennessey and his family.

[42]   Although both offenders had worked for Roszko, Mr. Hennessey was also involved in a criminal enterprise with him. Mr. Hennessey told Mr. Cheeseman that he needed Mr. Cheeseman's help because there were RCMP officers at Roszko's farm and Mr. Hennessey was involved in the marijuana grow operation located on that property. Mr. Hennessey knew that Roszko intended to burn down the Quonset. This act by Roszko would have benefitted Mr. Hennessey. It would have destroyed evidence of Mr. Hennessey and Roszko's criminal grow operation, effectively obstructing the investigation and the enforcement of the law. The burning of the Quonset while police officers were involved in an active investigation of it could, in itself, have put the officers at risk of life threatening injuries.

[43]   I infer from the facts that Mr. Hennessey had control over the rifle which his grandfather had given him. Before giving it to Roszko, he wiped it down, presumably to remove his own fingerprints.

Page: 12

[44]   There was clearly an element of self-interest in Mr. Hennessey's actions, which were all directed at distancing himself from anything that could link him to Roszko and the marijuana grow op. There was some discussion during the sentencing hearing as to the extent of the offenders' involvement in the drug trade. Defence counsel acknowledges that Mr. Hennessey sold small quantities of marijuana to family and friends, but argues that there is no clear evidence that destroying evidence of the grow operation was a motive in their involvement.

[45]   Several questions are left unanswered by the Agreed Facts. One such question is why the rifle was a necessary component of the plan to burn down the Quonset. Roszko did not ask for gasoline or a match. If a firearm was a necessary part of that plan, why were two firearms required? Whatever the answers to these questions, Mr. Hennessey had to know that Roszko, in his enraged and heavily armed state, was a serious danger to the police officers who were already on his property.

[46]   Mr. Hennessey persuaded the younger Mr. Cheeseman to come home to help him deal with Roszko and his concern over the grow op. He also persuaded Mr. Cheeseman to accompany him and Roszko in his car. Mr. Hennessey involved Mr. Cheeseman out of his own self-interest.

[47]   It was Mr. Hennessey who drove the vehicle. After dropping off Roszko at his property, Mr. Cheeseman suggested calling the police. Mr. Hennessey discouraged that idea, apparently on the basis that Roszko would then come after them. Again, Mr. Hennessey acted in his own self-interest. At that point, when it was evident the police were already on the property, there was no likelihood Mr. Hennessey would have been blamed by Roszko for instigating an investigation. The investigation was in progress. There was no good reason not to alert the police to the danger.

[48]   Mr. Cheeseman's involvement in the matter was quite different. He came home at Mr. Hennessey's request to support him in the situation with Roszko and the marijuana grow op. There is no suggestion in the Agreed Facts that he played any part in the decision to provide the rifle to Roszko. He took it upon himself to retrieve a pillow case in which he put the rifle. He accompanied Mr. Hennessey and Roszko, at Mr. Hennessey's request, in Mr. Hennessey's car. He suggested they warn the police after they dropped off Roszko.

[49]   Apart from providing the pillow case, the Agreed Facts suggest that Mr. Cheeseman was little more than a bystander with knowledge of the danger to the police posed by Roszko. He apparently had no involvement in the grow operation. His involvement appears to have stemmed from a fear of Roszko combined with a willingness to support his brother-in-law. While there is little to suggest any self-interest in his involvement, it appears that he initially agreed to participate, and then continued his involvement, to help Mr. Hennessey do whatever Mr. Hennessey felt necessary to aid Roszko in burning down the Quonset. That is, he agreed to participate in the unlawful act of burning down the Quonset to help protect Mr. Hennessey.

[50]   Defence counsel emphasized that these two offenders are convicted only on the basis of being parties who ought to have foreseen the possible consequences of the events. Counsel urged

Page: 13

the Court to carefully consider *Laberge* and the two forms of *mens rea*, subjective and objective, arguing that there was no subjective intention on the part of these offenders to inflict harm upon the officers.

[51]   The *Laberge* analysis addresses both subjective and objective *mens rea* at paras. 13 and 14:

> 13   Even though only objective *mens rea* need be proven, subjective intent may also have been established in a given case. Where subjective intent has been established, that might well be braided together with objective intent at a different culpability level. Perfect symmetry between the two may not exist. Nor need it.

> 14   Despite the fact that the Crown need not prove that an offender knew or intended that his conduct would put his victim at risk of injury in order to ground a conviction for manslaughter, whether this additional level of subjective intent has been established is important in assessing the offender's blameworthiness for sentencing purposes. That is because our criminal justice system is based on the premise that, all other things being equal, the more an offender's "intention" or "awareness" approaches the point that he knew or was wilfully blind to the fact that his unlawful act was not only likely to put the victim at risk of death, but indeed to cause death, the more culpable he is. Similarly, even absent proof of subjective *mens rea*, the more that the offender's conduct, on an objective basis, approaches the point where it can be said that he ought to have known, had he proceeded reasonably, that his unlawful act would be likely to cause life-threatening injuries as opposed to simply putting the victim at risk of bodily injury, the more culpable he is. In other words, the offender's moral blameworthiness and in turn the gravity of the offence are functions of the degree of fault.

[52]   Both Mr. Hennessey and Mr. Cheeseman knew that armed confrontation with the police was a real possibility and that the situation was clearly trouble. On the ride to Roszko's property, he "ranted and complained about the RCMP, and threatened to get even with them." He said he was going to burn down the Quonset. Mr. Cheeseman described his rantings as "devil talk". Importantly, Mr. Cheeseman and Mr. Hennessey could see the lights from the police cars when they dropped off Roszko. They witnessed Roszko pull socks over the outside of the boots he was wearing, grab the Winchester rifle from the back seat and proceed off in the direction of the police.

[53]   Mr. Hennessey's moral culpability does not reach the highest rung on the moral culpability ladder. He was neither present when the officers were killed nor did he fire a gun. He also did not concoct the original plan to burn down the Quonset and while the plan he did agree to and participate in was dangerous, it did not expressly involve the intentional infliction of harm. Defence counsel argued that there was no clear evidence that destroying the marijuana

Page: 14

grow op was a motive for Hennessey, but I believe that to be a logical inference to be drawn from the facts agreed upon. It is my view that Mr. Hennessey reaches the highest rung possible for a party to murder who did not participate in formulating a plan to murder, was not present and was not the shooter. While Mr. Hennessey may have been under some duress in his dealings with Roszko that night, he had another reason for assisting Roszko and his actions in doing so placed four RCMP officers at risk of life threatening injuries.

[54]   Mr. Hennessey may not have subjectively intended for officers to be injured or killed, but he either knew or was wilfully blind to the fact that his actions rendered this a real possibility. On an objective analysis, any reasonable person would have known that Roszko's return to his farm with weapons and ammunition in his agitated state created an extreme danger for the officers: a danger of receiving life threatening injuries; a danger that was ultimately and tragically realized. Mr. Hennessey appears to have been motivated exclusively by self-interest. The fact that he was fearful of Roszko reinforces the conclusion that he either knew or was wilfully blind to the threat Roszko posed to the officers.

[55]   As for Mr. Cheeseman, I find his moral culpability to be lower than that of Mr. Hennessey. As stated above, his actions put him in a position more similar to that of a bystander. However, at a minimum he involved himself in activities intended to lead to the burning of the Quonset. While acting in what he may have believed to be a noble cause of assisting his friend and brother-in-law avoid possible criminal prosecution, his actions were clearly intended to obstruct a legitimate RCMP investigation and subvert justice. He further knew or ought to have known that any assistance in furthering Roszko's plan to burn down the Quonset would contribute to creating a grave danger to the officers. His awareness of the danger is manifestly evidenced by his suggestion that they call the police.

[56]   Having considered the circumstances of their involvement in the events of March 3, 2005, I conclude that the actions of Mr. Hennessey and Mr. Cheeseman were particularly aggravating. The only factor that may be considered as mitigating the seriousness of their actions is the duress or fear they experienced in dealing with Roszko.

2.   The Killing of Police Officers

[57]   The discussion of the sentencing principles applicable to this case would not be complete without consideration of the fact that the victims in this case were RCMP officers.

[58]   The case law is replete with statements regarding the very serious impact of violence against police officers on our society. As a free and democratic country, we require certain individuals to take positions as police officers to help maintain a just, peaceful and safe society. By doing so, they accept the inherent risks and dangers. Police officers have a duty to protect members of the public. Their occupations are extremely dangerous, having regard to the persons with whom they are in frequent contact. Members of the public may flee trouble, but police officers must face it for it is their duty to enforce the law and to maintain law and order, often at

Page: 15

great risk to their own lives or personal safety. Due to their willingness to face danger for the public good, police officers are entitled to protection and to know that society demands that they be protected.

[59]   The public relies on police officers to provide safety and security. An attack on a police officer is an attack on society itself, and when a police officer is killed in the execution of duty, the community is understandably outraged. Members of the public must know that police officers acting in the course of duty are to be obeyed and respected, failing which heavy penalties will follow. It is impossible for police officers to maintain law and order unless they enjoy the support of the public and unless they are seen to have the solid backing of the courts when they are entitled to it. It is absolutely essential that all members of the public understand that violence against police officers in the course of their duties will be severely sanctioned. For law-abiding citizens, this knowledge enables them to conduct their affairs with confidence and assurance. For those who find themselves on the wrong side of the law, it is hoped that the severe consequences of engaging in violent acts against police officers will act as a deterrent.

[60]   It is for these reasons that denunciation and deterrence are primary considerations in sentencing an offender in relation to the killing of a police officer. The killing of a person whose obligation it is to maintain law and order carries with it added moral culpability and requires a heavier deterrent to protect the public interest.

[61]   With the exception of *Bell*, the sentencing cases cited earlier in which the offender did not directly kill the victim do not involve the killing of a police officer. In considering appropriate sentences in this case, I am guided by the range reflected in the case law, but must give consideration to the fact that the victims were police officers who were in the course of their duties at the time. These offenders knew or were wilfully blind to the fact that unknowing and unsuspecting police officers, engaged in a lawful investigation, were at risk of life threatening injuries at the hands of a heavily armed, volatile and dangerous individual.

[62]   Mr. Hennessey and Mr. Cheeseman failed to show respect for the law and for those who enforce it. Through their actions in furtherance of Roszko's plan, they let themselves and their own families. They let down four RCMP Constables who put their lives at risk while acting in the course of their duties as peace officers to serve and protect all, including Mr. Hennessey and Mr. Cheeseman. They let down the families of Constable Anthony Gordon, Constable Peter Schiemann, Constable Lionide Johnston and Constable Brock Myrol. They let down the communities where the officers lived, worked and served. They let down the country the officers unselfishly agreed to serve and where the offenders are privileged to live under the rule of law.

[63]   In imposing sentence, it is appropriate to reflect society's revulsion for this aspect of the offence.

Page: 16

3. Guilty Pleas

[64] The guilty pleas in this case must be given considerable weight. The guilty pleas by Mr. Hennessey and Mr. Cheeseman were not entered at the eleventh hour in the face of overwhelming Crown evidence as to inevitable guilt. In my view, the pleas were entered as early as it was reasonable to do so given the complexities of the case and the length of the investigation. In order to fully and properly consider the risks involved in proceeding to trial, it was essential for the accused and their counsel to obtain and review full disclosure from the Crown. It was also necessary for them to attend a preliminary inquiry to gain a full understanding of the nature of the Crown's case and some idea of the manner in which it would be presented. Indeed, it was also necessary for the Crown to conduct a preliminary inquiry so as to be in a position to assess the nature and quality of its evidence as well as its effect.

[65] The pleas were entered months before a scheduled 10 week trial. By pleading guilty, Mr. Hennessey and Mr. Cheeseman have saved the victims' families, the communities involved, the RCMP and the entire country from reliving a tragedy in microscopic and excruciating detail. The early resolution to this matter has also freed up resources in terms of the officers who would have been witnesses and the various other players in the administration of justice.

[66] Finally, the guilty pleas evidence a clear acknowledgement of responsibility and remorse on the part of both offenders. The pleas are an essential step on the road to rehabilitation.

[67] The mitigating effects and the resulting value of early guilty pleas in these criminal proceedings cannot be overemphasized.

4. Circumstances of the Offenders

Shawn Hennessey

[68] Shawn Hennessey is 29 years old. He was 26 years old at the time of the offences. He moved from Nova Scotia to Barrhead in 1994. He has two siblings: a sister in Barrhead and a brother in British Columbia. He graduated from High School in 1997 and has been steadily employed since then on oil rigs, then at Fountain Tire and Kal-Tire where he rose to the position of assistant manager, a position he held at the time of his arrest in 2007. On being released on bail in 2008, he found work with a construction company.

[69] Mr. Hennessey is married to Christine, and has two children, 8 and 5 years old. They own their own home south of Barrhead. Mr. Hennessey has enjoyed a great deal of family and community support throughout the proceedings. Over 100 letters were presented to the Court at the time of bail in support of his character. He is reportedly generous, helpful, a loving husband, father, brother, son, and friend. He is devoted to his family. He is a trustworthy, reliable, decent, hardworking employee.

Page: 17

Dennis Cheeseman

[70]   Mr. Cheeseman was 21 years old at the time of the crime. He has one sister, Mr. Hennessey's wife, Christine. His father died when he was two years old. He survived a serious car accident when he was four years old. His mother remarried when he was five years old. His step-father was in his life for five years, but was a heavy drinker and abusive. There was not much money in his home for extra-curricular activities. He was shy and quiet, and did not have many friends during his school years. He dropped out of school at the age of 16. His mother sold the farmland around the house. His sister started dating Mr. Hennessey. His mother left when he was 16 and Mr. Hennessey moved in. He has had contact with his mother only four or five times in the last nine years.

[71]   Mr. Cheeseman became very close to his sister and eventually with Mr. Hennessey. He was happy when they got married and had children. He looked up to Mr. Hennessey. He would babysit for Mr. Hennessey and Christine. He was happy living there.

[72]   Mr. Cheeseman became a full-time janitor at the age of 16 and then worked at a hardware store in Barrhead for two years. He then began working for Sepallo Foods where he remained until his arrest. Since his release he has worked with a door installer. He has completed a number of courses throughout his work history. He has worked hard at staying employed and trying to better himself. He got along well with his fellow employees and employer. He had no previous dealings with the police. He too has community support.

[73]   To summarize, both Mr. Hennessey and Mr. Cheeseman have been productive, contributing members of society who have enjoyed the support of those around them. Neither has a criminal record. The time each spent on bail under reasonably onerous conditions was unmarred by any violation. With respect to Mr. Hennessey, however, all of those mitigating factors stand in stark contrast to his partnership with Roszko in a marijuana grow operation and his participation in trafficking activities.

IV.   The Victim Impact Statements

[74]   Section 722 of the *Criminal Code* provides that for the purpose of determining the sentence to be imposed on an offender, the court shall consider victim impact statements describing the harm done to, or loss suffered by, the victim or victims of the offence. Thirteen such statements were read in open court during the sentencing hearing. The Court acknowledges the courage exhibited by those family members who spoke so candidly of the pain they have suffered at the loss of their loved ones, the four officers who prematurely lost their lives while courageously serving their country.

Page: 18

A.   Constable Anthony Fitzgerald Gordon

[75]   Constable Gordon was 28 years old in March 2005. His mother (Doreen Jewell-Duffy), step-father (John Duffy) and wife (Kimberley Gordon) all speak of the void and the physical, mental and emotional pain left by the loss of Anthony Gordon. Kimberley was pregnant with their second child at the time of Anthony's death. She grieves the loss of her husband and her children's father. She attests to the fact that despite tremendous support of family and friends, deep feelings of loneliness remain.

B.   Constable Peter Christopher Schiemann

[76]   Constable Schiemann was 25 years old at the time he was killed. His father (Donald), mother (Beth), brother (Mike), and sister (Julia Loughlin) provided statements. Their statements attest to the love and respect they and others held for Peter, and the devastating loss they have felt as a result of his death. Donald Schiemann states that the events of March 3, 2005 ripped the family's lives apart, inflicting a pain beyond words. His mother Beth writes of how difficult it is to experience family celebrations without Peter. Mike and Julia speak of the gaping hole left by the loss of a loved sibling.

C.   Constable Lionide Nicholas Johnston

[77]   Constable Johnston was 32 years old in March of 2005. His wife (Kelly) speaks to the great pain and loss in her life, the loss of dreams and plans she and her husband had formed together as a couple. His mother (Grace) speaks of the horror and devastation which the crime brought to herself and the extended family, including Constable Johnston's nieces and nephews.

D.   Constable Brock Warren Myrol

[78]   Constable Myrol was 29 years of age in March 2005. His father (Keith), mother (Colleen), sister (Kalhanie Stillings) and fiancée (Anjila Steeves Myrol) provided victim impact statements. They outline the toll which this crime has taken on those nearest to Brock. Keith states that it is like being given a life sentence of loneliness and suffering. He speaks of a hurt so deep words cannot tell. Colleen speaks of the emotional and physical toll on the family. Kalhanie speaks of the impact on her, but also on her children. Anjila speaks of the loss of the dream of a life and future together.

[79]   It is clear that the RCMP officers who were victims in this case were loved dearly by their families, and that they provided inspiration through their desire to serve and protect others by becoming RCMP officers. The fact that their promising lives were cut short has been devastating. Their families have experienced horrendous loss, the effects of which are strongly felt even after four years.

Page: 19

[80]   On March 3, 2005, these four RCMP officers were acting in the course and scope of their duties to protect and serve the communities in which they lived and worked. They died in the course of those duties. These four men were Canadian heroes and will forever be remembered as such.

V.   Calculation of Sentence

[81]   This brings me to the determination of the appropriate sentences in this case.

A.   The Starting Point

[82]   The Crown submits that a sentence in the upper end of the range of 10 to 15 years, before considering credit for time served, is an appropriate starting point for determining the overall sentence for each offender. Counsel for Mr Hennessey submits that an appropriate starting point for his sentence should be 5 years, less credit for his guilty pleas and for time served. Counsel for Mr. Cheeseman argues that his client is less culpable than Mr. Hennessey and suggests a starting point of 4 years imprisonment, less credit for his guilty pleas and for time served.

[83]   As indicated earlier, I consider the moral culpability of Mr. Hennessey to be as high as it can be for an individual who did not pre-meditate a murder, was not at the scene of the murders and did not fire a gun. While I accept that he was under some duress in facing Roszko, I believe he was principally motivated by a desire to have the evidence of his partnership with Roszko in an illegal marijuana grow operation destroyed by Roszko. When he solicited the assistance of Mr. Cheeseman, he told him of the presence of the RCMP at Roszko's farm and his own involvement in the grow operation.

[84]   While Mr. Hennessey's stated understanding was that Roszko simply intended to destroy evidence by burning down the Quonset, he provided Roszko with a .300 Winchester rifle knowing that Roszko was already in possession of a Luger handgun. Though he may not have known that Roszko owned an assault rifle, he knew that the weapons already in Roszko's possession could cause life threatening injuries. Further, while Roszko never used the Winchester rifle, he obviously felt it was needed for him to accomplish whatever he intended to accomplish. Mr. Hennessey also prompted the involvement of Mr. Cheeseman to aid him in furthering Roszko's plans to destroy evidence.

[85]   Mr. Hennessey rejected Mr. Cheeseman's suggestion after dropping off Roszko that the police be called and warned. He says that he was afraid that if Roszko evaded the police, he would then come after them. The difficulty I have with that suggestion is that these men knew that the police were already on Roszko's property. A phone call warning police that Roszko was on the property and armed would simply have allowed the police to properly meet the situation. Indeed, armed with that knowledge, the RCMP officers would undoubtedly have taken a different approach to securing the Quonset and their own safety. It is difficult to understand

Page: 20

precisely what deduction Mr. Hennessey was fearful Roszko would make from the fact that the police who were already present on the property happened to be properly prepared for an armed confrontation.

[86] It is also important that the tragic consequences of Roszko's actions and Mr. Hennessey's assistance not be forgotten: four young RCMP Constables were murdered. These offenders pled guilty to four separate acts of manslaughter arising out of one series of actions. That series of actions put a number of police officers at risk of life threatening injuries. While the tragic consequences cannot unduly distort determination of the appropriate penalty, they must still be taken into account in considering the proportionality of the sentence and the need for denunciation and deterrence.

[87] In my view a fit and proper sentence to impose upon Mr. Hennessey, before considering the mitigating effect of the guilty pleas and credit for pre-sentencing custody, is 15 years imprisonment.

[88] I consider the moral culpability of Mr. Cheeseman to be lower than that of Mr. Hennessey. While Mr. Cheeseman also suggests that he was under some duress as a result of the fear and intimidation by Roszko, there does not appear from any of the agreed facts that Mr. Roszko made any demands of Mr. Cheeseman nor threatened him in any way. Again, it appears that Mr. Cheeseman was acting on a request by Mr. Hennessey to help Roszko obstruct justice. Seemingly without prompting, he provided Roszko with a pillowcase to hide the rifle given to him by Mr. Hennessey, though the benefit of this to Roszko is unclear. He also willingly participated in the transportation of Roszko to his property whereupon the danger to the RCMP officers present was obvious. While his suggestion of contacting the police after dropping off Roszko may appear commendable, his acquiescence to the refusal by Mr. Hennessey is not. Finally, and as in the case of Mr. Hennessey, the horrific consequences of Roszko's actions and Mr. Cheeseman's assistance cannot be ignored, though neither can they unduly distort consideration of the appropriate sentence.

[89] In my view, a fit and proper sentence to impose upon Mr. Cheeseman, before considering the mitigating effect of the guilty pleas and credit for pre-sentencing custody, is 12 years imprisonment.

B.   The Effect of the Guilty Pleas

[90] Mr. Hennessey and Mr. Cheeseman gave up their constitutional right to a fair trial. As indicated earlier, the positive impact of those guilty pleas on the families of the victims, the communities involved and the administration of justice must be recognized. In my view, Mr. Hennessey and Mr. Cheeseman are each entitled to a reduction of 3 years in their sentence to recognize the significance of their guilty pleas, their acceptance of responsibility and the evidence of remorse. This effectively reduces Mr. Hennessey's sentence to a further period of

Page: 21

incarceration of 12 years, and Mr. Cheeseman's sentence to a further period of incarceration of 9 years.

[91]   While I recognize that giving each the same credit for the guilty pleas gives a greater proportionate benefit to Mr. Cheeseman as his starting point is lower than that of Mr. Hennessey, I feel it to be appropriate as a further recognition of the different levels of moral culpability of the two offenders in the events of March 3, 2005.

C.   Credit for Time Served

[92]   The Crown and Defence have agreed that Mr. Hennessey and Mr. Cheeseman should each receive credit for the time they have served on a 2 for 1 basis. As of today, Mr. Hennessey has spent about 9 months and 3 weeks in remand, while Mr. Cheeseman has spent about 10 months and 3 weeks in remand.

[93]   The *Criminal Code* provides in s. 719(3):

> 719(3) In determining the sentence to be imposed on a person convicted of an offence, a Court may take into account any time spent in custody by the person as a result of the offence.

[94]   Sentencing Judges ordinarily exercise the discretion provided in s. 719 by giving credit to a convicted person for pre-trial and pre-sentencing custody. A judge should not deny credit without good reason, since the incarceration of an individual for any period of time prior to trial is a denial of that person's liberty before any final determination is made as to his guilt [*R. v. Rezaie* (1996), 112 C.C.C. (3d) 97 (Ont. C.A.)].

[95]   In Alberta, credit is usually given on a 2 for 1 basis for that period of time spent by an accused incarcerated at a Remand Centre pending trial or sentencing. This is because the time spent in remand is commonly considered "dead time": first, the time spent in pre-trial or pre-sentencing custody is not considered in the legislative provisions for parole eligibility and statutory release; second, the Remand Centre does not provide those educational, retraining or rehabilitation programs available to an individual in the prison system. (*R. v. Rezaie, supra,* and *R. v. Wust* [2000] 1 S.C.R. 455). The conditions in the Remand Centre are harsh and are not suited to long term detention.

[96]   I find that there is no good reason in this case to deny credit to each of the offenders on a 2 for 1 basis for the time they have spent in custody prior to sentencing. Accordingly, Mr. Hennessey shall receive credit on a 2 for 1 basis for a total credit of 19 ½ months. Mr. Cheeseman shall also receive credit on a 2 for 1 basis for a total credit of 21 ½ months.

Page: 22

D.   Credit for Time on Bail

[97]   Mr. Hennessey was on bail for approximately 9 months, and Mr. Cheeseman was on bail for approximately 8 months before they pled guilty. They each want full credit (that is, credit on a one for one basis) for the time spent on bail as they were under onerous conditions, essentially amounting to a form of house arrest. While both were entitled to work while on release, that was the only time they were allowed out of their homes and in their community unless in the company of a surety. They were allowed no contact with each other and no contact with any person named as a potential witness in the case.

[98]   The Crown opposes the suggestion that they should receive any credit for the time spent on bail as they had the clear benefit of being out of the Remand Centre and with family.

[99]   Mr. Hennessey and Mr. Cheeseman rely on the decisions of the Alberta Court of Appeal in *R. v. Lau*, 2004 ABCA 408, 193 C.C.C. (3d) 51 and *R. v. Hilderman*, 2005 ABCA 249, 199 C.C.C. (3d) 561. In *Lau*, the Court noted that the sentencing judge may take into account strict bail conditions and treat them as akin to custody. Whether or not to give credit, and how much, is a matter within the judge's discretion having regard to factors such as the intrusiveness of the bail terms (*Lau* at paras. 15 and 16; *Hilderman* at para. 18).

[100]   In my view, pre-trial interim release without any house arrest type provisions would not justify any credit being given. On the other hand, bail conditions amounting to a full house arrest of an accused might well justify a 1 for 1 credit as such a condition would essentially fully deprive an accused of his liberty.

[101]   Where an accused is under a partial house arrest in the sense that he is allowed out of the house for only a limited time (to work for example) and his liberty is severely restricted, consideration may be given to some credit between the two extremes. For example, where an accused is only allowed out of his home to work and is otherwise confined to his house at all other times, a court might well consider some compromise, such as credit on a 1 for 2 basis, that is, credit amounting to one half of the time on release.

[102]   The offenders in this case were released on reasonably onerous conditions. They had strict reporting conditions and were subject to a curfew. However, they were both allowed to work. They were both allowed out of the house when accompanied by a surety. Obviously, their release conditions were markedly better than the conditions in the Remand Centre.

[103]   The onus is on an offender to provide sufficient information for the Court to properly assess the impact of the pre-trial release conditions so as to consider their mitigating effect (*R. v. Downes*, 208 O.A.C. 324). While these offenders suggested that their release conditions were onerous, no evidence was provided to the Court as to the adverse impact on them personally beyond the apparent inconvenience of having a surety accompany them outside of their homes and some restrictions on their communications with potential witnesses.

Page: 23

[104] I have considered the time spent on judicial interim release and the conditions of the release order as mitigating factors in determining the appropriate starting points for the offenders and am not prepared to consider granting the offenders any further credit.

E.   Eligibilty for Parole

[105] The *Criminal Code* provides in s. 743.6 that the Court may order that the portion of a sentence that must be served before the offender is eligible for parole be one-half of the sentence or 10 years, whichever is less. The Crown has indicated that it is not seeking such an order from this Court.

[106] Section 743.6(2) provides that the paramount principles which are to guide the Court considering an order to delay parole are denunciation and specific or general deterrence, with rehabilitation of the offender being subordinate to those principles.

[107] The two offenders were on Judicial Interim Release and working in the community for a period of time before sentencing. It has not been suggested that they acted in any way contrary to the terms of release and even the Crown has suggested that an order to delay parole eligibility cannot be justified on the basis that it will be necessary as part of the rehabilitation of either of the offenders. I agree.

[108] Further, I am satisfied that the sentence I have imposed herein, with a starting point of 15 years for Mr. Hennessey and 12 years for Mr. Cheeseman adequately recognizes and emphasizes the principles of denunciation and specific and general deterrence. The fact that they will each serve less than the time I have determined to be fit sentences for each merely reflects the appropriate credit each is to receive.

[109] Accordingly, there will be no order under s. 743.6(2).

VI.   Conclusion

[110] Please stand Mr. Hennessey:

> Mr. Hennessey I have determined that a fit and proper sentence to impose upon you for having committed four acts of manslaughter in relation to the deaths of four RCMP Constables is 15 years imprisonment. I have also determined that it is appropriate for you to receive 3 years credit for having entered guilty pleas to the charges and 19 ½ months credit for pre-sentencing time spent in custody. The balance of your sentence is 10 years plus 4 ½ months in jail.

Page: 24

[111] Please stand Mr. Cheeseman:

I have determined that a fit and proper sentence to impose upon you for having committed four acts of manslaughter in relation to the deaths of four RCMP Constables is 12 years imprisonment. I have also determined that it is appropriate for you to receive 3 years credit for having entered guilty pleas to the charges and 21 ½ months credit for pre-sentencing time spent in custody. The balance of your sentence is 7 years plus 2 ½ months in jail.

[112] Pursuant to s. 109 of the *Criminal Code*, Mr. Hennessey and Mr. Cheeseman are each prohibited for life from possessing any firearm, including a prohibited firearm or restricted firearm, crossbow, restricted weapon, ammunition and explosive substances.

[113] Pursuant to, and in accordance with s. 487.051 of the *Criminal Code*, Mr. Hennessey and Mr. Cheeseman will each provide samples of bodily substances reasonably required for the purposes of forensic DNA analysis.

[114] Victim fine surcharges are waived.

Heard on the 19th day of January, 2009.
Dated at the City of Edmonton, Alberta this 30th day of January, 2009.

Eric F. Macklin
J.C.Q.B.A.

Appearances:

David A. Labrenz, Alberta Justice
    for the Crown

D'Arcy Depoe - Fleming Depoe Banks Gubbins
Edmond Joseph O'Neill - Beresh Cunningham
    for Shawn Hennessey

Peter Northcott and Bradley Thomlinson
Peter G. Northcott Professional Corporation
    for Dennis Cheeseman

Acknowledgements

Al's Cab, Barrhead, AB

Armstrong, S/Sgt. (ret.) William, Dundas, ON

Arthur, Charlotte, Mayerthorpe, AB

Barlow, Eliza, *Edmonton Sun*

Baysville Horticultural Society, Baysville, ON

Begg, Don, Cochrane, AB

Begg, Shirley, Cochrane, AB

Bennett, Dean, Canadian Press

Callaway, Tim, *Christian Week*

Campobasso, Cpl. Mike, Burlington, ON

Carson, Magdalene, Manotick, ON

Cheliak, Chief Supt. Marty, Iqaluit, Nunavit

Chichakian, Lynne, CBC, Toronto, ON

Christians (née Dennis), Cst. Cindie, Leduc, AB

Coffey, Andrew, *Barrhead Leader*, Barrhead, AB

Coffey, Stephen, *Barrhead Leader*, Barrhead, AB

Collins, Michelle, *Edmonton Journal*

Coogan, Sue, Iqaluit, Nunavut

Cook, Tim, Canadian Press

Cotter, John, Canadian Press

Cormier, Ryan, *Edmonton Journal*

D'Aliesio, Renata, *Edmonton Journal*

DePoe, D'Arcy, Edmonton, AB

Dowell, Glenn, Dundas, Ontario

Drouillard, Phil, Streetsville, ON

Dunn, Peter, Dundas, ON

Duplessie, Wanda, Lac Ste. Ann County Office, AB

Dwyer, Lorraine, Mayerthorpe, AB

Edwards, Peter, *Toronto Star*

Farnalls, Carol, Barrhead, AB

Fowler, Bill, Dundas, ON

Garlatti, Andy, Windsor, ON

Gordon, Kim, Sherwood Park, AB

Greenspoon, Ira, Dundas, ON

Guiry, Jim, Lindsay, ON

Hall, Jamie, *Edmonton Journal*

Harding, Katherine, *Globe and Mail*

Haven Inn Hotel, Mayerthorpe, AB

Helland, S/Sgt. (ret.) William, London, ON

Hennessey, Barry, Barrhead, AB

Hoogestraat, Cst. Garret, Edmonton HQ, AB

Inkpen, Ross and Heather, Waupoos, ON

Johnson, Ken, QC, Port Elgin, ON

Johnston, Kelly, Airdrie, AB

Johnston, Cpl. Lee, Ottawa, ON

Karchmar, Jane, Editor, Kingston, ON

Klaus, Christine, Lac Ste. Anne County Office, AB

Knuckle, Elizabeth, Editor, Dundas, ON

Krevesky, S/Sgt. (ret.) Mike, Kelowna, BC

Kyle, Dr. John, Mayerthorpe, AB

Letal, Cst. Julie, Peace River, AB

Lotholz, Rev. Arnold, Mayerthorpe, AB

Lynden Canoe Club, Lynden, ON

MacIntyre, Asst. Commissioner Al, Vancouver, BC

MacIntyre, Linden, CBC, Toronto, ON

MacDougall, S/Sgt. (ret.), Joe, Winnipeg, MN

MacLeod, Sgt. Blake, Whistler, BC

Macleod, S/Sgt Carl (ret.), Burlington, ON

Mahar, Don, Ottawa, ON

Martel, Sgt. Mike, Mayerthorpe, AB

Martin, Haley, Mayerthorpe, AB

Martin, Sgt. Jim, Spruce Grove, AB

Masterson, Kevin, Windsor, ON

Matthews, Jan, Calgary, AB

McDermid, Doug, Mayerthorpe, AB

McKillop, Colette, Mayerthorpe, AB

McLaughlin, Joe, *Red Deer Advocate*

McLean, Archie, *Edmonton Journal*

Nicholson, Sgt. Ron, Markham, ON

Oakes, Cpl. Wayne, Media Relations Officer, Edmonton AB

O'Neil, Katherine, *Globe and Mail*

Plunkett, Ian, Brooklin, ON

Preugschas, Jurgen, Sangudo, AB

Reid (née Gogan), Andria, Spruce Grove, AB

Romeo, Dianne, Mayerthorpe, AB

Romeo, Bruce, Mayerthorpe, AB

Schalm, Albert, Mayerthorpe, AB

Seguin, Cst. Clayton, Claresholm, AB

Staples, David, *Edmonton Journal*

Mathias, Sgt. Mark, Whitecourt, AB

Steeves–Myrol, Anjila, Red Deer, AB

Thibault, Margaret, Mayerthorpe, AB

Tweedie, Barbara, Ancaster, ON

Tweedie, Tom, Ancaster, ON

Vanderwell, Tanya, Lac Ste. Anne County Office, AB

Vigor, Cpl. Steve, Edmonton HQ, AB

Weber, Bob, Canadian Press

Wheeler, Lori, Barrhead, AB

Whipple, Cpl. Jeff, Stony Plain, AB

Wiebe, Rev. Wendell, Mayerthorpe, AB

Wilcox, Linda, *Whitecourt Star*

Williams, Supt. Robert, Edmonton, AB

Windsor Group, Windsor, ON

Wingrove, Josh, *Globe and Mail*

Zabjek, Alexandra, *Edmonton Journal*

Barrhead Leader

CBC Toronto

Calgary Herald

Calgary Sun

Canada.Com

Canada Space

Canadian Press

Christian Week

CTV

Edmonton Journal

Edmonton Sun

Global Television

Globe and Mail

Grande Prairie Herald–Tribune

Guelph Mercury

Hamilton Spectator

Mayerthorpe Freelancer

McMaster University Library

National Post

Neighborhood Inn, Barrhead, AB

News 880 AM

Q107, Calgary

Red Baron Restaurant, Barrhead, AB

Red Deer Advocate

Royal Canadian Mounted Police

Toronto Star

Western Catholic Reporter

Special thanks to

    Tim Gordon, Publisher, Renfrew, ON

    Jane Karchmar, Editor, Kingston, ON

    Staff Sgt. (ret.) Carl MacLeod, Burlington, ON

    Sgt. Jim Martin, Mayerthorpe, AB

    Cpl. Wayne Oakes, RCMP Media Relations, Edmonton, AB

    Margaret Thibault, Mayerthorpe, AB

AUTHOR'S INTERVIEWS

Begg, Don, Cochrane, AB

Begg, Shirley, Cochrane, AB

Campobasso, Cpl. Mike, Burlington, ON

Cheliak, Chief Supt. Marty, Iqaluit, Nunavit

Christians (née Dennis), Cst. Cindie, Leduc, AB

Coffey, Andrew, *Barrhead Leader*, Barrhead, AB

DePoe, D'Arcy, Edmonton, AB

Dowell, Glenn, Dundas, ON

Drouillard, Phil, Streetsville, ON

Dunn, Peter, Dundas, ON

Duplessie, Wanda, Lac Ste. Ann County Office, AB

Dwyer, Lorraine, Mayerthorpe, AB

Farnalls, Carol, Barrhead, AB

Fowler, Bill, Dundas, ON

Gordon, Kim, Sherwood Park, AB

Greenspoon, Ira, Dundas, ON

Guiry, Jim, Lindsay, ON

Garlatti, Andy, Windsor, ON

Helland, S/Sgt. (ret.) William, London, ON

Hennessey, Barry, Barrhead, AB

Hoogestraat, Cst. Garret, Edmonton HQ, AB

Johnson, Ken, QC, Port Elgin, ON

Johnston, Kelly, Airdrie, AB

Johnston, Cpl. Lee, Ottawa, ON

Krevesky, S/Sgt. (ret.) Mike, Kelowna, BC

Kyle, Dr. John, Mayerthorpe, AB

Lotholz, Rev. Arnold, Mayerthorpe, AB

MacIntyre, Asst. Commissioner Al, Vancouver, BC

MacIntyre, Linden, CBC, Toronto, ON

MacDougall, S/Sgt. (ret.) Joe, Winnipeg, MN

Macleod, S/Sgt. (ret.) Carl, Burlington, ON

Mahar, Don, Ottawa, ON

Martel, Sgt. Mike, Mayerthorpe, AB

Martin, Haley, Mayerthorpe, AB

Martin, Sgt. Jim, Mayerthorpe, AB

McDermid, Doug, Mayerthorpe, AB

McKillop, Colette, Mayerthorpe, AB

Nicholson, Sgt. Ron, Markham, ON

Oakes, Cpl. Wayne, Media Relations Officer, Edmonton AB

Preugschas, Jurgen, Sangudo, AB

Reid (née Gogan), Andria, Spruce Grove, AB

Romeo, Dianne, Mayerthorpe, AB

Romeo, Bruce, Mayerthorpe, AB

Schalm, Albert, Mayerthorpe, AB

Seguin, Cst. Clayton, Claresholm, AB

Steeves–Myrol, Anjila, Red Deer, AB

Thibault, Margaret, Mayerthorpe, AB

Tweedie, Barbara, Ancaster, ON

Tweedie, Tom, Ancaster, ON

Vigor, Cpl. Steve, Edmonton HQ, AB

Wheeler, Lori, Barrhead, AB

Whipple, Cpl. Jeff, Stony Plain, AB

Wiebe, Rev. Wendell, Mayerthorpe, AB

Williams, Supt. Robert, Edmonton, AB

Wolch, Hersh, Calgary, AB

Index

About the Author

ROBERT KNUCKLE was born and raised in Windsor, Ontario. He received his B.A. from the University of Windsor in 1957 and M.Ed. from the University of Toronto in 1968. He began writing fulltime in 1992. Prior to that, Mr. Knuckle was an English and Latin teacher and a secondary school vice-principal with the Hamilton Board of Education.

Robert Knuckle is the author of eleven books, three of them for children. Most of his other books are about true crime or tales of the Royal Canadian Mounted Police. He has written for radio, television, and cinema and won an ACTRA writing award for his radio script *I Am Not a Legend*, the story of legendary football coach Vince Lombardi. Three of his stage plays have been produced at major venues in Ontario.

Robert Knuckle resides in Dundas, Ontario, with his wife, Elizabeth. They have four children and seven grandchildren.

Other Books by Robert Knuckle

In the Line of Duty: From Fort Macleod to Mayerthorpe
The Flying Bandit
Beyond Reason
Murder at Eglinton Square
Molly of the Mounties
Black Jack: America's Famous Riderless Horse
Top Secret — an educational booklet
True Crime — an educational booklet
In the Line of Duty, Volume II: From Fort Macleod to Mayerthorpe
A Master of Deception: Working Undercover for the RCMP

THE

MAYERTHORPE

STORY

FROM AMBUSH TO AFTERMATH

ROBERT KNUCKLE

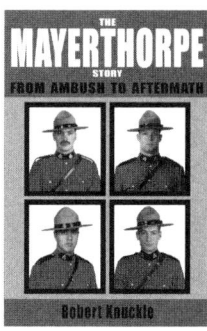

TO ORDER MORE COPIES, CONTACT:

General Store Publishing House

499 O'Brien Road, Box 415
Renfrew, Ontario, Canada K7V 4A6
Tel 1-800-465-6072 • Fax 1-613-432-7184
www.gsph.com